Carnival Is Woman

CARIBBEAN
STUDIES
SERIES

Anton L. Allahar and Natasha Barnes
Series Editors

Carnival Is Woman

Feminism and Performance in Caribbean Mas

Edited by Frances Henry and Dwaine Plaza

University Press of Mississippi / Jackson

The University Press of Mississippi is the scholarly publishing agency of
the Mississippi Institutions of Higher Learning: Alcorn State University,
Delta State University, Jackson State University, Mississippi State University,
Mississippi University for Women, Mississippi Valley State University,
University of Mississippi, and University of Southern Mississippi.

www.upress.state.ms.us

The University Press of Mississippi is a member
of the Association of University Presses.

First printing 2020
∞

Library of Congress Cataloging-in-Publication Data available

LCCN 2019030132
Hardback ISBN 978-1-4968-2544-5
Trade paperback ISBN 978-1-4968-2545-2
Epub single ISBN 978-1-4968-2546-9
Epub institutional ISBN 978-1-4968-2547-6
PDF single ISBN 978-1-4968-2548-3
PDF institutional ISBN 978-1-4968-2549-0

British Library Cataloging-in-Publication Data available

Contents

Preface

This book was born from a panel on Carnivals in the Caribbean presented at the meeting of the Caribbean Studies Association in New Orleans in 2015. Interest in the content of this panel was substantial as it attracted a large, attentive audience and an animated discussion and question period. Publishers present at the conference expressed interest in screening a manuscript and as a result, Frances Henry, who was one of the speakers, approached panel members with the idea of developing an edited book.[1]

This volume, likely the first of its kind to concentrate solely on women in Carnival, normalizes the contemporary Carnival, especially as it is played in Trinidad and Tobago, by demonstrating not only their numerical strength but the kind of *mas'* that is featured. The bikini-and-beads, or bikini-and-feathers, or "pretty *mas'*," is often decried by traditionalists. They hark back to the days of massive historical *mas'*, huge and elaborate costuming clothing, and real-life figures of the past tell their stories with most having little or nothing to do with history of the Caribbean. They criticize the behavior of the women in their scanty costumes who seem only intent on enjoying themselves, and who therefore do not tell a story. What is missed in this form of criticism is what the players of today, mainly women, signify and symbolize in this form of *mas'*, that is, their own newly discovered empowerment as females and their resistance to the older cultural norms of male oppression. This volume therefore provides a feminist perspective to the understanding of Carnival today.

Carnival Is Woman

Introduction

—Frances Henry and Dwaine Plaza

While the literature on Carnivals is fairly substantial, especially in the Americas, the subject of women in Carnival as a serious topic of inquiry is relatively new. While the glamour of skimpily clad young and very beautiful women celebrated in the Rio Carnival makes annual headlines, increasingly similarly dressed women in the Caribbean Carnivals also attracts media attention. One of the main differences between the Rio Carnival and those in the Caribbean and its diaspora is that in the former those who are chosen to head the glamorous floats are always young, slim, beautiful, and invariably white. The current Caribbean Carnivals, on the other hand, celebrate ordinary women of all ages, all skin colors, all ethnicities, and most of them are far from slim. As the numbers of women have grown in recent years to about 80 percent of the participants, this phenomenon has caught the attention not only of the media but also of scholars. The growth of feminist research, especially in the social sciences, has spurred on scholars to more closely examine the reasons for this growth in numbers as well as what these large ranks of women are actually expressing as they wine and carouse in very skimpy bikini-and-beads types of costumes (Hosein 2017; Reddock 1997; Barnes 2000). In this introduction, we briefly review the history of Carnivals in the Caribbean with emphasis on the Carnival in Trinidad. Second, we provide a theoretical lens for examining Carnival, focusing on the work of Mikhail Bakhtin (1994). Finally, we end this introductory chapter by discussing the main individual chapters contained within the book.

Overview of Caribbean Carnival History

All Carnivals seem to share a similar quality in that they are characterized by a series of performances or routinized events. This often includes costuming, oral performances, burlesques and farces, aggressive but controlled threats, drunken revelry, licentious and provocative promenading, quasi-street theatre, and transvestism (Green and Scher 2007). Carnival traditions in the Caribbean were developed primarily in Trinidad and Tobago and then spread to other islands and out to the diaspora where Caribbean people have migrated. Carnival in Trinidad is a two-day festive event preceding Ash Wednesday. The spectacle of Carnival usually consists of two days of singing, dancing, parading through the streets, drinking, and indulging in normally restricted behaviors. Carnival today provides a space for revelers to express their sexuality and places greater emphasis on the body and its attractive functions.

Carnival celebrations were brought by French colonizers to Trinidad and Tobago in the eighteenth century and heavily influenced by the Catholic traditions. Balls, concerts, dinners, hunts, and other festive events were held from Christmas until the preceding Ash Wednesday. During their pre-emancipation Carnival activities, the colonizers often costumed themselves as Negues Jadin (Garden Negroes) and mulatresses. They also re-enacted the cannes brulées (burning canes), the practice of rounding up slaves to put out fires in the cane field. These masquerade balls were witnessed with great amusement by enslaved Africans who began to have private celebrations of their own incorporating sacred traditions, particularly masking and funerary rituals. They also used these occasions to mock and lampoon the lascivious conduct of the masters and their wives. When the British took over Trinidad and set up their own colonial rule in 1802, the French Carnival tradition continued.

After emancipation in the early 1830s, participation in Carnival by Trinidadians of African descent increased dramatically, and African retentions in music, dance, costume, and ritual became even more predominant. By 1834, Carnival took on the characteristics of a celebration of deliverance rather than a European-inspired nature festival. Former slaves, who numbered in the tens of thousands, celebrated their newfound freedom by marching together, along with those already free. In the earliest period, masqueraders were predominantly male as Trinidad society was patriarchal, and women, important for upholding the values of society, were marginalized (Mason 1998). During this time, their costumes were used to express their social grievances (Liverpool 2001). Specifically, when the slaves fight for freedom became a national movement, costumes conveyed very aggressive meanings via personalities like the Midnight Robber, a Pierrot (i.e., French character that performs poetic rhetoric about societal issues), and stick fighters. Men dominated masquerade such that if there was a female role to be played, males sometimes cross-dressed to perform the role, as in Dame Lorraine (Franco 2007, Hill, 1972, Mason 1998).

Women began to participate in Carnival, primarily as yard "chantwells" or lead singers (the forerunners of calypsonians). In between the stick fighting contests held by men in the yards, women sang "carisos" or Carnival songs which continued the African practice (with added French and Spanish elements) of using praise and derision to describe the contenders. The women also danced to the songs in what some observers described as "obscene, lewd, and erotic" manner (Mohammed 2002), whereas men glorified their physical prowess, courage, and skill (Noel 2009). From the late nineteenth century until the mid-twentieth century, the poor black woman who defied standards of propriety and retaliated against her dehumanizing position in society was referred to as the "Jamette" (Green and Scher 2007). When Jamettes violated the conservative rules of etiquette in everyday life and during Carnival, they prompted a re-evaluation in Trinidadian society of the ways in which women appeared and behaved in public (Noel 2009).

By the nineteenth century, economically deprived people and their subculture dominated Carnival. They had continued developing their skills in stick fighting, their sharpness of wit in conversation and song (bragging especially about their sexual accomplishments), their talent in dance and music, and their indifference to colonial law and authority. The legacy of the "Jamette" label still exists today as a hegemonic unconscious cognitive bias within patriarchal Trinidadian society. However, the difference today is that there is new negative language policing the boundaries of morally acceptable behavior for women who participate in Carnival. The new diction includes terms like "Jagabat," "sketele," "skank," or "slut." Mohammed (2002) notes that despite the impact of Victorianism in the prohibition of women's active participation in Carnival during the early 1900s, the Jamettes openly expressed their sexuality and contributed greatly to the evolution of Carnival.

Although women were marginalized as masqueraders, they still played an integral role during Carnival. Women who were brave enough to participate did so in the dirty *mas'* celebrations (Franco 2007). Covering themselves with mud and oil and parading in the darkness of the predawn hours provided them with anonymity. Although the literature discusses the exclusion of women in regards to playing costumed masqueraders, it should be noted that their presence was important to the success of the men's performances (Green and Scher 2007). That is, the males needed an audience to legitimize their costumed identities.

Explaining Carnival: Theoretical Considerations

A number of theories attempt to explain the role of Carnival in society. David Gilmore's book *Carnival and Culture* (1998) provides a summary of four distinguishable but overlapping approaches to the study of ritual and social action.

First, the "Structural-Functionalist Approach" derived from Emile Durkheim viewed Carnival as a safety valve for letting off steam by the masses and therefore as a necessary celebration for maintaining social solidarity.

Second, the "Dynamic Equilibrium" rituals of rebellion approach put forth by Turner (1969) are examined by Gilmore. This approach is based on a modification of the safety valve thesis which asserts rituals of rebellion on the streets during Carnival are expressions of conflict between the various segments of a society that have the effect of enhancing social cohesion.

Third, the "Marxist Culture of Resistance" takes the viewpoint that popular festivities such as Carnival may be seen as sources of class unity through the ritualized re-enactment of resistance to the ruling class (Cohen 1993).

Fourth, the "Interpretive-Symbolic Approaches" where rituals are seen as a symbolic text requiring interpretation. Within this category one may include the semiotic approaches of writers such as Mikhail Bakhtin (1984).

Bakhtin used the term "Carnival" to apply to the varied popular festival life of the Middle Ages and the Renaissance. For Bakhtin, Carnival was celebrated in order to provide temporary liberation from the social order. In studying the work of French writer Rabelais, known for his work on the grotesque, Bakhtin became aware of how Carnival (carnivalesque) exemplified the grotesque, especially that of the body and its functions. In *Rabelais and his World* (1984), Bakhtin describes Carnival as a social institution within a culture that involves performers and spectators. The two-day celebration is neither an extension of reality nor real life; it becomes an alternate form of reality. Bakhtin understood Carnival to be a time in which all rules, restrictions, and inhibitions that society normally applies to human behavior, are suspended. Everything is permitted except violence, and it is a time of extreme excess. It is an alternate space where social boundaries are blurred, and everyone is supposed to be free and equal. All normal social rules can be broken, and people can ape or mock their "betters" and make them look ridiculous. He especially noted that all forms of social and political hierarchy can be upended. All people who take part in the carnival "live it," but it is not an extension of the "real world" or "real life"; instead, as Bakhtin puts it, it is "the world standing on its head," the world upside down (180). This event is unique in that rules, inhibitions, restrictions, and regulations that determine the course of everyday life are suspended, including hierarchical structures such as social class and political order (Bakhtin 1984).

According to Bakhtin, there are four dimensions in the "carnivalesque" world:

- Free and close interactions between people.
- Acceptable and eccentric behavior which is normally frowned upon becomes acceptable in Carnival and the hidden sides can be shown.

- Carnivalistic misalliances . . . that which is normally separated can become connected, the new and the old, the high and the low, the sacred and the profane.
- Sacrilegiousness—Carnival is a place for blasphemy, profanity, and parodies of things that are normally held sacred.

Bakhtin's (1984) theory of the Carnival sometimes allied with the grotesque also includes the self, which to him is really the body. It is a body "robust, curious, fertile, grotesque that is on holiday" (58). This body is also warm, friendly, cheerful and "free from shame and embarrassment . . . and it requires neither discipline nor control" (63). It expresses an irreverence toward life and is especially distrustful of all hierarchies. The laughing face of Carnival is "all mouth with barely any eyes and the carnivalized body is all lips, cheeks, breasts, and buttocks . . . Like these protuberances it is outward and other oriented" (Grodon et al. 2012, 36).

Emphasis is placed on basic needs and the body, and on the sensual and the senses, counterpoised to the commands of the will, bringing the spiritual and the abstract down to the material level of living. The good life is lived, not through inner thought or experience, but by the whole person, in thought and body. It affirms that the necessities, norms, and systems of daily life are temporary, historically variable and relative, and one day will come to an end. In Carnival, everything is rendered ever-changing, playful, and undefined. Hierarchies are overturned through inversions, debasements, and profanations, performed by normally silenced voices and energies (Robinson 2011).

Bakhtin's perspective on Carnival has had great influence partly because of its simplicity in that it emphasizes the reversal of normal life and displays affective, emotional, and expressive forms of behavior which are easily observable in Carnival. It also prioritizes the fleshly body as its primary instrument. Of major importance is his theory that promotes change because he views Carnival's reversal of the dominant structures of society as a form of resistance; the carnivelesque represents a separate reality and contains the possibility of liberation from an overly structured hierarchy (Mason 1998).

Bakhtin's account of Carnival is criticized by many. For example, anthropologist Max Gluckman (1963) is known for his theory of rituals of rebellion which are brief transitory events against a dominant societal structure, are temporary in nature, and act as a release for the tensions created by rigid hierarchical structures. However, these alone are not transformative in nature. For Gluckman (1963) and his followers, such as Victor Turner (1969), who developed the concept of liminality and liminal spaces, rituals or temporary events do not necessarily lead to social change. Such theorists understand Carnival merely as a safety valve that allows people to harmlessly express their pent-up feelings and emotions without seriously attempting to upset the social order (Robinson 2011).

Bakhtin's approach to Carnival is also criticized by Eco (1983) who rejects the idea of Carnival as liberation. For Eco, in order for one to enjoy Carnival, rules and rituals must be parodied and already be recognized and respected as without a valid law to break, Carnival is impossible. Eco goes on to further state that "humor" is a form of social criticism, but Carnival is not. Eagleton (1981) argues that Carnival is a licensed affair, a permissible rupture in hegemony and ineffectual as a revolutionary work of art.

More recently, critics contend Bakhtin's interpretation of Carnival may not be pertinent to such celebrations today. Schechner (2006) notes that as Trinidad Carnival continues to develop in the twenty-first century, its cultural complexity multiplies. Trinidad Carnival has become both a centripetal hub and a centrifugal force for Carnival, musical, and masking styles that flow inward to the islands of Trinidad and Tobago and radiate outward from them to the world at large. This kind of complexity confounds Bakhtinian theory. Trinidad Carnival both critiques official culture and supports it. It is an event both "of the people" and "of the nation" (Schechner 2006, 27). Others question the validity of Bakhtin's theories because of the organized nature of Trinidad Carnival events. One such theorist is Eagleton (1981), who believes that Carnivals are often organized by the government of a country and are so vivaciously celebrated that the necessary political criticism is not correct. Eagleton's point is that the powerful still determine the structure and order of Carnival events.

Another perspective studies Carnival by examining the context of the social and political environment in which they occur (Liverpool 2001; Van Koningsbruggen 1997). Still others examine Carnival through the lens of gender, race, and social class (Alonso 1990). The most illuminating analysis of the festival takes place through the perspective of social transformations that affect the Carnival identity, the practice and meaning, and the social location of key actors involved in the cultural debates (Brereton 1975; Trotman 2005; Noel 2009). A common approach to the analysis of Trinidad Carnival examines the controversies over the nature of Trinidad's cultural heritage that arises during the Carnival season (Cohen 1993; Green 2002; Burman 2001). In these studies, Carnival is an important platform in which cultural conflicts are expressed.

Whilst theoretical approaches to Carnival differ they are not necessarily in contradiction. All suggest the ambivalent nature of Carnival in that it may both subvert and reinforce existing boundaries, hierarchies, and moralities. In addition, all agree that Carnival may contribute to social unity.

Themes and Discussion

Several themes emerge in these chapters on the changing role of women in Trinidad and diaspora Carnivals today.

One of the most interesting developments in the recent study of women in Trinidad Carnival and its derivatives are the two competing ideologies of what the surge in scantily clad bikinis-and-beads women signifies. One the one hand, there is the often-repeated complaint that traditional Carnival has been superseded by these women who do not play *mas'* but merely play to have a good time and to pleasure themselves rather than recreating a theme or telling a story. They see no value in this presentation and bemoan the good old days when fully fashioned, often complete replicas of historical figures were the dominant *mas'* being played by women and men alike. They lament the passing of the real Carnival, which featured real costumes signifying fantasy, history, and the imagination of the band leader. Some critical observers believe that the increasing fetishization of the female body within Carnival has halted social progress within the movement. In their view, images of Carnival increasingly concentrate on bikinis, bosoms, and bling and women in *mas'* are represented as accommodating themselves to stereotypes of male desire (Hosein 2017).

In some instances, the criticism also includes a condemnation of the women who display sexualized erotic bodies that actually objectify women and lead to a reinforcement of their misogynistic treatment by men. Jeff Henry (2008) has described the contemporary Carnival as "superficial and empty of direction." Henry further laments the replacement of the masquerade by the artificiality of Carnival. Dwaine Plaza, one of the editors of this volume supports this view of pretty *mas'*. He writes in a later chapter that

> the constant overrepresentation of the female Carnival body on the band web sites and throughout the popular press media, often excessively sexualized, has many implications. Not only does this practice support patriarchy, and the objectification and misogynistic treatment of women, but it also persuasively affirms the Caribbean as a sexualized paradise where certain exotic Caribbean women are available and willing to denigrate themselves in order to be noticed and celebrated.

There is, however, a counter theory to this perspective, one contending that women are "revaluing their formerly owned and colonised bodies." Perkins, for example, maintains that Caribbean women have "subverted and continue to subvert" negative interpretations of the female body, in particular those found in the Christian traditions of Lent, which, she argues, "devalue the physical being and often times view it as a site of sinfulness and temptation" (2011, 368). Furthermore, she maintains that criticism of bikini-and-beads *mas'* or skin *mas'* should be seen as a knee-jerk reaction by men to female empowerment—a reaction to a growing sense of panic as women are taking over *mas'*, setting the pace, and no longer being content to remain in the shadows playing adjunct to men. Henry (1995) also believes that the masquerade of sequins and bikinis is in fact a progressive one—one which celebrates the female body in public through bodily transgressions, and assaults conservative notions of a woman's "proper place."

During the period of formal slavery, the black female body was the site of violence, ownership, and reproduction. Today, daughters, mothers, and grandmothers dancing wildly on the streets in revealing clothing are making a direct challenge to the construction of the black female body as property, as a symbol of Christian virtue, or as child-bearer and mother (Farrar and Zobel 2017). Through their transgressive acts, they are reclaiming agency over their own bodies. As Gabrielle Hosein (2017) has argued, the bikini-and-beads masquerade:

> Should not be seen as undermining or counter to feminist political activism. Rather, Carnival is the largest movement of women in Trinidad and Tobago seeking autonomy and self-determination around their sexuality and their bodies, in opposition to a particular kind of respectability politics . . . purely for the joy and pleasure they experience.

Samantha Noel (2009) supports this theory that women masqueraders use their bodies as a vehicle to have agency over patriarchal structures in society. She notes that "women's bodies, their presentation, and their acknowledgment of the body's potential for non-verbal articulation impacted the evolution of performance practices and the costume aesthetic in Trinidad Carnival" (1119). She goes on to say that "what has dramatically changed in the way in which women play 'mas' in the modern Carnival is that they are using and displaying their bodies to convey a message about women's new roles in modernizing societies" (125). Their increased economic power allows them more freedom to express themselves by emphasizing their bodies as a performance tableau. Indeed, women *mas'* players interviewed by Plaza (2017) in Toronto's Caribana say, "playing myself gives me confidence, it feels good about yourself, gives you an internal boost." Another said, "it's beautiful, women of color celebrating . . . you can even see bigger women, but they kill that costume!"

This changing role of women in Carnival represents an urgent need of women to "manipulate the body as an aesthetic medium and site of subversion"

(Noel 2009, 202). Belinda Edmondson (2009) uses the term "performance" to describe women's popular culture rituals and behaviors in the public sphere. In that, "performance suggests a physical gesture made with a physical body for a passive viewing audience" (55). "Performance" implies agency, an act meant to do particular kinds of work or make particular kinds of statements.

In a similar vein, Cooper (1996), analyzing the dancehall culture of Jamaica, notes that in dancehall, "affirmation of the pleasures of the body, which is often misunderstood as a devaluation of female sexuality, also can be theorized as an act of self-conscious female assertion of control over the representation of her person" (p. 24).

The emergence of bikini-and-beads costuming, and its revealing wining of the body therefore seem to suggest more than a new costume style, or a move away from heavily thematic Carnival portrayals of the past. It demonstrates the new power of women who can now afford costumes, however briefly, and in so doing demonstrate their agency and power by performing with their bodies. It also reveals a dramatic change of venue for viewing women. Traditionally, the domestic arena and its space is the domain of women, whereas it has long been held that public space and the performances within that space is the domain of men (Rezeanu 2015).

The move away from thematic *mas'* bands—where themes were played out by men and some women wearing heavy-cloth costumes usually adorned with jewels, sequins, and other materials—to very large bands mainly made up of bikini-and-bead-wearing women launched a new era. Instead of displaying elaborate costumes, women, and especially young women, chose to display their skin while making the erotic dance movements referred to as wining. These women play themselves rather than a pre-designed role. In so doing, they expose their bodies to performance.

Political resistance is a dominant part of the nineteenth-century development of Carnival expressed primarily in opposition to colonial power and the dominance of the remaining white planter class. By 1834, carnival took on the characteristics of a celebration of deliverance rather than a European-inspired nature festival. Former slaves resisted the shackles of bondage by marching down the road together in some type of costume that symbolized oppression. Their costumes were used to express their social grievances (Liverpool 2001) or to mock the position of the dominant European colonist.

By the 1870s, the so-called Jamette Carnival, especially its women, can be understood as symbols of rebellion and resistance especially to the dominance of men. The Jamettes used their agency to intentionally violate the conservative rules of etiquette in everyday life, and, during Carnival, they prompted a re-evaluation in Trinidadian society of the ways in which women appeared and behaved in public, thereby challenging control of their bodies by colonialism (Noel 2009).

Today, we examine how Carnival has changed for women while accounting for the powerful theme of resistance that is not expressed in political terms. Today, the bikini-and-beads or pretty *mas'* proclaims women's resistance to their personal status and against the constrained role that women have had to play vis-a-vis the patriarchal and religious dominance of men in Caribbean societies.

Philip Scher, who is featured in this collection, highlights the dominance of women in the cannes brulees protests. The cannes brulees became part of Carnival after abolition and remained as a symbolic gesture of resistance. It is significant that these riots or protests which became part of the Carnival in earlier times has re-emerged as part of the modern Carnival. Traditional female figures of the ole *mas'* such as Baby Doll and Dame Lorraine are highlighted by Henry and Henry in this book. They note that Baby Doll's appearance as a Carnival character symbolizes her oppressed status as an unwed mother who has been taken advantage of by men. The Carnival depiction is an act of resistance against the men who father children but do not assume responsibility for them.

In 2015, Destra Garcia joined the ongoing resistance movement through the song she sang entitled "Lucy." In the lyrics, Destra chides women to emancipate themselves from the "slut shaming" with her double entendre lyrics. Destra plays with the word "loose" as something she has agency over and she does not care about the indecent label that has troubled Caribbean women since the period of emancipation when European gender "ideals" became the coded standards. Destra's lyrics are not a unique call to gender emancipation in Trinidadian culture; they fall in line with a new generation of female soca artists that include Fay Ann Lyons-Alvarez, Alison Hinds, Patrice Roberts, Drupatee, and Nadia Batson. These fifth-wave feminists have been influenced by earlier feminist calypso artists who pushed the boundaries of "morality" policing. These pioneer, trailblazing women include Calypso Rose, Denise Plummer, and Singing Sandra (Noel 2009). The evolution of women's participation in Trinidad Carnival and its cultural industry has precluded the role and participation of Caribbean women in diaspora Carnivals in spaces like Toronto, New York, and Miami.

The third theme highlights the changing nature of Carnival within a modernizing materialistic culture in which corporate and governmental support, tourism, and its monetary value to the economy play dominant roles. Chapters by Plaza and DeCosmo note the importance of the impact of materialism on the modern Carnival. A number of chapters in this book deal with the way in which women's costuming and behavior has changed over the years. More specifically, these modern young scholars, many of them of Caribbean background, are attempting to explain the seemingly vulgar and open display of the female body. The current vogue of the feathers-and-beads, small bikini-type costuming can also be interpreted in economic terms. Some chapters discuss in detail the commoditization of Carnival in which sex is used to enhance tourism, providing striking visual images for magazines and websites. Several put the emphasis on the unveiling of the female body and the hip rolling sexual movements called "winin" or sometimes just "it" (as in "use your it"). What most of these chapters have in common, however, is the emphasis on the scantily clad female body and its movements and gyrations.

Another aspect of the modernity of the costumes is the way in which they are mass-produced by outsourcing the labor to China due to the economies of scale needed to make them. Many of the bikini, beads, and feather costumes are bought from an online catalogue and ordered directly from a factory in China. The latest trend tends to naturalize the stratification of the masqueraders who now pay various ranges of money for their costumes that include "Front Liners" and "Back Liners." This stratification is linked to skin color, social class, and race. The front-line costumes are interesting in that they are showgirl look-alike. The costume for the showgirl tends to be similar to the lingerie of Victoria's Secret. This is a fantasy lingerie-type costume.

In bands today, the women often express themselves through winin it and by displaying their bodies as a form of both female empowerment and resistance. Although the beads-and-bikini *mas'* do not make traditional political or historical statements, their importance lies in the rise of women in the society of Trinidad and Tobago. Today, more women earn significant incomes as a result of their increased access to education, resulting in higher paying jobs that will make many financially independent of men. Playing *mas'*, then, celebrates their enhanced social status but also affirms their beauty and sexuality. The women of today are thus empowered by their place in the managerial workforce as well as their femininity, beauty, and sexuality. This form of *mas'* provides a way of resisting the moral controls that society and especially its restrictions placed on women. The playing of bikini-and-beads *mas'* also signifies a powerful feminist movement, which is given a fun-loving cultural expression in this *mas'*. The emphasis in many of the chapters of this book examining the changing roles of women in Carnival can be read as a cultural studies reader in resistance and empowerment.

Outline of Chapters

Chapter 1—Dwaine Plaza and Jan DeCosmo: Women and the De-Africanization
of Trinidad Carnival: From the Jamette to Bikini, Beads, and Feathers

Based on participant observation over a period of nearly a quarter of a century, Plaza and DeCosmo maintain that Carnival is not an unlicensed orgy of overindulgence. Instead, it is a ritualized celebration of renewal that, for a limited period, provides space in the center for those typically on the margins of society. The broad participation typical of Carnival has the potential to break down barriers of race, class, gender, religion, ethnicity, age, and sexual orientation at least temporarily. Oppositions or dualities, such as male/female, white/black, young/old, rich/poor, and sacred/profane, can momentarily be suspended. However, by fostering a new consciousness, a new sense of identity, and a new sense of unity, the activities of Carnival contain possibilities for personal and social transformation. The vast majority of masqueraders dancing through the streets of Port of Spain on Carnival Tuesday in recent years are women. The cultural roots of their confident display of public abandon are to be found in the history of Trinidad. After examining the transgressions of gender, class, and race in its history, a feminist analysis of Carnival will be compared to that derived from an African-centered perspective.

Chapter 2—Frances Henry and Jeff Henry: Stories of
Resistance and Oppression: Baby Doll and Dame Lorraine

During the nineteenth and early twentieth centuries, two "ole *mas*" female characters played important roles in the Carnival festivities. These characters, now called "traditional," have largely disappeared from Carnival Tuesday, but still play prominent roles in J'ouvert. Traditional characters each have their own specific form and structure and the costume they wear and implements they carry have a particular purpose. Each character has its own manner of speech, physical portrayal, and demeanor. The costume design, music, and rhythms played are specific to each character and dictate the shape of the movements or dance steps, which allow the character to distinguish itself in form and intent. A storyline is attached to each performance and portrayal. Of particular relevance to this book are two rather prominent characters who are women: first, "Dame Lorraine," whose origin can be traced to the earlier French masques, and more recently, "Baby Doll," who probably originated toward the end of the nineteenth century. This chapter raises the question of who these characters were, where they came from, and more importantly what symbolic meanings are attached to them.

Chapter 3—Philip W. Scher: Jamette!: Women and Canboulay in 1881

This chapter provides a richly detailed description of the Jamette's character, environment, and artistic expressions. Scher aims to contextualize the Canboulay riots of 1881 in Trinidad, as well as to highlight the role that women played not just in the action itself but their relationship to the early form of Carnival often referred to as the Jamette Carnival. This chapter highlights the centrality of women masqueraders, especially Jamettes, in these events. Instead of characterizing these "riots," the aim in this chapter is to focus on the context of the times and suggest that rather than riots, we may be able to re-characterize and reframe the disturbances as protests led by women.

Chapter 4—Samantha Noel: Taking the Queen to the Streets: The Jaycees Carnival Queen and the Pretty *Mas'* Aesthetic

The Jaycees Carnival Queen competition ritualized the celebration and idealization of women of European and mixed descent in the realm of Carnival. Noel's chapter provides a critical and important account of how the Jaycees Competition was conceived as a way of reinforcing the white standards of European femininity. During colonialism and the first decades of independence, the competition influenced how gender and class were presented in Carnival and in society. The first beauty pageant of its kind in Trinidad and Tobago, the show was part of a greater tradition of beauty pageants in the colonial English-speaking Caribbean. Colonial female subjects were expected to adhere to the models of beauty and femininity celebrated in the Jaycees Carnival Queen competition. The Jaycees Carnival Queen became a symbol of nationalism, representing the perfect beauty of the island nation and this "beauty queen" ideal still heavily influences contemporary women masqueraders. This chapter examines how the upper and middle classes, in upholding the Jaycees Carnival Queen in opposition to the black working-class aesthetic, began a national tradition promoting a Eurocentric archetype of the ideal woman. Jaycees Carnival Queen represented the antithesis of the working-class culture from which the Jamettes and the musical form calypso emerged. This new focus on physicality in costume design coincided with the masquerader's awareness of her body and its potential for creative expression.

Chapter 5— Adanna Kai Jones: Practicing Jametteness:
The Transmission of "Bad Behavior" as a Strategy of Survival

Caribbean bodies are sexually marked and recognized by their renowned abilities to roll their "its"—a skill informally learned at a very young age. This movement includes, at the very least, dexterous and vigorous rolls, gyrations, thrusts, and shakes of the hip, pelvis, and buttocks. It is colloquially known as winin' (or the wine) in Trinidad, Guyana, and Jamaica, and wukkin'-up in Barbados. The rolling "it" is sometimes recognized as a dance in and of itself (e.g., the dutty wine, from the dancehalls of Jamaica, or the bicycle wine, created and promoted by Trinidadian soca artist Denise "Saucy WOW" Belfon); or it can be a movement within a larger dance complex (e.g., the rumbas of Cuba). It is clear that rolling one's "it" not only plays a critical role in upholding the evolving iterations of Caribbean identities, but it also helps many Caribbean men and women ascertain an overall sense of self, especially in relation to other bodies who do or do not roll their "its." A winer's very identity is written into their wine, so much so that how they roll their "its" can be used as a gauge for deciphering where that person is from or not from, who they are, and what their intentions might be.

Chapter 6—Asha St. Bernard: "Thirty Gyal to One Man":
Women's Prolific Presence in the Trinidad Carnival

In this chapter, St. Bernard points to the level of dominance and consent that has taken over the Carnival celebrations and which perpetuate inequality in representation. This is particularly evident in the ways in which marketers privilege some racial and ethnic groups over others, especially on the basis of skin complexion and other physical attributes such as hair. This has become a prominent issue particularly with high levels of competitiveness among Carnival businesses, whose organizers in turn rely on cultural prejudices to stand out in the competition by highlighting valued notions of European beauty standards to endorse their brand. Despite these blatant practices, businesses manage to thrive and continue to attract growing numbers of participants each year.

Chapter 7— Darrell Gerohn Baksh: From Devi to Diva:
Indo-Caribbean Women Rising in Chutney

In this chapter, Baksh turns our attention to the East Indian population in Trinidad and especially women who explore their conflicts and complexities in how their Indo-Caribbean femininity has been defined. At a moment when the Indo-Caribbean woman is breaking away from embodiments of devi, traditional models of female representation are strongly tied to religious patriarchy, to diva, a contemporary persona publicly expressed in the realm of chutney soca, a popular form of Indo-Caribbean music that has absorbed the Carnival aesthetic in Trinidad. Increasingly, Indo-Caribbean women were exposed to multiple historical influences and templates of female performance in the public spaces of Trinidad Carnival derived from several Afro-Caribbean archetypes: nineteenth-century Jamettes, twentieth-century calypsonians, and twenty-first-century "soca divas." The impact of South Asian culture—specifically, female folk performance in private Indo-Caribbean spaces and the Hindi cinema "item girl"—is discussed. This analysis suggests that such agency is a transgressive act that breaks traditionally held ideologies ascribed to the societal roles and behaviors of Indo-Caribbean women.

Chapter 8—Dwaine Plaza: Caribana in Toronto:
From Male Dominance to Female Agency

While women's participation in the Trinidad Carnival has vastly increased in the last years, as is demonstrated in several chapters of this book, similar changes have also taken place in diaspora Carnivals in Toronto, New York, Miami, and Notting Hill. This chapter focuses on one such Carnival, known as "Caribana," which first began in 1967. At that time, it was a showcase of Trinidadian Carnival music, culture, and art, including costume design and playing steel pan music. The evolution of the Caribana Festival in Toronto parallels the changing social, economic, and cultural role of women in the Trinidad Carnival, where bands are increasingly devoid of men as masqueraders, section leaders, or designers. The purpose of this chapter is to examine the current state of Caribbean women's participation in the Caribana Festival in Toronto. Caribbean-origin women in general have, over time, developed transnational identities that are a logical extension of their roles as modern, assertive feminist subjects who are employed full-time, juggle familial responsibilities, and are also actively participating in the Caribana cultural festival each year by helping to make *mas'*, dancing on the Lakeshore Boulevard, and provocatively expressing their agency and independence.

Notes

1. Our thanks go to all the contributors included in this volume. Our thanks also to Jan DeCosmo, whose idea of a Women in Carnival panel at the Caribbean Studies Association conference in 2014 served as the impetus for this collection. These chapters could not have been written without the help of the many persons, *mas'* makers, designers, and players who contributed their experiences, thoughts, and ideas to our researchers about their involvement in creating a Carnival.

Bibliography

Alonso, A. "Men in Rags and the Devil on the Throne: A Study of Protest and Interventions in Carnival of Post Emancipation Trinidad in Plantation Society in the Americas." In Thomas Fiehrer et. al., *Carnival in Perspective*, 1990.

Bakhtin, Mikhail. *Rabelais and His World*. Transl. Helene Iswolsky. Bloomington: Indiana University Press, 1984.

Barnes, Natasha. "Body Talk: Notes on Women and Spectacle in Contemporary Trinidad Carnival." *Small Axe* 7 (2000): 93–105.

Brereton, Bridget. "The Trinidad Carnival: 1870–1900." *Savacou* 11/12 (1975): 46–57.

Burman, Jenny. "Masquerading Toronto Through Caribana: Transnational Carnival Meets the Sign "Music Ends Here." *Identity* 1:3 (2001): 273–28.

Cohen, A. *Masquerade Politics: Explorations in the Structure of Urban Cultural Movements*. Abingdon: Oxford University Press, 1993.

Cooper, Carolyn. *Noises in the Blood: Orality, Gender and the "Vulgar" Body of Jamaican Popular Culture*. London: Macmillan Caribbean, 1996.

Eagleton, T. *Walter Benjamin: Towards a Revolutionary Criticism*. London: Verso Press, 1981.

Eco, Umberto. *Carnival!* New York: Mouton Publishers, 1983.

Edmondson, Belinda. *Caribbean Middlebrow Leisure Culture and the Middle Class,* New York: Cornell University Press, 2009.

Farrar, Max, and Emily Zobel. "The Leeds West Indian Carnival is Fifty: Marking its African, Asian and European Heritage." *Leeds African Studies Bulletin* 79 (Winter 2017/18): 125–37.

Franco, Pamela. "The Invention of Traditional Mas and the Politics of Gender." In *Trinidad Carnival: The Cultural Politics of a Transnational Festival*, eds. G. Green and P. Scher, 25–47. Bloomington: Indiana University Press, 2007.

Gilmore, David. *Carnival and Culture: Sex Symbol & Status in Spain*. New Haven and London: Yale University Press, 1998.

Gluckman, Max. *Order and Rebellion in Tribal Africa: Collected Essays with an Autobiographical Introduction*. Abingdon: Oxford University Press, 1963.

Green, Garth. "Marketing the Nation: Carnival and Tourism in Trinidad and Tobago." In John Gledhill and Stephen Nugent." *Critique of Anthropology* 22, no. 3 (2002): 283–304.

Green, Garth, and Phillip Scher. *Trinidad Carnival: The Cultural Politics of a Transnational Festival*. Bloomington: Indiana University Press, 2007.

Groden, Michael, Martin Kreiswirth, and Imre Szeman. *Contemporary Literary and Cultural Theory: The Johns Hopkins Guide*. Baltimore: Johns Hopkins University Press, 2012.

Henry, Frances, and Wilson, Pamela. "The Status of Women in Caribbean Societies: An Overview of their Social and Economic Status." *Social and Economic Studies* 1.24, no. 2 (1995).

Henry, Jeff. *Under the 'Mas': Resistance and Rebellion in the Trinidad Carnival*. Trinidad: Lexicon, 2008.

Hill, Errol. *The Trinidad Carnival; Mandate for a National Theatre*. Austin: University of Texas Press, 1972.

Hosein Gabrielle. "In Trinidad and Tobago, Carnival goes Feminist (Bikinis and Feathers Included)." *Huffington Post*, March 16, 2018. https://www.huffingtonpost.com/entry/in-trinidad-and-tobago-carnival-goes-feminist-bikinis_us_58cacda3e4b0537abd956ec4.

Liverpool, Hollis. *Rituals of Power and Rebellion: The Carnival Tradition in Trinidad and Tobago, 1763–1962*. Trinidad and Tobago: Research Associated School Times; Frontline Distribution, 2001.

Mason, Peter. *Bacchanal!: The Carnival Culture of Trinidad*. London: Latin American Bureau; Philadelphia: Temple University Press, 1998.

Mohammed, Patricia, ed. *Gendered Realities: Essays in Caribbean Feminist Thought*. Kingston, Jamaica: University of the West Indies Press; Mona, Jamaica: Center for Gender and Development Studies, 2002.

Noel, Samantha. "Carnival is Woman!: Gender, Performance and Visual Culture in Contemporary Trinidad Carnival." Unpublished dissertation, Department of Art, Art History and Visual Studies, Duke University, 2009.

Perkins Kasifi, Ana. "Carne Vale (Goodbye to Flesh?): Caribbean Carnival, Notions (Goodbye to Flesh?): Caribbean Carnival, Notions of the Flesh and Christian Ambivalence about the Body." *Sexuality and Culture* (2011): 373–84.

Reddock, Rhonda. "Transcription of Discussion in Caribbean Dialogue: Special Issue on Calypso." In Ryan Selwin, ed. St. Augustine, Trinidad: ISER, UWI, 1997.

Rezeanu, Cătălina-Ionela. "The Relationship between Domestic Space and Gender Identity: Some Signs of Emergence of Alternative Domestic Femininity and Masculinity." *Journal of Comparative Research in Anthropology and Sociology* 6, no. 2 (Winter 2015).

Robinson, Anthony. "In Theory Bakhtin: Carnival against Capital, Carnival against Power." *Ceasefire*. https://ceasefiremagazine.co.uk/in-theory-bakhtin-2/,2011.

Scher, Philip. *Carnival and the Formation of a Caribbean Transnation*. Gainesville: University Press of Florida, 2003.

Schechner, Richard. *Performance Studies: An Introduction*. London: Routledge, 2006.

Trotman, David. "Transforming Caribbean and Canadian Identity." *Atlantic Studies* 2, no. 2 (2005): 177–98.

Turner, V. *The Ritual Process: Structure and Anti-Structure*. London: Routledge, 1969.

Van Koningsbruggn, P. *Trinidad Carnival*. London: MacMillan, 1997.

Chapter 1

Women and the De-Africanization of Trinidad Carnival: From the Jamette to Bikini, Beads, and Feathers

—Dwaine Plaza and Jan DeCosmo

In 2010, Bunji Garlin sang a calypso entitled "De African." This song followed a long line of twentieth-century calypsonians who regularly paid homage to Africa's struggles for independence and the positive African influence on the culture of Trinidad.[1] This Afrocentric position was in direct opposition to the many centuries during which the white slave masters made concerted efforts to destroy every aspect of African cultural, social, and religious traditions. These were intentionally replaced by a Eurocentric value system. The legacy of this hegemonic value system continues to affect Caribbean people's hearts and minds. There still remains a deep-seated psychological desire for things European while at the same time seeing things African as inferior, heathen, backward, and evil.[2] In spite of these deeply embedded psychological values, many aspects of African culture survive and continue to influence the contemporary dance, music, food, religion, language, living arrangements, and family structures in Trinidad and Tobago.[3]

The purpose of this chapter is to examine the evolution of Carnival traditions in Trinidad and Tobago as they relate to the historical context in which Carnival evolved from European traditions with distinct African customs as part of its DNA. The chapter seeks to examine the evolving African content in the annual Carnival celebrations from the 1950s to the present. We provide evidence to show that current trends across most Carnival bands in Trinidad and the diaspora have been moving away from epic theatrical productions with deep cultural meaning to themes and costumes that are superficial, homogenous, and intimately interwoven with the sexual objectification of

female masqueraders. These trends are most apparent in the de-Africanization of *mas'* bands.

Carnival in Nineteenth-Century Trinidad

European Carnival celebrations came to Trinidad in the eighteenth century
with the French, who were invited by the Spanish, by then the governors of
Trinidad. The French planters in Trinidad in the late eighteenth century began
their Carnival festivities at Christmas and ended them on Ash Wednesday.
Balls, concerts, dinners, hunts, and other festive events were held in the coun-
tryside. Of course, these French settlers brought with them their cultural bag-
gage. As the French Creoles set up great houses and businesses in Trinidad,
they held elaborate pre-Lenten masked balls. These elaborate balls continued
even though the island changed ownership by force from Spain to Britain in
1797. The pre-emancipation Carnival saw whites costume themselves as Negues Jadin (Negres Jardin—Garden Negroes-French) and mulatresses.[4] They
also reenacted the cannes brulées (burning canes), which were best described
as the practice of rounding up slaves to put out fires in the cane field (Green
and Scher 2007). The masquerade balls were witnessed with great amusement
by the enslaved Africans, who began to have private celebrations of their own
incorporating their own sacred traditions, particularly masking and funerary
rituals. They also used these occasions to mock and lampoon the lascivious
conduct of the masters and their wives. The slave celebrations also included
stick fighting (a ritual of dance-like movement also known as the *kalinda*),
dancing, singing, and drumming. They also performed little shows or plays,
organizing themselves into regiments led by individuals wearing costumes
representing king and queen (Green and Scher 2007).

The conditions of slavery forced Africans of different ethnic groups to
come together to construct a cultural identity that was distinct from that of
the white planter class. Unable to perform the masquerades of their home-
lands, Africans turned to participation in European-based celebrations in
which their Creolized masquerades' primary concerns were self-representation and symbolic repositioning.[5] The result has been a unique style of masquerade, one that departs from the canonical configuration of secrecy, total
transformation, obligatory masking, and men as the preeminent performers
(Franco 2000).

Even when the British took over Trinidad and set up their own colonial
rule in 1802, the French Carnival tradition continued. The governor gave
masked balls, and members of the upper classes would drive their carriages

through Port of Spain going from house to house in masked disguises. Free persons of color could wear masks, but they were not allowed to join the festivities alongside the privileged (Franco 2000).

As Mervyn Alleyne (1988, 83) has argued, religion and rebellion were closely linked in the Caribbean. Well aware of the connection, colonial slave masters in Trinidad, as elsewhere, repeatedly attempted to outlaw the most important instrument in African ritual, the drum. Without drums, the command by spirits or deities to overthrow colonial masters could not be heard. However, enslaved Africans continued to make music using anything readily at hand, including biscuit tins, bottles, and sticks. In fact, the tambour-bamboo bands, in which members strike differing lengths of bamboo on the ground to make a percussive sound, originated as a result of banning the drum and can still be found in Carnival today.

After emancipation in the early 1830s, participation in Carnival by Trinidadians of African descent increased dramatically, and African retentions in music, dance, costume, and ritual became even more predominant. At that point, Carnival took on the characteristics of a celebration of deliverance rather than a European-inspired annual nature festival. Former slaves, who numbered in the tens of thousands, celebrated their newfound freedom by marching down the road together, along with those already free. As the years passed, Chinese and South Asian Indian immigrants began to arrive and slowly join the festivities. At the same time, the French Creole elite began to describe Carnival using such phrases as "wretched buffoonery," "an orgy indulged in by the dissolute," "annual abomination," "wild excess," and "diabolical festival," and subsequently attempted to have it banned (Green and Scher 2007).

One English visitor to Carnival in 1847 reported that "nearly naked" Negroes daubed in black varnish joined forces in groups of ten to twenty, some wearing chains around their feet to symbolize slavery. As one observer wrote, others masqueraded as whites: "Every negro, male and female, wore a white flesh colored mask, their woolly hair carefully concealed by handkerchiefs . . ." (Lee 1990, 25). Other groups paraded as the king and queen of England, the angel Gabriel, pirates, Turks, the strange and exotic Highlander, Indians of South America, and the personification of Death (a white skeleton painted onto a black covering). "I noticed that whenever a black mask appeared it was sure to be a white man," wrote the visitor (Lee 1990, 26). All the while, bands played what was described as "execrable music," making a "tremendous uproar" (Lee 1990, 25). During both of these phases of Carnival, both before and after emancipation, switches in racial and ethnic identity were common.

From the moment the newly emancipated Africans began to openly participate in the Carnival, the newspaper editorials became hostile, critical of the inclusion of anything African. That would include African dances and masking. What follows is a letter written in 1838 by "A Scotchman" [*sic*] in the *Port of Spain Gazette* that gives an indication of the feelings of some of the whites at that time for all things African:

> We will not dwell on the disgusting and indecent scenes that were enacted in our streets—we will not say how many we saw in a state so nearly approaching nudity, as to outrage decency and shock modesty—we will not describe the AFRICAN custom [emphasis mine] of carrying a stuffed figure of a woman on a pole, which was followed by hundreds of negroes yelling out a savage Guinea song [we regret to say nine-tenths of these people were Creoles]. . . . But we will say at once that the custom of keeping Carnival, by allowing the lower order of society to run about the Streets in wretched masquerade, belongs to other days and ought to be abolished in our own.

The white plantocracy in Trinidad deeply resented and resisted any measure that appeared to favor blacks. They made their powerful influence felt in every sphere of Trinidadian society. Harsh vagrancy laws were implemented that punished Africans and later South Asian Indians who were not attached to any plantation. During the Carnival period, those in power repeatedly called for the imposition of martial law. The Trinidadian plantocracy's paranoia was fueled by the fact that the African population still retained a strong African consciousness. In spite of the slavery, in spite of the "seasoning" processes, and especially in spite of the religious and secular education imposed upon them, many Africans still identified themselves with things African. They even went so far as to create African-centered support groups, secret societies, and so on (Green and Scher 2007).

The English traveler Charles Day was one of the first to document women's masquerade in Trinidad. In his 1847 eyewitness account of the "Negro Carnival Day," he described a band of "little girls dressed *a la jupe*" (1852, 316). The Martinican dress, as this costume was popularly called in Trinidad, comprised of two distinct styles: the *a la jupe* or *chemisette et jupe* and the *douillette* or *la grande robe* (Riggio 2004, 33). The Martinican dress was one of "high affect," juxtaposing highly contrasting colors and designs. Traveler Lafcadio Hearn (1923 [1890]) noted that, by the late nineteenth century, Afro-Creole Martinican women had devised an elaborate program of color coordination in their costumes. Based on the complementarity of the cloth and darker skin tones, the costumes created a radiant effect. For example, a *capresse*, or a very fair

Afro-Creole woman, reportedly looked her best in a yellow robe accented with a blue scarf. The darker *negresse* looked her best in either white or "any violent color," like red (Hearn, 329). According to Lafcadio Hearn, the visual effect was further intensified by the brilliance produced by the brooch-bedecked calendered turban and the masses of jewelry worn around the neck and arms.

Most likely, this French Creole dress was introduced into Trinidad Carnival by Afro-Creole Martinican women in the late eighteenth century, via the drum dances, performances in which the drum is the primary musical accompaniment. John Cowley explains that drum dances in the French Caribbean islands were frequently organized by "black dancing societies" (1996). Trinidadian historian Pierre-Gustave-Louis Borde notes that, by 1797, the Afro-Creoles' dance repertoire included French Creole dances like "the *calinda*, the *jhouba*, and the *bel air*" (1982 [1883], 313). In the nineteenth century, these dance performances were held throughout the year to mark such events as funerals or wakes and saints' days. They were also a popular form of entertainment. Elaborate drum dances, sometimes referred to as "dignity balls" or bouquets (n3), were popular Carnival events and often featured a king and queen.

After emancipation more women began to participate in Carnival, primarily as yard "chantwells" or lead singers (the forerunners of calypsonians). In between the stick fighting contests held by men in the yards, women sang "carisos" or Carnival songs, continuing the African practice (with added French and Spanish elements) of using praise and derision to describe their contenders. The women also danced to the songs in what some observers described as an "obscene, lewd, and erotic" manner. Apparently, carisos were sung exclusively by women. While the male stick fighters did not become chantwells, some of the women chantwells did become stick fighters, especially during the next phase of Carnival.

This next phase, from 1860 to the early 1880s, is known as Jamette Carnival. "Jamette" was a term which referred to the "other half" or "the underworld." By this time, the economically deprived subculture had taken over Carnival. Trinidadian Jamettes had continued developing their skills in stick fighting, their sharpness of wit in conversation and song (bragging especially about their sexual accomplishments), their talent in dance and music, and their indifference to colonial law and authority. As expected, the authorities set out to curb these excesses. This was especially the case with the "pissenlit," a direct translation from French which meant "bed-wetters" or "stinker" bands, which entailed an interesting gender reversal. These bands were made up of men dressed in women's transparent nightgowns carrying what appeared to be menstrual cloths stained with blood and singing obscene songs.

During this phase of Carnival, women chantwells not only sang fighting songs to encourage male stick fighters as they prepared to do battle, but even joined gangs themselves. Many were labeled prostitutes—whether they were in fact or not—and were arrested for indecent behavior, disorderly conduct, and for using obscene and profane language. According to Anna S. Gottreich (1993, 11), "calypsos survive which refer to these female underground characters, well-known for their brawling, drinking, and especially singing and dancing." She described one group of women called the "Mourcelines" who in 1864 fought against another group, the "Don't Care a Damns." She wrote that "both groups were armed with stones, knives, and razors. They fought each other, 'with their frocks tucked up' in a battle which led to the arrest of twenty women, 'being unlawfully assembled and arrayed in a warlike manner'" (Payne 1990, 13). Many of these women took on men, as well. But these groups of women did not exist for the sole purpose of engaging in violent activities. As Gottreich (1993, 11) claimed, they functioned as sororities that "served as friendship and support networks in the often difficult and alienating urban environment of the time."

Gendered Twentieth-Century Carnival Trends

The early twentieth century saw women's participation in Carnival as a highly regulated event. Concurrently, regulatory groups like the 1919 Carnival Deputation Committee (CDC) and the 1938 Carnival Improvement Committee (CIC) devised ways to "clean up" the festival—in other words, to remove what they perceived as obscenities and other undesirable aspects of *mas'*. They encouraged costume competitions that were organized by the local merchants. They also offered guidelines for "appropriate" Carnival costumes, the majority of them targeting female masqueraders. For example, in 1919 the CDC supported the government regulation "against the wearing of clothing to disguise the sexes." The CDC had several lists of Carnival costumes they deemed appropriate for women. The list included such characters as Lorraine Peasant, Fish Girl, Goat Girl, Flower Girl, and Charity Girl. Judging from the characters, the CDC apparently endorsed peasants and non-authoritarian disguises as being suitable for women. These lists were not intended simply to prohibit cross-dressing but to ensure that women adhered to the tenets of womanhood as defined by the larger society. Despite the liminal nature of the festival, women were bound to uphold these laws.

Many Afro-Creole women accepted the external trappings associated with the local construction of womanhood, but they were able to present their concerns by using them as an encoded masquerade. The Bajan Cook (Bajan meaning "from Barbados") was one such women's *mas'* costume. By 1911, it was well established and very popular. The masqueraders wore simple white dresses with aprons, in a style similar to nurses' uniforms. They did not wear face masks. A decade later, this costume had evolved into calf-length white dresses with high necklines and long sleeves over ankle-length underskirts, decorated with lace and fancy edging. The layering and decorations of the underskirts reflected a hybrid Martinican costume. Acceptable Martinican costumes consisted of a headscarf, cotton skirt, and an embroidered madras blouse.

During the First and Second World Wars, numerous Jamettes in Port of Spain continued to participate through their involvement with the steel bands and sailor *mas'* costumed bands. The presence of the many American soldiers who resided at naval bases only accelerated the challenges to traditional moral codes already pursued by the Jamettes and badjohns (Reddock 1994). Furthermore, the American soldiers' validation of the calypso art form matched their attraction to the Jamettes. The fact that some middle-class women also had liaisons with the American soldiers may have had some impact on their desire to participate.

After World War II, the genre of historical *mas'* encompassed European, biblical, and mythological narratives. In this genre, "looking good" privileged a European dress aesthetic. Its hallmarks were tailored costumes using yards of rich materials such as satins and velvets—hence historical masquerades are often known as "cloth *mas'*"—and accuracy of character portrayal.

In the historical *mas'* bands, men usually disguised themselves as kings, princes, high priests, warriors, gladiators, and knights. Women, who composed one-third to one-half of the band, portrayed queens, high priestesses, wives, dancers, and slaves. However, Mrs. Evelyn Houlder, one of the most prolific female band leaders in the 1950s, did not construct her *mas'* band according to character hierarchy. Instead, female members dressed in costumes that were identical in color and style. This can be seen in her 1953 portrayal of Queen Elizabeth and Sir Walter Raleigh. In this band of approximately 125 women and 25 men, the women wore Victorian-style gowns with hoop skirts. A white ruffle framed the face. Gloves, fake pearls, and other jewelry accented the dress. Masqueraders wore wigs coiffed in the style of the period and topped with a crown. A wire-screen mask and fan completed the costume.

In the historical *mas'* bands, Afro-Creole women's "dressing up" also addressed a sociocultural problem: the stereotype of black women as promiscuous. In 1950s-era Trinidad, promiscuity was exemplified by the Jamette woman, whose *mas'* of choice was the male-dominated military band or the Indian (Native American-inspired) band. Her costume featured trousers or, sometimes, a very short skirt, both of which drew attention to her lower extremities, or what Mikhail Bakhtin (1941) terms her "sexualized" body. If long skirts, which hid a woman's lower body and restricted her movements, signified femininity, trousers, which permitted the freest of movements, were unfeminine. Therefore, the Jamette woman's public acknowledgment of her preferences classified her as the antithesis of respectability—an anti-ideal. To counteract this image, some Afro-Creole women opted for participation in the historical *mas'* bands, where they were "less inclined to fear the accusation of sexual promiscuity" (Franco 1998). In addition, their costumes with very full, long skirts concealed or contained all signs of their sexuality.

In the 1950s, the majority of the Carnival participants in Trinidad were black (Franco 2007). Ironically however, the *mas'* band portrayals were overwhelmingly based on non-African and non-Caribbean historical narratives. In 1957, the first Carnival following the Peoples National Movement political party victory, the festival organizers created a new competition category called "The Band of the Year." In 1957, George Bailey won the coveted prize with his band's portrayal of "Back to Africa." It portrayed Africa as the ancestral land for black folks in Trinidad.[6] Prior to 1957, Carnival representations of Africa had frequently been based on a spurious Western and Hollywood perception of the African continent as primitive and uncivilized (Franco 2007). Bailey's depiction of Africa veered away from the stereotypical images of Africa as primitive, savage, and backward to a view of Africa as "elegant and dignified." Bailey achieved this by historicizing the African continent alongside the great European civilizations like Greece and Rome (Franco 2007). Bailey's depiction of both women and men's costumes flaunted this stereotype by drawing on the elaborate pomp usually associated with bands depicting the history of Europe. Bailey's meticulously researched African costumes asked masqueraders to think of a regal heritage rather than savagery. Bailey's 1957 representation of Africa singlehandedly changed the Trinidadian *mas'* culture that up to this time had negatively associated Africa with being primitive compared to Roman or Greek cultures (see images 1 and 2 in the appendices). George Bailey's portrayal of Africa was described by historian Michael Anthony as:

> Bailey's band Back to Africa made a stunning and immediate impact and straightaway changed the then current viewpoint towards African masquerade. People had been accustomed to seeing the fierce looking Zulu, the prancing Watusi, and the crocodile loving Zambesi. They had never seen an elaborate, elegant, dignified, and at the same time wondrously colorful display of African

masquerade, and they had never dreamt that any African masquerade could reach such heights of splendor so as to challenge the classic styles of Greece and Rome. (Franco 2007, 28)

The effect on the lower class was even more potent by the 1960s, since Trinidad Carnival began to embrace the cultural and corporeal practices of the working class. The black masses, whose cultural contributions were "nativized" during the anti-colonialist independence movement, were now seen as symbolizing the "essence" of Trinidadian culture. Since Carnival was no longer required to pay obeisance to the European colonial discursive legacy, it now became a "We ting." It was supposed to reflect this newly constructed indigeneity. Bailey would again launch an African-positive theme in his 1969 portrayal entitled: "Bright Africa." This presentation was produced in response to the "Black Power" movement that began in the United States. Trinidadians like Stokely Carmichael and Jamaicans like Marcus Garvey were instrumental in influencing George Bailey's positive Pan-Africanist approach to organizing his band. "Bright Africa," was Bailey's assertion of both his heritage and his imagination.

In the 1970s, there was a gradual yet consistent modification in gender dynamics as more women masqueraded in the streets during the festival. Fantasy-oriented themes attracted greater numbers of women of various classes and ethnicities to the costumed bands. More and more women started to work outside the home, and the disposable income for some began to rise and thus allowed women to play *mas'*. As the decade unfolded, Carnival was increasingly recognized as a viable economic resource, and more people, both men and women, were attracted to the festival. The increase in the number of masqueraders in costumed bands reflected this. New bands continued to emerge, with women now dominating their *mas'* camps (Barnes 2000). During this period, the two-piece or the bikini became the basis for most costumes. The desire to exhibit oneself in the public domain was an alluring element that attracted more women to masquerade in this costume aesthetic regardless of race, class, or age (Barnes 2000). Bandleader Edmund Hart even noted that he knew of people in his band who "cut up their costumes to make them further scanty." Apart from wanting to show as much of their bodies as possible, there seemed to be what can be perceived as a yearning by women immersed in the various Carnival activities to deploy their corporeality in a sexually suggestive way (Franco 2000).

By the 1980s, there continued to be a great deal of anxiety expressed by the public in newspapers that seemed to echo those of late nineteenth-century Trinidad. There was a tendency in the 1980s for women to wear bikini-based costumes (Franco 2000). The launch of Peter Minshall's presentation for Carnival in 1988 called Jumbie emphasized the fact that his designs for costumes were always over wear and that the masquerader could freely improvise underneath. The night of the band's launching, the focus was taken away from Minshall's aesthetic and, instead, a few of the female masqueraders in his band wore G-strings and other high-cut leotards (Franco 2000). The next morning, a number of newspapers featured on their front pages photographs of these female masqueraders. A letter to the editor from a popular television personality initiated the attack on the band launch. In it she exclaimed:

> Bare bottoms and revealing vaginas have their place (they already desecrate our beaches), but what message are you giving to the young when you show them a horde of non-thinking half-naked people, "wining" and rubbing bouncing derrieres across a Savannah stage and on our streets? (*Trinidad Guardian*, January 20, 1988, 8)

Reflections from the 1988 Carnival in the newspapers included concerns that "women were expressing themselves in dance that is nothing short of scandalous" and recounted how women "in skimpy outfits, which apparently some of them still found to be too cumbersome, gyrated wildly by themselves, with and against one another and occasionally with men." One writer angrily compared women masqueraders to prostitutes charging that "many of our women are lost, beyond redemption, and seemingly content to be branded with the image of sluts and loose-morale individuals" (Franco 2000).

The 1990s was similar to the previous decade in terms of the way in which women's activity during Carnival was policed by the media. During the 1994 celebration, the *Daily Express* of February 16 published a complaint in anticipation of what was soon to occur in Port of Spain. The article protested that the Lenten season would "unfortunately [be] ushered in by an explosion of sensuality, over-indulgence and self-gratification awash in intoxicated pleasures, in the worldwide celebration of Carnival which proceeds it" (*Daily Express*, February 16, 1994).

The vast majority of masqueraders dancing through the streets of Port of Spain in 1994 on Carnival Tuesday were women. The impression was soon to be confirmed by newspaper accounts. One caption under a photograph of masqueraders in the *Express* newspaper of February 15 read: "in or out of costume, [women] dominated" (*Daily Express*, February 15, 1994). What was striking to this writer was that, despite attire that clearly revealed less-than-perfect bodies, none of the women appeared to be in the least self-conscious about their shape, size, age, or race as they danced down the streets of Port of Spain.

The 2000s were dominated by the band leader and *mas'* maker Brian McFarlane.[7] McFarlane, like Peter Minshall before him, was a man of European Caribbean origin. Both men over the years attempted to represent African themes in a positive way in the *mas'* they built. McFarlane attempted to appeal to the broad base of the black middle class in Trinidad. His *mas'* brought a sense of theatrics to the streets and the Trinidadian imagination (Noel 2009). McFarlane found himself not only bringing in new styles and influences, but also catering to the growing audience of women. The numbers of women on the road during Trinidad Carnival in the mid-2000s had resounding consequences in the overall development of the festival and generated new debates about the role of Carnival in the national consciousness, especially as women were perceived to be engaged in inordinately "lewd" behavior in public (Noel 2009).

In 2009, McFarlane produced a band entitled "Africa—Her People, Her Glory, Her Tears." This band was reminiscent of George Bailey's 1957 *mas'* band "Back to Africa," which gave Africa a dignified place. McFarlane's presentation was not about the cheery beads, feathers, and bikinis that had become the norm by the 2000s, but it was instead focused on the somber topic of the Transatlantic slave trade (Noel 2010). McFarlane did a great deal of research in bringing out his band, and the various sections of McFarlane's band reflected the real places, cultures, and countries in Africa. The sections included Cameroon's Elephant Mask Dancers, Zambia's Sachihango Hunters, and Ghana's Shai Womanhood. McFarlane made a great effort to represent all three corners of sub-Sahara Africa, including the most popular cultures and countries, and not just one monolithic stereotypical version of one aspect of the continent (see image 3 in the appendices for an example of McFarlane's representation of Africa).

McFarlane has said that his work is more of an artistic presentation than "senseless bikini and beads mas." This is the type of presentation that he dislikes. McFarlane notes that this "kind of Mas is just senseless, just wine and drink and get up the next morning" (Noel 2010). He further notes that his costumes have the ability to influence behavior, and that his work brings "discipline and consciousness" rather than the typical "wine and jam attitude" displayed on the streets during Carnival in the 2000s.

The De-Africanization of Carnival

In the last section of this chapter, we examine a case study of the practice of cultural appropriation of things African by current Carnival *mas'* band leaders. We use Louis Saldenah's band "Outta Africa," which was presented in the Caribana Festival in Toronto in 2016, as an example of the practice of using African cultural objects or names for commercial purposes but not going much deeper in the presentation of the band. In both the Caribbean diaspora and Trinidad, Carnival has moved away from theatrical meaningful band performances to what Peter Minshall calls "pretty *mas*'" because this is more financially lucrative for band leaders. In pretty *mas*', the costumes have become more akin to showgirl-type displays.[8] These costumes are often referred to as "bikini, feathers, and beads." The disdain some people have for this new and popular type of costuming comes from the belief that the authentic creativity of past costume designers is now replaced by generic mass-produced designs which are only differentiated by color or the number of beads and feathers.

To carry out the analysis, we will be relying on our own experiences with Caribana and Carnival as *mas*' event promoters, annual masqueraders, and individuals who have spent decades working behind the scenes at Caribana and Carnival events in Toronto, Tallahassee, and Trinidad. We will also undertake a visual and textual analysis of the costumes on the Saldenah website.[9] The purpose behind this content analysis is to uncover the encoded messages that masqueraders receive when they view and sign up for their costumes. This type of visual and textual analysis could be carried out on virtually all current Carnival websites in places like New York, Miami, London, Trinidad, or Jamaica.

The Caribana Festival in Toronto began in 1967, when Canada was celebrating its centennial. At that time, the West Indian community was asked by the federal government to make a contribution which would enhance the celebrations of Expo '67. The festival was originally meant to showcase the mosaic of Carnival music, culture, and art, including costume making and steel pan playing throughout the Caribbean region. The reality was that the festival in Toronto was dominated by the Trinidad and Tobago cultural influence (Trotman 2005). The highlight of the Toronto Caribana Festival has been the annual street parade. Participants in the annual Caribana parade are organized into masquerade "bands" (there were ten big bands in the 2016 parade), each of which was accompanied by live music (usually a DJ). Each masquerade band expresses a particular theme (be it historical, satirical, political, or fantasy) and is led by a "king" and "queen" who appear on the most lavish twenty-foot float-like costumes that they pull along the parade route. This organization parallels what happens each year in Trinidad in terms of costume colors, designs, and traditions (Trotman 2005).

The Caribana Festival like the Carnival events in Trinidad has evolved into business ventures that are dominated by an ever smaller number of transnational cultural entrepreneurs. Band leaders, event organizers, party promoters, and the local organizing committees in Trinidad and the diaspora often become involved in the Carnival activities because they stand to make a significant profit. Hence, the festivals in Trinidad and in the diaspora are being packaged mainly for economic gain, unlike earlier days when the Carnival functioned more as a time for political activism in the form of opposing hierarchal order and social norms, through dance and songs. Although the elements have not been entirely lost to entrepreneurial aspirations, they have dwindled away (Ho and Nurse 2005).

Saldenah Mas K Club is an archetype for popular contemporary Carnival bands throughout the diaspora. As an incorporated events company, they provide Carnival social events throughout the year in Toronto (fetes, soca music shows, and boat cruises) but are primarily known for their presence during the Caribana season, when they operate a *mas'* camp in Toronto. Mas K Club attracts persons of all races, ethnicities, and social classes as seen at their events throughout the year and by the masqueraders in their band on Caribana Saturday. Saldenah's band is an exemplar of the popular contemporary Caribana Festival in Canada. The first thing one sees on Saldenah's website is imagery of young women in shiny, skimpy costumes, a scene reminiscent of the annual Victoria's Secret Fashion Show, which features sexy lingerie and sleepwear. The models on the website are mainly female, and vary in shades—mostly light browns, and are made-up to perfection. These are not people who look like they are part of the working class; these people represent what Belinda Edmondson (2009) calls the "Caribbean Middlebrow." This Euro-centric ideal is a legacy of the slavery period manifesting itself in the hearts and minds of the current generations of Caribbean people who live in the region or in diaspora spaces. Even on the band websites today, there still remains a deep-seated psychological desire for things European while at the same time seeing things African as ugly, undesirable, and evil.

Within a predominantly patriarchal, heteronormative10 space, and with the common perception that "sex sells," it is no surprise that the female body has come to symbolize the Caribana Festival. Likewise, with the increase in Caribana's commercialism, it is not surprising that the event and a display of sexuality are intimately interwoven. There is a connection between heterosexuality and the female body in almost every element of Caribana, whether it is the soca music, masquerade, other social events, and especially through its promotional material (Noel 2009).

The constant overrepresentation of the female Carnival body on the band websites and throughout the popular press media, often excessively sexualized, has many implications. Not only does this practice support patriarchy, and the objectification and misogynistic treatment of women, but it also persuasively affirms the Caribbean as a sexualized paradise where certain exotic Caribbean women are available and willing to denigrate themselves in order to be noticed and celebrated.

The images on the 2016 Saldenah website also show the women masqueraders in ways that the men simply are not shown. On all of the imbedded web pages at the Saldenah website, there are close-up pictures of the models' breasts, buttocks, mid-sections, and legs, further eroticizing already sexualized images. The buttocks of the female models are consistently shown in ways that would not be expected of male models. The male models are typically shown from the front or slightly angled. This in effect maintains a notion of heteronormativity, in which female subordination is naturalized. Obviously these costume models have a function, and that is to show-off the costume the best they can. This is the denotative function. The connotative function is to sell a heterosexual male fantasy of unbridled sexual availability of exotic nubile women. Hence, it makes sense that Saldenah, from a marketing perspective, would use these erotic photographs and even zoom in on some parts of the costume/body in order to convey to their potential masquerader customers that by choosing their costume they can have the "ideal" body that will be noticed on Caribana Day. By following prescribed exotic and Eurocentric beauty "ideals," this has the effect of excluding many types of women who would feel uncomfortable in the band—the majority being older women, people who are not slim or athletically built, darker-skinned individuals who one might consider more African in terms of ethnic presentation of self.

Men in costume on the website are less visible than are women. Men typically have very few choices in their costume. A typical male costume consists of long shorts, a minimal head piece, a neck piece, and wristbands or armbands. Most men's costumes are not customizable or additive. In essence, the men's costumes are boring and are usually designed to be just the same color as the women's costumes, so that they will match in the section. What is interesting about the male models used as archetypes for the band is that they are often selected for their youthful physique. This physique usually consists of males who have six-pack abdominal muscles, toned biceps, and/or well-maintained dreadlocks. Many of the male models, like the female models, are light- or brown-skinned, suggesting that they are of mixed ethnicity. Very few of the males smile; most use the "cool pose," which is a tough, unapproachable black male image as the norm when they are presented in group photos

(Messner 1989). This image also has the effect of conveying a preponderance of heterosexuality to the viewer. This is particularly important since the act of dancing and wining in the streets, wearing the male version of a pretty *mas'* costume for the amusement of the spectators, might be perceived as an activity for effeminate men. The males on the website have to overcome this possible conflict with their sexuality and present themselves as overtly heterosexual and in some ways hyper-masculine.

Although the name and theme of the band is supposed to be "Outta Africa," this is only reflected in the name attached to the various sections. Ironically, the sixteen sections in Saldenah's 2016 band presentation incorporate an African theme by name only. The sections include such exotic-sounding names as Ashanti, Serengeti, Birds of the Congo, or African Golden Jackal. One would imagine that these sections would reflect some aspect of an African theme, but what is most disappointing is that these sections have virtually no connection to an authentic African cultural look (see images 4 and 5 in the appendices). Despite having an opportunity to do something different in 2016, Louis Saldenah's band followed the global trend of producing evocative shiny "bikinis, beads, and feathers" costumes that are meaningless and hollow. The only thing that differentiates each of the sixteen sections was the colors used by the section leaders and the differing amounts of sequins, feathers, and beads on each costume. Virtually all of the costumes are interchangeable from the previous years in terms of style and cut. They are similar to the costumes found in the large bands in Trinidad and Tobago, such as Tribe, Yuma, Bliss, or Harts. All of these big bands have "normalized" the notion that a Carnival costume is "beads, feathers, and skimpy bikinis." A complicated, epic theatrical theme has been dropped for the sake of the simplicity of mass-producing the costumes. These heterogeneous mass-produced costumes today make enormous profits for the band leaders who have to put very little creative energy each year in bringing out their bands. Part of the profit also comes from the selling of additional services for masqueraders on the road, like an all-inclusive food-and-drinks package or creating exclusive front line sections within the band.

Conclusion

Trinidad Carnival today is a multifaceted festival that emerged out of the African slavery experience as well as European religious traditions. African cultural themes have been part of Carnival in Trinidad as both a form of memory, pride, and recollection. Nothing typifies this African influence more

George Bailey 1957 Presenation "Back to Africa."

than the dawn Jouvert pre-Carnival celebration that ushers in the *mas'* on Monday and Tuesday in Trinidad. The traditional masquerader, emerging from slavery and oppression in the nineteenth century, used his/her costume, dance moves, and singing as a vehicle to rebel against the European status quo. Along with rehearsed rhetoric, the appearance of the costumed masqueraders provided the voice for the character being mimicked, whether Dame Lorraine, the Peasant Girl, Pierrot Grenade, Midnight Robber, or Fancy Sailor.

Since the colonial period, women have been part of the Carnival events in Trinidad. Not surprisingly, women's participation in Carnival has always been scrutinized and overly policed by the conservative societal norms for what is acceptable for women to wear and do on the public streets. The strict boundaries women must follow have always been influenced by the conservative Judeo-Christian value system that hegemonically shapes Caribbean cultural ideals. Despite these socially constructed boundaries, Caribbean women have continued to find their own ways of manifesting agency in public spaces and have come to enjoy participating in Carnival events, while avoiding promiscuous Jamette, Jakobat, or Wabeen labels. This can be seen in the Carnival costumes women have worn on the streets of Port of Spain in the early celebrations, circa the eighteenth century, as well as the Carnival costumes that are worn today.

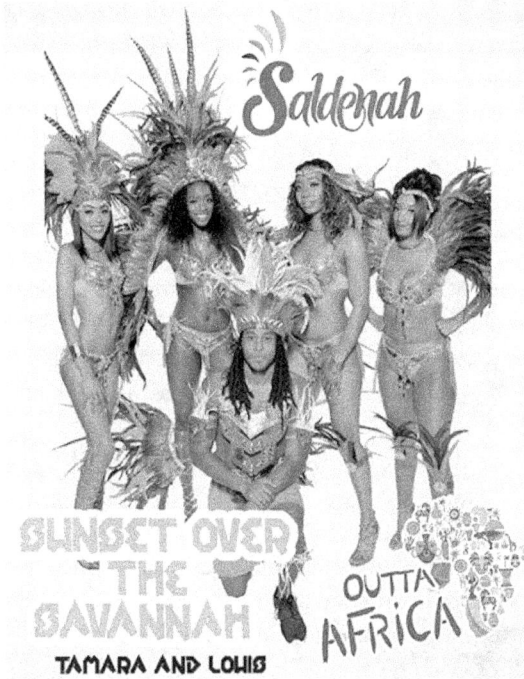

Louis Saldenah Presentation
Outta Africa 2016.

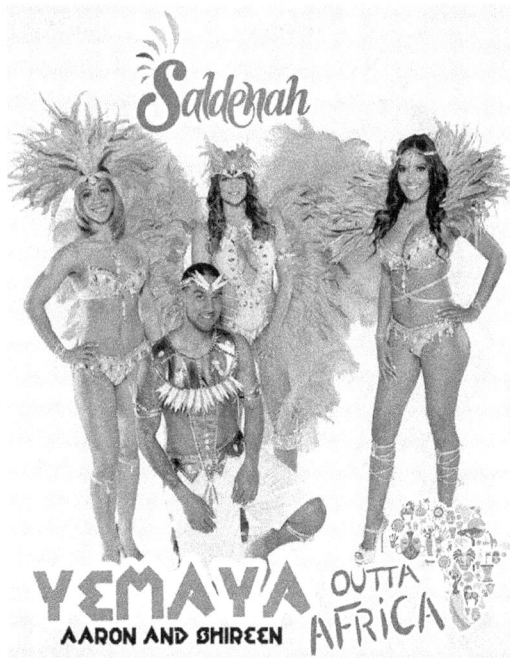

Louis Saldenah Presentation
Outta Africa 2016.

Ever since the 1950s, the majority of the Carnival *mas'* band portrayals were overwhelmingly based on non-African and non-Caribbean historical narratives. The big band leaders like Edmund Hart, Wayne Berkeley, and Steven Lee Heung brought out *mas'* bands that were themed along mythical exotic fantasies that included Romans, Amazonians, Greeks, Aztecs, Chinese, Atlantis, Mayans, and so on. There have been few exceptions to this non-African trend. The most notable exception to these ahistorical and minor themes was George Baily, who intentionally created bands that had very positive African themes. Other notable big band leaders who intentionally portrayed Africa in a positive light include Brian McFarlane and Peter Minshall.

Most recently, Louis Saldenah, a diaspora band leader, put forth an African theme for his 2016 Caribana band. Although Saldenah's "Outta Africa" theme may have been a genuine attempt to venerate African history, society, and culture, the reality is that Saldenah followed the "pretty *mas'*" trend whereby the costumes were more akin to showgirl-type displays. The prettier the costumes became, the less inclined men were to join the band and play *mas'* for fear of looking too effeminate in shiny and bedazzled costumes. Women, on the other hand, pushed band leaders for ever prettier costumes that made them look like exotic goddesses. The decline in the African cultural forms in *mas'* bands had the effect of opening the door over time to the greater participation by Indo-Trinidadians. Since the period of indenture ship, Indo-Trinidadians had regarded Carnival as an Afro-Trinidadian sacred space to be respected and avoided. With the decline in African band themes and content, Indo-Trinidadians came to find a new space for themselves in contemporary Carnival bands. Indian cultural forms now play a significant role in the ongoing process of shaping the Carnival events in Trinidad as well as in the diaspora. This Indian participation likely would not have happened if the African cultural forms and traditions had not declined.

Long gone are the grand theatrical band presentations that were designed to inform the spectators of some aspect of history vis-a-vis a *mas'* costume Any hope of having an authentic African cultural presence in the band has also been lost because of lack of desire by the band leaders and the masqueraders to portray a complicated theatrical *mas'*. The band leaders' main interest is economic gain while the masqueraders interest often lies in simply having a carefree and fun time. There has been a distinct McDonaldization of the Carnival, the costumes, and the *mas'* itself (Ritzer 2009; Pieterse 2009). The female Carnival costume today is more about fashion and as a means to display the body rather than as a vehicle to be theatrical, educational, or a culturally significant theme The theme of authentic African content was lost in Saldenah's 2016 band presentation because the costumes were simply various colored feathers, beads, and bikinis. The only culturally significant and educationally important aspect of Saldenah's band was in the naming of each costumed section after well-known geographical location, proverb, or myth that originated on the African continent. This gave each section the false sentiment of exoticness and authenticity.

Notes

1. Some of the earlier calypso pioneers of Afrocentric music include Ella Andall—"Hello Africa" (1976), the Mighty Sparrow—"Love African Style" (1980), Crazy & the Kalico Band—"Tarshika" (1982), Black Stalin—"Sing for the Land" (1986), Mighty Duke—"How Many More Must Die" (1986), "Bally-Shaka Shaka" (1988), David Rudder—"Down at the Shebeen" (1990), and, most recently, Machel Montano and Kerwin Du Bois—"Possessed" (2013).

2. In the colonial relationship, everything associated with the colonized is portrayed as negative and inferior in comparison to the colonizer. Thus, the colonizer should be emulated while the colonized should be despised. In this light, it is perhaps not surprising that European social and cultural values seem to dominate, shaping language, thinking, beauty, and other ideals, and cultural practices (Fanon 1967).

3. African slaves never forgot about where they came from and passed along their memories to each subsequent generation through oral history and reminisces. After emancipation in 1834, there was an initial desire among some African Caribbeans for a physical repatriation to the African continent. This was certainly the case for Mandingoes from Trinidad, who sought repatriation to the Gambia, and the Congolese from Cuba, who sought repatriation to the Congo (Williams 1971).

4. A mulatress is a female mulatto woman with one black and one white parent.

5. Creolization has been defined by Edward Kamau Brathwaite (1971, 6) as a cultural process which may be divided into two aspects of itself: ac/culturation, which is the yoking (by force and example, deriving from power/prestige) of one culture to another (in this case the enslaved/African to the European); and inter/culturation, which is an unplanned, unstructured but osmotic relationship proceeding from this yoke. The creolization that follows (and it is process, not a product), becomes the tentative cultural norm of the society.

6. During his fifteen years as a Carnival bandleader, George Bailey's presentations won the coveted Band of the Year Award six times (1957, 1959, 1960, 1961, 1962, 1969) and the People's Choice Award ten times (1957, 1959, 1960, 1961, 1962, 1966, 1967, 1968, 1969, 1970).

7. Mac Farlane entered the Carnival arena in the late 1990s and is well-known for his "Theatre Mas." He has won the National Band of the Year title many times, including the record for doing so seven times consecutively with "India—the Story of Boyie" (2007), "Earth—Cries of Despair, Wings of Hope" (2008), "Africa—Her People, Her Glory, Her Tears" (2009), "Resurrection—The Mas" (2010), "Humanity-Circle of Life" (2011), "Sanctification—In Search Of" (2012), and "Joy—The Finale" (2013).

8. Keith Nurse (1999, 661) notes that globalization has brought about the expansion of Trinidad Carnival into diasporic transnational festivals that are culturally similar. The

"periphery is greatly influenced by Trinidadian Carnival at the centre, but the reverse is also the case."

9. The main method used to carry out this study is a visual textual analysis of the costumes on the 2016 Louis Saldenah Caribana website. Visual textual analysis is a qualitative research technique which provides the researcher with an abundance of information in the form of encoded messages that are later decoded and analyzed for their perceived meanings, and can help in showing how culture is produced, transmitted, and interpreted, and, most importantly, the political messages inherent to many cultural images and texts. The images and texts that were examined constitute a purposive sample as they each contribute to notions of popular, contemporary Carnival (McKee 2003).

10. Heteronormativity is the belief that people fall into distinct and complementary genders (man and woman) with natural roles in life. It assumes that heterosexuality is the only sexual orientation or only norm, and states that sexual and marital relations are most (or only) fitting between people of opposite sexes. Consequently, a "heteronormative" view is one that involves alignment of biological sex, sexuality, gender identity, and gender roles. Heteronormativity is often linked to heterosexism and homophobia.

Bibliography

Alleyne, Mervyn. *Roots of Jamaican Culture*. London: Pluto Press, 1988.

Alleyne, Mike "Mirage in the Mirror: Album Cover Imagery in Caribbean Music." In *Caribbean Cultural Identities*, ed. Griffith. Ontario: Rosemont Publishing & Printing, 2001.

Bakhtin, Mikhail. *Rabelais and his World.* Bloomington: Indiana University Press, 1941.

Barnes, Natasha. "Body Talk: Notes on Women and Spectacle in Contemporary Trinidad Carnival." *Small Axe 7* (2000): 93–105.

Brathwaite, Kamau. *The Development of Creole Society in Jamaica, 1770–1820,* New York: Oxford University Press, 1971.

Brereton, Bridget. "The Trinidad Carnival: 1870–1900." *Savacou* 11/12 (1975): 46–57.

Burman, Jenny. "Masquerading Toronto Through Caribana: Transnational Carnival Meets the Sign 'Music Ends Here.'" *Identity* 1:3 (2001): 273–328.

Cohen, C. B. "Trinidad Carnival Today: Local Culture in Global Context." *Anthropology Quarterly* 80, no. 3 (2007): 897–902.

Cooper, Carolyn. *Noises in the Blood: Orality, Gender and the "Vulgar" Body of Jamaican Popular Culture*. London: Macmillan Caribbean, 1996.

Day, Charles. 1852. Cited in Milla Riggio, ed. *Carnival: Culture in Action—The Trinidad Experience*. New York and Abingdon: Routledge, 2004, 74.

Dudley, Shannon. *Carnival Music in Trinidad: Experiencing Music, Expressing Culture*. New York: Oxford University Press, 2004.

Edmondson, Belinda. *Caribbean Middlebrow Leisure Culture and the Middle Class*. New York: Cornell University Press, 2009.

Espinet, Ramabai. "Caribana: A Diasporic Dub." *Fuse* 22 (1999): 18–25.

Fannon, Franz, *Black Skin, White Masks*. New York: Grove Press, 1967.

Franco, Pamela. "Dressing Up and Looking Good: Afro-Creole Female Maskers in Trinidad Carnival." *African Arts* 31, no. 2 (1998): 62–67.

Franco, Pamela. "The Invention of Traditional Mas and the Politics of Gender." In *Carnival: The Cultural Politics of a Transnational Festival*, eds. G. Green and P. Scher, 25–47. Bloomington: Indiana University Press, 2007.

Franco, Pamela. "The 'Unruly Woman' in Nineteenth-Century Trinidad Carnival." *Small Axe* 7 (2000): 60–76.

Gottreisch, Anna. "We She Go Do" Women's Participation in Trinidad Calypso." Unpublished paper delivered at the Caribbean Studies Association Conference in Kingston and Ocho Rios, Jamaica, May 24–29, 1993.

Green, Garth. "Marketing the Nation: Carnival and Tourism in Trinidad and Tobago." In *In Critique of Anthropology*, eds. John Gledhill and Stephen Nugent, 238–304. Thousand Oaks, CA: Sage Publications, 2002.

Green, Gart, and Phillip Scher, eds. *Trinidad Carnival: The Cultural Politics of Transformational Festival*. Bloomington: Indiana University Press, 2007.

Guilbault, Jocelyne. "Music, Politics, and Pleaure: Live Soca in Trinidad" *Small Axe* 31, no. 14 (2010): 16–29.

Hearn, LaFcadio. *Two Years in the French West Indies Travel and Exploration*. New York: Harper and Brothers, 1923.

Ho, Christine, and Keith Nurse. *Globalization, Diaspora Caribbean Pop Culture*. Kingston: Ian Randle, 2005.

Lee, Simon. "The Development of Carnival in Trinidad and Tobago." In *20 Years of Trinidad Carnival*, ed. Noel Norton, 20–32. Port of Spain, Trinidad and Tobago: Insurance Limited, 1990.

Liverpool, Hollis. *Rituals of Power and Rebellion: The Carnival Tradition in Trinidad and Tobago, 1763–1962*. Trinidad and Tobago: Research Associated School Times, 2000.

Manning, Frank. "Overseas Caribbean Carnivals: The Arts and Politics of Transnational Celebration." In *Caribbean Popular Culture*, ed. J. Lent. Bowling Green, OH: Bowling Green University Popular Press, 1990.

McKee, A. *Textual Analysis: A Beginner's Guide*. London: Sage, 2003.

Messner, Michael. "Masculinities and Athletic Careers." *Gender and Society* 3, no. 1 (1989): 71–88.

Noel, S. "De jamette in we: Redefining Performance in Contemporary Trinidad Carnival." *Small Axe* 31 (2010): 60–78.

Noel, Samantha. "Carnival is Woman!: Gender, Performance and Visual Culture in Contemporary Trinidad Carnival." Unpublished dissertation, Department of Art, Art History and Visual Studies, Duke University, 2009.

Nurse, Keith. "Globalization and Trinidad Carnival: Diaspora, Hybridity and Identity in Global Culture." *Cultural Studies* 13, no. 4 (1999): 661–90.

Payne, Nellie. "Grenada Mas' 1928–1988." *Caribbean Quarterly* 36, nos. 3–4 (1990): 75–94.

Pearse, A. "Carnival in Nineteenth Century Trinidad." *Caribbean Quarterly* 4, nos. 3–4 (1956): 4–42.

Pieterse, Jan Nederveen. *Globalization and Culture: Global Melange*. Lanham, MD: Rowman & Littlefield, 2009.

Ritzer, George. *The McDonaldization of Society*. Los Angeles: Pine Forge Press, 2009.

Scher, Phillip. "Carnival and the Formation of Caribbean Transnation." Gainsville, FL: University of Florida Press, 2003.

Schaffner, Raimund. "Carnival, Cultural Identity, and Mustapha Matura's 'Play Mas.'" *New Theatre Quarterly* 18, no. 2 (2002): 186–95.

St. Bernard, Asha. *Happiest People Alive: An Analysis of Class and Gender in the Trinidad Carnival*. Unpublished master's dissertation, University of Western Ontario, Graduate Program in Media Studies, 2015.

Trotman, David. "Transforming Caribbean and Canadian Identity." *Atlantic Studies* 2, no. 2 (2005): 177–98.

Williams, Eric. *From Columbus to Castro: The History of the Caribbean, 1492–1969*. New York, Harper & Row, 1971.

Chapter 2

Stories of Resistance and Oppression:
Baby Doll and Dame Lorraine*

—Frances Henry and Jeff Henry

Several chapters in this book deal with the changes that have taken place in the Trinidad Carnival and the Carnivals which now are also found in other countries to which Caribbean people have migrated. This Carnival stems from the earlier period of colonization when the Spaniards and then the French brought this form of entertainment to the islands. It is to be expected that as time went by these islands faced momentous changes through modernization, development, and independence. Many areas of culture, including Carnival—their most famous form of entertainment—would also change, and this book includes some examples. But what of earlier eras? What was Carnival like in Trinidad in earlier historical periods in these islands?

This chapter deals with an important period in the history of the Carnival, especially as it relates to the participation of women. During the nineteenth century, and into the twentieth, two "ole *mas*"[1] female characters played important roles in the festivities. These characters, now called "traditional," have largely disappeared from Carnival Tuesday but still play prominent roles in J'ouvay or J'ouvert on Monday morning opening celebrations and they are also remembered in the various theatricals that take place during the Carnival period. The role of gender in earlier periods of history and the development of what are now called "traditional" characters playing the "*mas*" will be explored (Crowley 1956). In this earlier period, there were fewer large bands of players, and more emphasis was placed on individuals playing certain traditional characters derived from African and European folklore and traditions. Each such character had a specific form and structure symbolized by their costumes, the implements they carried, speech, song and dance styles, behavior, and demeanor. The costume design and the music and rhythms played were specific to each character and dictated the shape of the movements or dance steps, costume, and design that allowed the character to distinguish itself from that of others. A storyline was attached to each performance and portrayal, letting the spectators know who they were and what they were doing. While many of these traditional characters were male, two very important ones were women, and these are of interest to the themes in this book. First, Dame Lorraine, whose origin can be traced to the earlier French masques; and more recently, Baby Doll, who probably originated towards the end of the nineteenth century. Who were these female characters, where did they come from, and more importantly, what symbolic meanings can be attached to them?

Historical Background of "Dame Lorraine"

The Carnival in Trinidad and Tobago is based on the earlier concept of Masquerade brought by the French who took over the islands from the earlier Spaniards. As Roman Catholics, they celebrated the pre-Lenten period by holding elaborate balls. These sophisticated balls continued even though Trinidad changed ownership by force from Spain to Britain in 1797. Enslaved Africans who worked on the estates were taught to dance European dances as African dances and rhythms were thought to be too barbarous.

Full-time duty during the holidays, and at parties of gay abandonment, provided the enslaved with the opportunity to keenly observe their owners' behavior and depravities. It is well known that during the enslavement period, the plantation masters were always under scrutiny by their slaves (Hill 1972). In fact, Mitto Sampson writes about "Ofuba the Chantwell," an enslaved African who sang of "neg deye potla," which literally means "the nigger behind the door." The characterization of the Dame Lorraine demonstrated that on every possible occasion, the enslaved Africans had their masters under scrutiny. After their tasks at the balls, the enslaved returned to the barracks or compounds with exciting information on the proceedings. They related, in ritual and presentational form, their observations of the hypocrisy and pretense of these supposedly great people. During this period, the upper classes did not themselves do physical work, instead spending much of their time indulging in drinking and eating. These excesses may have led to the development of illnesses such as gout, diabetes, rheumatism, high blood pressure, and heart problems, indicators of overeating, excessive drinking, and lack of proper exercise. In the eyes of the enslaved workers, their masters were inept, depraved, and physically grotesque. The men were also sexual predators of teenage African enslaved women. These balls and celebrations were witnessed with great amusement by their enslaved Africans, who began to have private celebrations of their own. They used these occasions to mock and lampoon the lascivious conduct of the masters and their wives. "Little did the 'estate planters' masters realize that their erstwhile pupils would change the form into an elaborate and grotesque parody of the way the elites conducted themselves at their stylish balls" (Hill 1972). A central theme of this older form of the masquerade was the creation of special lascivious characters named in patois after protuberant body parts of the human body. These included Misie Gwo Toti or Gwo (Mr. Big Penis), Misie Gwo Koko (Mr. Big Balls), Ma Gros Tete (Madame Big Breast), Ma Gwo Bunda (Madame Big Bottom), and Ma Chen Mun (Miss Frigid).

As the period of French aristocracy waned and Trinidad became a British colony, and especially with the abolition of slavery in 1834, this masquerade took a different turn. Freed slaves took to the streets to begin a Carnival tradition of their own—the masquerade—and turned to "playing *mas*," which was done on the streets, in tents, and in stage presentations. An important part of *mas*' became the playing of some of the earlier French characters as well as new ones. African songs, dance movements, and other influences played a significant role in their celebrations. The liberated slaves recreated these costumes, copying the elaborate hats and fans by using materials available to them such as rags and pillows. Male and female players alike were masked, dancing to tunes played by cuatro and bandol groups.[3] Specific tunes became associated with the characters being played. (The tune associated with the Dame Lorraine still exists and is played whenever "she" appears in groups, at cultural events, or during Carnival events.)

Of special interest to this book was a female character named Dame Lorraine, a large black woman with grossly exaggerated huge breasts and buttocks, wearing a brightly colored ankle-length dress, high-heeled shoes, and a large and very fancy hat. She would, as did most of the traditional characters, wear a mask of some sort to partially cover her face. Dame Lorraine's history harks back to a phase in the French period when two ribald characters named Ma Gwo Bunda (Madame Big Bottom) and Ma Gros Tete (Madame Big Breasts) were especially popular.

Dame Lorraine was never played as a band on the streets during Carnival Tuesday *mas*' but appeared in the Monday-morning J'ouvert. She did, however, become highly popular in the various theatricals that took place around Carnival time. During the late nineteenth century, performances usually were held in a tent with a small stage; the audience sat on its three sides. The performance consisted of a short characterization of the ole *mas'*.[4] In the late nineteenth century, it was also used as entertainment in *mas'* camps where small groups of people were responsible for bringing out bands and building various kinds of costumes. After midnight before J'ouvert, as costumes neared completion, supporters came to the camps to give a "pull through" or assistance to make sure the band got on the road in time. Light refreshments, coffee, cheese, crackers, and rum were served with much "ole talk" and "picong."[5] It was within this close-knit community that the Dame Lorraine ensemble was presented for entertainment. Later, in the mid-nineteenth century, when the calypso tents became popular and in vogue on Sunday night, Dame Lorraine was presented for a paying audience. The show sometimes ran until next morning, and ole *mas'"* bands exploded onto the streets on J'ouvert. Later in 1948, this final night of entertainment was replaced by the more formal Dimanche Gras show, which included more entertainment but the ole *mas'* and especially the Dame Lorraine characters usually appeared there and in private festivities throughout the city. Today, many new forms of entertainment such as Vieu La Couy,[6] a recreation of older traditional characters, have been developed, but the Dame is still featured.

On the surface, the character of Dame Lorraine and the other traditional characters are huge, overdressed, larger-than-life figures who are usually saying and doing comedic things. Their performances are explained as comedy, and the more outrageous they appear, the more laughter swells in the audience. At the same time, mockery of former French colonists is presented as comic mockery to hide other more significant messages.

These characters, and especially the large Dame Lorraine, are in the first instance symbols of the resistance of slaves who in private mocked, jeered, and grossly exaggerated their masters and enlarged body parts with pillows and other stuffing. By poking fun at their masters, the enslaved were able to proclaim, at least among themselves, that they were as good if not better than their masters. They did not respect them nor did they try to emulate them in these dances. The importance of the Dame Lorraine character (and others of her time) was in the use of parody and mimicry by the enslaved. Originally male slaves enacted this character as it was probably thought that men playing large women presented greater wit. (Later, women took on the role, but even today there remain a few men who play the Dame.) These characters demonstrated that the enslaved used thought, imagination, and artistic skills to develop their own entertainment, which consisted largely of showing what they really thought of their masters and their lifestyles. What turned into ole *mas'* characters eventually actually began as statements of resistance.

The Baby Doll

As previously noted, most of the traditional ole *mas'* characters emerged from the French-style balls held in the colonial period. However, there was one character which had a different history, and which was influenced by the sexual servitude of female slaves during the earlier period of enslavement. Baby Doll is usually interpreted in a simplistic fashion as that of a single mother of African descent with an infant in her arms, desperately searching for the father of her child. She is depicted as a young, shallow, unthinking, promiscuous female who has a child with a man she has only briefly met. The tryst was committed on the spur of the moment and now she is a confused young mother unable to care for her child. She wanders the streets during Carnival time holding a white baby (doll) in her arms and accosts men with the phrase "mind yuh baby" as she demands money.

The character of the Baby Doll has a complex and interesting history that has not been explored in terms of its sociological and political origins. Today, Baby Doll is recognized and celebrated as a prestigious traditional character. She is simply portrayed, but the female Baby Doll character is, in fact, a symbol of the status of young black women from the time of enslavement and down through centuries of exploitation. Rather than being simply a poor but cute young woman searching for the father of her child, Baby Doll is the ultimate symbol of the oppression of African women. As such, playing out this oppression in a Carnival character can be understood as a symbol of resistance to the historical and even contemporary societal forces that kept African women in servitude, disadvantaged, and poverty stricken.

The History of the Baby Doll on the Streets of Port of Spain

When exactly the Baby Doll character started to parade the streets of Port of Spain is unclear and the subject of debate. Some people believe her debut was influenced by the American military during the Second World War. This argument gained strength with the calypso from that period entitled "Brown Skin Girl Go Home and Mind Baby." The calypso reflected the American military sojourn on the island that resulted in temporary liaisons and subsequent pregnancies. However, written documents that have surfaced relatively recently have provided evidence of earlier origins.

In a book entitled *The De Limas of Frederick Street* by Arthur de Lima, a founder of the well-known De Lima family of jewelers in Port of Spain, he noted that in 1925 his father Jack related a story to his grandson Alfonso (Arthur's nephew) about the 1885 masquerade:

> It was called Masquerade in those days and it kept that name for long years. Inner city streets such as Duncan, Nelson, Duke, Prince, George, Piccadilly, Besson, and Queen were referred to as the Masquerade Zone. With three friends he went down to Tamarind Square from Charlotte street on J'ouvert morning of 1885: "suddenly, I felt an elbow in my ribs and I fell flat on the ground. A big hulking woman was holding me down. "You can't love me and leave me! Pay up or reap the consequences!" "I delved my hands in my pocket and the shilling I gave her came to my rescue." "I did not enjoy the 'ole mas' women with cloth babies in their arms who stopped to claim me every time as a father of their child. They embarrassed me, and I quickly paid up the shilling they demanded. Six children were pinned on me by these money makers." (DeLima 1925)

In 1930, the same character was listed for the first time in Michael Anthony's *Parade of the Carnivals* under "old mas" and was described this way: "mothers with babies in their arms seeking 'fathers'" (Anthony 1930).

The first time the character was listed in a newspaper report as participating in a masquerade competition was 1930. Twenty-six years later, there was no name attached to this character and no detailed description of costume. As late as 1956, Dan Crowley (*Caribbean Quarterly*, 200) was informed that, in earlier times, this character was referred to as: "Ladies with babies in search of father." This nameless character was known by the doll she held, her pursuit of defaulting fathers, and her poignant pleas:

"You can't love me and leave me"
Or
"Mind yuh baby."
Or
"Ladies with babies in search of a father"

Even today, the last request—"mind yuh baby"—remains the phrase this character shouts as she solicits support from the alleged delinquent fathers.

The Collusion between Church and State

The Baby Doll character in its earlier manifestation was probably played by women (and men) to reflect some of the changes taking place in Trinidadian society just before the turn of the century. Yet why is Baby Doll depicted as a black-skinned female with a white-skinned blue-eyed doll? What was this character communicating? The answer explains why Baby Doll was and is one of the most explosive of the traditional characters in the Trinidad masquerade. The characterization symbolized the sexual exploitation of women from the days of bondage when slave owners saw it as their right to demand sexual favors from their bondwomen. These women had no rights under the law and submitted to the sexual demands of their masters or estate overseers. Many children were born under these circumstances. As these children had lighter skin, they were considered, even by the victims, to be of a superior class and to, therefore, have a better opportunity for survival in the society.

After emancipation, the economic oppression under colonialism followed a similar pattern, and young females in service to upper-class families were not only victimized by the masters of the house but also by their sons. These young women had come from the country districts to the city to find jobs and had to live with their employers in back rooms on the premises. They were at the beck and call of their employers, and many of these women were unsophisticated, unschooled, and far from parents or elders. They could not openly challenge the advances of their unscrupulous masters or their masters' sons. The wives of these colonial masters probably knew of their husbands' indiscretions, but given their own lowly position and the strong patriarchy of the times, chose to turn a blind eye.

Other societal and especially political conditions of the times influenced the meaning of the Baby Doll. By the nineteenth century, illegitimacy was widespread, especially among the African-derived population. Moreover, Hindu and Moslem marriages were not considered legal unless they were registered in the court. Given their poverty, many Indian couples relied solely on their religious marriage rite, and since they were not Christian and did not register under the colonial law, their unions were not legitimate and their offspring were demeaned as bastards. Even the small Chinese population in Trinidad at this time also suffered from this form of degradation. However, in their hypocrisy, the Christian elites denigrated all non-European females. As Trotman (1986, 246) notes:

> The female Chinese immigrants were said to be picked up in the streets of Hong Kong and Canton and said to be the lowest class of Chinese. East Indian immigrants were said to be of the lowest caste, morally worthless because they had been brought by the recruiter and consigned to the highest bidder.

Thus, every female group except the Europeans was demeaned in this manner. However, it was the black-skinned African female who faced the greatest attack not only on her morality but on the very essence of her existence. These women were often described as lascivious, basically sexual animals whose very purpose was defined by their sexual appetites. Moreover, this uncontrollable need for sex was portrayed as racial in origin. Children were born in this environment, but there was no family unit. Relationships were transient, fathers were absentee, and single mothers had to fend for themselves and their children. The men were described as lazy sexual predators who preened themselves and strutted around to attract many females to take care of them as they lived their privileged lives.

There were also the elite white French Creole men who were considered upstanding citizens in the society. They had the means to live the privileged married life but were secretly having children from different relationships. They subjected these African women to the role of concubine. In need of providers for their children, the women kept the liaisons secret. Without exception, everyone conformed to these practices, and it can almost be understood as an understanding between elite men, their wives, and their lowly concubines. As Trotman notes,

> This wide spread illegitimacy was defined by the elite as the result of the unbridled sexuality of the masses and evidence of their immorality.
>
> The elite also linked the high level of infant mortality in the nineteenth century to this illegitimacy. Infant deaths cut across race and class lines; the white upper class and the colored middle-class elite were equally affected by the infant mortally rate. (239)

Alarmed by the unhealthy social situation in the colony, the Colonial Office in London took action. Earlier in 1880, a Bastardy Ordinance was legislated in the colony of St. Vincent, and a governor was sent to Trinidad to introduce this same legislation forcing fathers to pay child support to their illegitimate children. The governor, however, supported by the archbishop of Port of Spain, as well as numbers of elite white men, considered such legislation inadvisable as concubinage was so widespread and was a deliberate choice of the women involved. This may have been true for women, especially mixed-race women, who, failing to find husbands, did consider concubinage as their only economic alternative. The archbishop criticized the ordinance because it would be of no "service to those living in an orderly and decent manner" although unmarried. He also stressed that the neglect of children was not a major problem (Brereton 1979).

It is interesting that the archbishop took such an extreme position in the debate on the Bastardy Ordinance of 1888, which compelled fathers of illegitimate children to support them out of a "social necessity because a high proportion of lower-class men regarded paternity so casually" (Brereton 1979) However, the real reason was that upper-class elite men could be called to court and that known prostitutes could be called to name the father(s) of their children. What is particularly noteworthy is the archbishop's callous attitude to the people who were affected, the most vulnerable of his flock: the black-skinned masses. The Bastardy Ordinance was the bastion of high moral standards, particularly those involving family values, because it complemented church values and church laws. Probably the only reason for the archbishop's double standard was the result of the possible repercussions, which were the complication of lives of the white elite men in that patriarchal society. In a bold shift of the church's teaching and values, he advocated that laws and morals should be compromised.

The Bastardy Ordinance was defeated; the matter was shelved. However, six years later, in 1888, under the term of Governor William Robinson, the same ordinance was passed. Governor Robinson had to use his casting vote as the unofficial nominated members, the French Creoles, voted in a block against the motion. Dr. De Verteuil said in his presentation that he would have supported the bill if "married men were exempted." He claimed that a child born from an adulterous relationship should not be placed on the same footing as one born from the union of unmarried parents. Moreover, he contended that because of the ordinance, wives would become aware of the adulterous relationships of their husbands. It should be noted that Dr. De Verteuil, a descendent of a prominent and influential French family, was mayor of Port of Spain, a member of the legislative council, and author of an important book on the geography of Trinidad! His position in the debate was supported by the archbishop.

Dr. De Boissiere, a planter, doctor, and longtime member of the legislative council, also spoke on behalf of the French Creole elite. He attacked the women, the unmarried mothers, claiming "they were the root cause of the problem, there were no deserted children . . . Desertion presupposes seduction, and seduction, in the full meaning of the word, is rare in our midst" (Trotman 212). Moreover, he continued, "Some of them, were neither prostitute, nor reported to be such nor known to be of immoral character but have managed so well that they have had intercourse clandestinely with several men" (Trotman 249). He was afraid that some of these lower-class women would blackmail any man with wealth or social position who may have had casual intercourse with them.

This argument is a good example of what is referred to as "blaming the victim." De Boissiere clearly stated the women had clandestine intercourse with several men, but did not point out these men were husbands and fathers and pillars of society who were also having clandestine intercourse with women. The entire argument of these learned gentlemen had nothing to do with morality: they told tall tales to their wives and children, hypocritically going to church each week and receiving the sacraments. None of these points were included in the debate. They were mainly concerned that the "outside" women would falsely accuse the men of paternity and prosecute them for support under the "bastardy law." These pillars of church and society, protectors of law and order, were supported by the honorable archbishop who did not debate the cause, only the effect. (Trotman 1986)

The white privilege the planters De Boissiere and De Verteuil defended had a long tradition, with roots in the slave society. It had been the right of the slave owners to exploit female chattels and to demand sexual favors. Support and recognition of the offspring of these relationships depended on the whim and fancy of the father and was used as evidence of the slave owner's power. These barons could withhold or deliver punishment at whim to prove their oppressive power or magnanimity. Such were the social conditions in colonial Trinidad, where people of African descent were the victims of the white Creole power elite aided by British derived laws. Young females of African descent in Trinidad in 1856 lived without laws and a social infrastructure.

The disenfranchised African women found their voice "behind the mask" and used the masquerade of Baby Doll to protest their situation. Displaying an obviously phenotypic white baby made the point as they protested, showing dissatisfaction with the debate that was exploding around and beyond them. The masquerade was used to express their frustration with the dominant males, first against the white male elite and later, as society changed, against the black males who also became absentee fathers.

The character in its original form was a demonstration of protest. What De Lima experienced as a young man in 1885 when he entered the "masquerade zone" was ordinary women telling the tale of the young women living in the community. From 1885 to 1929, this type of masquerade character was an important component of what was called the masquerade zone.

The 1930s were the height of the Depression. By that time, it was common knowledge that delinquent fathers encompassed all ethnicities and religions. The Baby Doll character turned inward to tell the tale of African men and their lack of support for their offspring. At this time, slum clearance took place in this zone, which demolished the long rows of barrack rooms in which poor people lived. This meant all barrack rooms in the areas of the masquerade zone were demolished. In the process, communities, which although poor but tightly knit, were broken up. No new recreational spaces were provided, and new housing was not designed for community living. People were moved around and displaced.

The Second World War became a factor in further exacerbating the upheaval. American military forces arrived, which created challenges for the working class. The American influence began to replace the British profile through its presence on the streets and interactions with the populace. Movies took on a new meaning, one called *Baby Doll* (1956) directed by Elia Kazan from a screenplay by Tennessee Williams. This movie was extremely popular in Trinidad and influenced the masquerade character. The traditional Baby Doll costume, a long white dress, was replaced by a shorter dress with frilly sleeves, and she began to assume a coquettish flirtatious demeanor. The blonde, blue-eyed Baby Doll remained in defining the characterization but "mind yuh baby" took on another connotation. The modern masquerade mother of the baby abdicated her vulnerable role as an exploited female and became much more sexually appealing and assertive.

What did this Baby Doll character symbolize? The doll figure denoted virginity and innocence, that is, an attraction to the male sex. The white costume denoted innocence, while the dress to the knee created a sexual image around this innocence—a comment on the male sexual desire. The white, blonde, blue-eyed baby exposed the sexual liaison, the exploitation of the vulnerable African female by the white male. The search for the father depicted the helplessness of the African female, coupled with a lack of voice to articulate the poignancy of the situation. She was alone, without a support system, to be pitied or ridiculed. The result was that the victim became the buffoon, as men ran when she approached them for help to support her baby. Spectators ridiculed and laughed uproariously at her situation.[7]

Conclusion

These traditional female characters closely associated with the history and development of Carnival in Trinidad were, and to some extent still are, sources of amusement and gaiety to the crowds on the streets and in entertainment venues. The one displaying her grotesque figure clearly grew out of the French-inspired costume balls of the eighteenth century, and the Dame's mockery of her masters provided comic relief for overburdened, exploited, and enslaved men and women. At the same time, however, the ability to perform in this manner demonstrated their own sense of themselves, and their identity as humans rather than mere slaves to powerful masters. Baby Doll challenges the authority of men as she demonstrates her victimhood and misery. She attempts to gain the sympathy of onlookers while, of course, demanding money for the upkeep of her child. She becomes the symbol of oppressed woman: at first in relation to exploitation during the colonial period and, more recently, in relation to the promiscuous and irresponsible behavior of local men.

Notes

* An earlier version of this chapter appeared in Jeff Henry's book, *Under the Mas*.

1. "Ole *mas*" refers to the traditional *mas'* as played in the 1800 hundreds. It is mainly used to distinguish it from the modern contemporary *mas'*.

2. The beginning of Carnival: an early Monday morning celebration.

3. Musical instruments like banjos.

4. Ole *mas'* takes place at J'ouvert, where people are costumed to lampoon and poke fun at other people or incidents that have taken place.

5. "Ole talk" refers to lose talk or banter. "Picong" is patois for the name of a competition that two calypsonians engage in by singing words, sometimes insults, back and forth at each other. "Picong" can also refer to a back and forth banter between friends.

6. French patois meaning "the old yard," the name of a celebration developed some years ago to preserve the old Carnival characters.

7. The Baby Doll was indeed a tragic figure. Her story is a metaphor for the history of the African female in society. She has even entered into fictional literature. *Night Calypso*, a novel written by expatriate English writer Lawrence Scott, tells the story of a French Creole family. The substance of this local story is that Dr. Vincent Metivier finally tells his new wife Madeleine (an ex-nun who was born in Europe) of his teenage romance with Sybil, the daughter of Odetta the servant of the Metivier household. This secret tryst produced a son who, now eighteen years old, whom he has never seen. Madeleine, his foreign-born wife, is not schooled in the complexities and nuances of race and color of Curacol (the island on which the story takes place). She is taken aback that Vincent had not told her of his son after all this time together. Baby Doll also appeared in a famous movie of that title directed by Elia Kazan from a screenplay by Tennessee Williams in 1956. The movie influenced the masquerade character. Changes began to take place—an adaptation of the name "Baby Doll" was not enough. A costume that suited the sexuality of the term "baby" was reflected in dress of the adult character, who was originally displayed as an ordinary female. Frills were added to her sleeves and the bottom of her skirt, and the skirt itself was shortened. The "lady" sexualized herself. The costume began to go through a process of gentrification, and color was added to the fashion. Fortunately, the blonde, blue-eyed Baby Doll remained a constant fixture in defining the characterization. However, "mind yuh baby" took on another connotation. The modern masquerade mother of the baby abdicated her vulnerable role as an exploited female and became much more sexually appealing and assertive.

Bibliography

Anthony, Michael. *Parade of the Carnivals of Trinidad, 1839–1989*. Port of Spain: Circle Press, 1989

Brereton, Bridget. *Race Relations in Colonial Trinidad, 1870–1900*. Cambridge: Cambridge University Press, 1979.

Crowley, Daniel J. "The Traditional Masques of Carnival." In *Trinidad Carnival: A Republication of the Caribbean Quarterly Trinidad Carnival Issue*, ed. Andrew Pearse, 42–90. Port of Spain: Paria Publishing, 1988 (1956).

De Lima, A. *The DeLimas of Frederick St.* Imprint Caribbean, 1981.

Henry, Jeff. *Under the "Mas" Resistance and Rebellion in the Trinidad Masquerade*. Trinidad and Tobago: Lexicon, 2008.

Hill, D. R. *The Trinidad Carnival; Mandate for a National Theatre*. Austin: University of Texas Press, 1972.

Trotman, David Vincent. *Crime in Trinidad: Conflict and Control in a Plantation Society, 1838–1900*. Knoxville: University of Tennessee Press, 1986.

Chapter 3

Jamette!: Women and Canboulay in 1881

—Philip W. Scher

She was, she recalled, in a tree when it happened. Frances Richard (recorded sometimes as Frances Edwards) was an eyewitness to the Canboulay riots in 1881. Her recollections were gathered by Tobagonian Folklorist J. D. Elder in the 1950s when Frances was in her nineties.[1] She described a quiet and stealthy scene, in early morning darkness in a part of Port of Spain that would normally have been bustling during the day, and raucous on a Carnival Monday night/Tuesday morning. Frances's memories provide an extraordinarily unusual subaltern view of the riots, most of the information for which comes through the accounts of the police, journalists, and government officials. In any case, her account is haunting and evocative.

Near midnight, before Carnival Monday, rows of stick fighters, drummers (their drums quieted) and torchbearers (their torches dark) crept quietly along the streets, heading eastward and southward from what was known as Medical Corner (now known as Green Corner), down St. Vincent Street to Park Street. They would have moved in this way about five blocks or so to the head of Piccadilly Street, possibly down towards Duke Street. At the head of the group was a woman who, in the darkness, called out to Captain Arthur Baker in patois. According to an interview given by Lennox Pierre to theatre director (and later early organizer of the Canboulay Riots reenactment) Tony Hall, the woman shouted, "Messiers, Captain Baker et tout l'homme au cour de la rue!" With that the torches were ignited, the drums began, and the stick fighters (batonye) advanced.

It was a battle, but a quick one, as the police were overwhelmed, driven back and sent into retreat. In all, thirty-eight out of the 150 police were injured in the fray (Brereton 2002, 171). The police fell back to their barracks and the revelers continued into the morning. Later the governor, Sir Sanford Freeling, addressed them and promised they could continue with their carnival, but pleaded for order and peace, which was granted. This chapter will briefly contextualize the Canboulay riots and highlight the role that women played not just in the action itself, but also in the life of what is commonly referred to as the Jamette Carnival. I conclude with the suggestion that we might re-imagine these activities, at least in part, as political protests rather than simply riots.

Canboulay (from cannes brulées, or burnt canes) was, as performed by people of African descent in Trinidad, a festive processional commemorating emancipation through the symbolism of bearing torches, drumming, and marching with a coterie of stick fighters, chantuelles, and other performers. The festival was initially held on August 1 to celebrate emancipation in 1834. The suppression of Canboulay led to its revitalization during the Carnival season, which had been restricted to a two-day affair in the 1840s. Canboulay is also identified as an origin point for calypso music. Specifically, Canboulay was meant to recall the frantic activity surrounding a fire in the cane fields. In the event of a fire in the fields, which were often purposefully set at night by saboteurs, slaves were rushed from their quarters and driven with whips to extinguish the flames. Fires were also sometimes set by planters in order to drive rats into the center of a cane field where they were then exterminated. This practice was, prior to emancipation, parodied by upper-class citizens of Trinidad during Carnival season. Women would dress as their Creole or "mulatto" domestic slaves and/or servants while men dressed in a costume known as the "neg jardin" or garden slave. According to a contemporary account, the procession of whites, masquerading as blacks during a cane fire emergency, was intended to be a "take off" of "slave life on a plantation," even including "the driver with a whip pretending to drive the people before him to extinguish a night-fire in the cane-piece." Furthermore, this observer notes, there would be the "slaves tramping in time and singing a rude refrain, to a small negro-drum and carrying torches to light their way down the road" (quoted in Cowley 1996, 21).

After emancipation (1834, with an "apprenticeship period" ending in 1838), Canboulay developed into an opportunity to reclaim the parodic performances of white and colored elites and quickly developed, ultimately, into a festival for liberated African laborers[2] and freed slaves who had been banned (with varying degrees of success) from participating in the masquerade Carnival events prior to emancipation. The event was successfully suppressed during the emancipation celebrations held on August 1, prior to the late 1840s, but reemerged as part of Carnival and grew along with the rise of what came to be known as the Jamette (or underworld) Carnival of the late 1800s.

By the 1870s, the so-called Jamette Carnival (despite how this term is generally written today, it was often written by contemporary observers as "diametre") was on the rise and was characterized by the presence at Carnival time of poor and working-class Trinidadians, the ranks of whom were swelled by poor migrants from the smaller islands of the Eastern Caribbean. The barracks and barrack yards as well as the inner-city slums were overcrowded and unsanitary and many residents struggled to earn a living through both legal and illegal means. Carnival became a time when these residents, whose presence was both dangerous and an affront to the upper classes and the authority structures they maintained, spilled out into public view. This included stickmen, drummers, prostitutes, badjohns, matadors (sometimes these were former prostitutes or madams, many of whom were involved in stick fighting), and obeahmen and obeahwomen. These groups controlled the streets of Port of Spain during Carnival, especially in the working-class neighborhoods to the east and west of downtown. Neighborhoods, in turn, were controlled by bands whose names reflected their alignment to any of the variety of identities that cut across Trinidadian Society, even within the same social class, such as French/patois- versus English-speaking communities. Women, who took a prominent role in the Jamette Carnival from the very beginning, heavily populated these bands. By 1881, the Canboulay celebrations were the opening explosion of Carnival revelry into the streets and avenues of Port of Spain. As John Cowley (1996) notes, the general modern form of the festival was established. Thus, Carnival Monday mornings featured the Canboulay processions with stick fighters, chantuelles, drummers, dancers, followed by a kind of Monday *mas'* of partial costumes and informal processions. By Monday night and into Tuesday, the "elegant and picturesque" costumes of the middle and upper classes began to appear. Except for the stricter class delineations implied in this description, this is very much what contemporary Carnival looks like, with Canboulay having been replaced by what is now known as "J'ouvert" or "Jouvay." Indeed, with the gradual transition to J'ouvert, which contains the spirit of many of the activities of Canboulay, but adds other elements, such as steel pan (which was invented in the twentieth century), the historical connections to Canboulay became somewhat murky, at least for much of the broader public.

The term "Jamette," referring not only to the lower classes of Port of Spain but to a distinct "criminal" element within that community, also came to be used as the shorthand to describe the celebratory activities of those Trinidadians. As such, the Jamette Carnival is a common way of referring to the historical period of Trinidad Carnival, falling roughly between emancipation (1838) and the middle-class Carnival reform movements of the late nineteenth century. This period is characterized by the democratization of Carnival activities and the increase in public participation in the festival by the newly emancipated slave population, as well as the relatively recent arrivals from India and China. In short, emancipation brought with it not simply a legal change in the condition of slaves, but an opportunity to seize control of the colony's largest and most visible festival.

What is interesting about the emergence of the Jamette Carnival and, indeed, the Jamette culture of this period, is the emphasis that contemporary observers (mostly European and male) put on specifically women's activities, appearance, and authority within this supposed demimonde. That is, although the term "Jamette" can be used to describe a collection of sociological identities including race and class, it has often been glossed as synonymous with race and gender, i.e., lower-class black women. In Richard Allsopp's *Dictionary of Caribbean English Usage* (1996), the word "Jamette" (where it is spelled "djanmet" or "djamet") gets two entries. One definition is given as people of a "low and disreputable class, belonging to the slums," while the second definition notes that it is most commonly used to refer to women of that class, with particular reference to their "morality" (Allsopp 1996, 194–95).

The world of the Jamette was created, as would be expected, by particular historical circumstances. Much excellent work has been done on Jamette culture and specifically its manifestation in Carnival in the late nineteenth century (Trotman 1984, Crowley 1996, King 1999) and on the broader context of Trinidadian society during this period (Brereton 1979, Reddock 1994). Furthermore, many scholars have written about the Jamettes in relation to issues of power and race as well as gender and class, paying special attention to the bodies of the Jamettes and their performances (Franco 2000, Noel 2010, de Freitas 1999, King 1999, Barnes 2000). This chapter is indebted to this work and seeks to build on these insights investigating the public and political dimension of Jamette activities. My aim here is to focus on the context of the Canboulay riots of 1881[3] and to contextualize both the centrality of women masqueraders in the events themselves and suggest that rather than riots, we may be able to, historically speaking, re-characterize and reframe the disturbances as protests. I make this distinction modestly, but with the aim of suggesting a degree of purpose, agency, and political consciousness that I believe previous authors rightly suggest. For example, Rosamond King, writing in 1999, tells us:

> Jamette performances embodied, embraced, and performed the stereotype of
> Black women's bodies as "unruly sexuality, untamed and wild" because to blur the
> lines between male and female is to create the possibility for alternate, "unruly"

and "wild" sexualities (i.e., those which are not monogamous, marital, hetero-sexual, or otherwise sanctioned). (King 1999, 206)

King emphasizes that these transgressive performative actions were signifi-cant for their "possible disruption of the gendered and raced political and economic hierarchy of Trinidad (King 1999, 207). The symbolic, expressive acts of Jamette women during Carnival were not, as King argues persuasively, acts of reversal or transgression limited to the streets of Port of Spain for a few brief moments a year. Women had been central to slave rebellions in the West Indies (Beckles 1990), instrumental in establishing a tradition of protest against profoundly exploitative work practices (Turner 2002), and key to the formation of independent constituencies in the post-emancipation colonies (see, for example, Mintz 1974). Patricia de Freitas (1992) has suggested that the awareness of the central role of women in *mas'* suffered during the rise of postwar nationalism in Trinidad and that women's roles were representation-ally marginalized during the fight for independence and beyond in the mid-twentieth century. My own work has in the main supported this conclusion (Scher 2002). Thus, I believe current research has highlighted a much more integral and purposeful role for women in the formation of independent Creole communities in both pre- and post-emancipation Caribbean societ-ies, and to this we might add that public forms of cultural expression are not to be seen as ancillary to politics, but as a kind of political action themselves.

In Trinidad, it would appear, Creole and African women continued the practice of pursuing independent economic activity and guarding against exploitation and slavery "by other means," after the formal period of slav-ery ended in 1838. Women were, in the post-Emancipation world of Trinidad and specifically Port of Spain, well represented in the population of that city's inner core (Trotman 1984, 60) yet were subjected to wide ranging forms of exploitation and discrimination. In 1881, the year of the Canboulay distur-bances, women comprised over 50 percent of the population of Port of Spain as compared to 46 percent in the broader population of Trinidad (Trotman 1984, 60). In addition to their large numbers, the population of urban women in 1881 were young, with a high percentage being between the ages of eighteen and forty. Another helpful snapshot taken from the 1881 census shows us that these women were largely unmarried. This condition itself was almost cer-tainly another legacy of slavery and the social and economic conditions that persisted after emancipation. As Rhoda Reddock notes:

. . . movement towards marriage was slow . . . slaves did not simply have an underdeveloped European middle-class mentality, but rather, based on their own

material and historical experiences, had come to their own understanding of
what their relationships should be. (Reddock 1994, 24)

But this did not mean an absence of ties of kinship or other forms of part-
nering. Although very few women of this class established what might be
considered "nuclear families," networks of relationships suited to the social
and economic conditions of their circumstances were actively established
and maintained (Reddock 1994, 24–25). The 1881 census also gives some indication of the occupations of urban women. Of the over 21,000 jobs listed for
women, well over half were domestic workers and seamstresses with the rest
predominantly identifying as washers/laundresses and "hucksters," or small-
scale traders of goods. The vast numbers of seamstresses and domestic workers may reflect something else:

> Many of those who mentioned such occupations to census takers were prob-
> ably expressing vocational preferences rather than actual occupations, for urban
> women had few job choices. Some rural re-migration occurred during the reap-
> ing season, but women had to develop a variety of urban survival strategies, espe-
> cially during the economic crisis of the late nineteenth century. More often than
> not, the price women paid for independence from the plantation was economic
> marginality. (Trotman 1984, 61)

By the 1880s, a degree of economic distress in Trinidad led to increasing numbers of women turning to prostitution either as a full-time occupation or as a
way to supplement income. Indeed, even as the general economy rebounded
towards the latter nineteenth century, women remained in the profession for
the larger income it produced and, in some cases, the independence it provided. The rise and visibility of prostitutes in Port of Spain did not escape
the attention of upper-class observers (nor certainly, their patronage). With
regard to the former, for example, the historian and former Chief of Police
L. M. Fraser was particularly focused on the expansion of the profession.
He expressed concern not only for the moral decline of the young women
engaged in the trade, but, almost equally, for the financial support prostitutes
gave to their male partners, thus allowing them to eschew regular employment and participate in other criminal activities (Fraser 1891, 1892).

    With regard to the latter, middle- and upper-class men almost certainly
frequented the brothels, taverns, and barrack yards to solicit the services of
prostitutes. Indeed, the lure of the "entertainments" available in the Jamette
quarters of Port of Spain produced what came to be called "jacketmen," or
Lom Kamisol. These were the members of the "respectable" classes who often

went masked to hide their features, but remained dressed in "jackets" as emblems of their class position. Many of these jacketmen maintained long-standing relationships with women in the brothels and barrack yards of Port of Spain and were later key figures in the institutionalization of the calypso tents in the early twentieth century.

If certain women were a central feature of the Jamette world, indeed to the point of being synonymous with it, the social-geographic center of their world was the barrack yard. The barrack yards were created by the construction of barrack buildings around a central, open space. Such barracks provided housing for laborers in and around Port of Spain and consisted of a long, low building with small rooms divided from one another but under the same roof. The barracks themselves were unsanitary, crowded, and hot. The barrack yards were communal and often held a single, shared water source, but provided some respite from the heat and were an important space for social interactions. As Andrew Pearse described them:

> The barrack yard community, which still exists in Port-of-Spain, has a certain character. Accommodation is such that there can be little privacy, and the yard in the centre becomes a common living place. Water and latrines are common facilities, and there is competition for their use. Deep antagonisms develop which burst out at times, but are largely restrained. A sensitive public opinion develops in the yard and expresses itself sharply. Few actions escape its scrutiny. An order of domination is built up in a series of encounters between rivals. (1988 [1956], 38)

Barrack yards became associated with the world of the Jamettes. They are identified as the source and performance center for many masquerade types including such enduring types as the Baby Doll, which form the core of the older masquerade types that appeared later during J'ouvert and which frequently burlesqued the sexual relationships and consequences between members of different classes (Green and Scher 2007, 227). It was in the barrack yards where Jamettes and their "bad john" partners socialized and where calypso, stick fighting, and other expressive forms central to the Carnival were rehearsed and developed. The barrack yards were not the only places that gave rise to the many masqueraded forms that developed in the late nineteenth and early twentieth centuries, and indeed, neighborhoods across the city developed their own identities, creative forms, and, perhaps not surprisingly, internecine rivalries.

The Jamette carnival, beginning in the 1860s or thereabouts and continuing into the reform movements of the early twentieth century, interwove expressive cultural forms (song, dance, drumming, and masquerading for example) with martial arts (calinda stick-fighting), and territorial rivalries. The origins of what are now the large colorful bands seen in Port of Spain at Carnival time grew from competitive, sometimes violent organizations whose roots lay deep in neighborhood pride and the protection of territorial integrity. These "bands" developed and evolved into, for example, steel band sides and their masqueraders.[4]

Early descriptions of these organized bands are frequently of women's masquerade groups. One of the earliest uses of the term "band" for a group of masqueraders appears in 1874, where men and women are decried by the *Port of Spain Gazette* as traveling in disreputable "herds" (cited in Pearse, 1988 [1956], 31). In 1877, bands were sufficiently coherent and well-known not only to have names but also to have those names be a point of pride and neighborhood identity. Twelve city bands are described in a newspaper editorial in February of 1877 each representing a particular area of the city:

> There were Free-grammar from Corbeau Town, the Bois d'Inde from Upper
> Prince Street, the bakers from east of the Market, the Danois . . . from Dry
> River, the Peau de Canelle from the Royal Jail area, the Corail from Newtown,
> the s'Amandes from the Wharves, the maribones from Belmont, and the Cerf-
> Volants from Duncan Street." (Brereton 1979, 167)

In addition to these bands, there were well-known women's bands, many of which were not only actively engaged with and charged in the aftermath of the Canboulay battles. These bands carried names that reflected both patois- and English-speaking members. For example, there were the Dahlias, nineteen of whom were charged for their involvement with Canboulay, the Mousselines, Magenta, Maribones, True-Blues, Black Balls, and Don't Care Damns. Court records note that many of the women had English names and therefore could have been immigrants from Barbados or other small islands, but both court witnesses and young Frances Richard/Edwards report women calling out in patois (Brereton 1979, 167). These bands of women were noted for fighting with each other and maintained rivalries that defended both their ethnic/ linguistic identities and the integrity of their territorial claims. Nevertheless, what emerges in in the later nineteenth century is not merely the turf battles of rival gangs, but the development of possible collaboration in the face of the repression or removal of the most important form of cultural expression available to this population: the Carnival itself. Brereton notes that in this period Carnival becomes the arena in which "class antagonisms were worked out" (1979, 169). Pearse echoes this perception as well, as he describes the pre-Canboulay riots Carnival as largely an opportunity for regional rivalries to burst out onto the street in moments of cultural competition and frequent violence. However, he suggests that Canboulay changed something: "And finally Canboulay, in 1881 and on a few other occasions, took on a class character, with the disappearance of band rivalries in united action against the police (Pearse 1956, 39). Crowley suggests in his essay, in the same special issue of *Caribbean Quarterly*, that the events of Canboulay of 1881 were in fact a sea change. He writes,

> . . . police intervention on Canboulay night brought to a head several different types of existing hostility to the administration, causing new social groups to identify themselves nominally [as] "the People" and the people's festival, so that Carnival began to be a symbol for a national sentiment shared by a broad section of the community, and in opposition to the administration, manned largely by British [i.e., "foreign" officials]. (Crowley 1988 [1956], 40)

If these historians are correct, as I think they are, the involvement of women and women's bands was central to a chain of events that lead to the Hamilton Commission, and ultimately the preservation and protection of the festival. It also led to the strong movement of reform spearheaded largely by the colored middle class that resulted in the decline of the Jamette-era celebrations and the rise of the more controlled and respectable Carnivals of the early twentieth century. That involvement itself was part of a broader effort on the part of the colored middle classes to make common cause with the largely African-descended working-class culture in an attempt to move towards greater political independence (Scher 2003, 36–43).

By the 1880s, the presence of bands was a fundamental feature of the Jamette Carnival, and women were central to them. Daniel Crowley notes in his description of the "Jamet" bands of the 1880s that they often featured women known as "matadors" (Ahye 1978), women sometimes reputed to be former prostitutes who gained some measure of wealth, generally wore flamboyant dress and jewelry, and were known to have many male admirers. Matadors often kept "sweetmen," individuals who lived off the largesse of the matador but who may have had their reputations as stick fighters, singers, and so on. They were also clearly entrepreneurial businesswomen, community leaders, and public figures. Within the local politics of the neighborhood, the barrack yards and the street played a significant role (Cummings 2004). It is telling that the names of many of these women survive (not all of them necessarily matadors it should be noted). Names such as Alice Sugar, Mossie Millie, Ocean Lizzie, Sybil Steele, Darling Dan, Ling Mama, Bodicea, and Piti Belle Lily are integrated into the lore and legend of the great figures of the

Jamette period. Their reputations were as fearless leaders, sometimes violent and uncompromising, but they were not without controversy as well. Some calypsos that endure from this period were harsh in their judgement. The chantwell Cedric Le Blanc composed these verses: "Bodicea first and then Petite Belle/The devil waiting for them in hell" (Pearse 1988 [1956], 162).

Port of Spain, 1870–85: Setting the Stage for the Canboulay Riots

As I have suggested above, the scene of the disturbances of 1881 was no stranger to unrest. The area from what was known as Medical Corner towards the east Dry River was a decidedly working-class neighborhood, and a frequent site for police surveillance and action. But for all its relative economic class uniformity, it was certainly not a culturally homogenous neighborhood. Former Trinidadian slaves and their families lived alongside free West African migrants; many of them settled in Trinidad after their liberation from slave ships operating contra British law. There were former black soldiers from the West India regiments, as well as freed American slaves who had fought for the British in the war of 1812. The neighborhoods surrounding what would become Woodford Square in central downtown Port of Spain were also teeming with Barbadian migrants who had been enticed by higher wages and the hope of available land after their own emancipation left them in an island with almost no available areas in which to settle freely (Brereton 1979, 110–12).

On the corner of Duke Street and what is now Charlotte Street (at one point called St. Ann's Road) there stood a Portuguese church, built to accommodate arrivals from Madeira who began arriving in the 1840s (Mavrogordato, 1977). A newer church was built shortly afterwards, up the road at Oxford Street. Peons from Venezuela also crowded into this dense cityscape during a time when indentured laborers from India and China were also present and visible in the cultural life of the colony. In addition to this cultural diversity was added an astonishing linguistic diversity that included English-speaking Barbadians and African-North Americans, patois-speaking Trinidadians, Spanish-speaking Venezuelans, and a number of West African languages, most likely including Yoruba and Fon but also Igbo, and Mandinka (Carr 1953), Portuguese, Hindi, and Cantonese. This vibrant mix of people did usually have one thing in common, which was a relatively low position in the class hierarchy of nineteenth-century Trinidad.

This sector of society, which included laborers, squatters, and the un- and underemployed, was largely excluded from the centers of official political power on the island. Moreover, they were often viewed culturally through

the exacting and prejudicial lens of Victorian social Darwinism and ethnic determinism that expected low social station from low "racial orders."
The term "Jamette" was applied, ultimately, to this portion of society, these
neighborhoods, and by extension, to the kind of Carnival they played. Tell-
ingly, the term "Jamette" is also most frequently applied to the women of this
demographic. Although men were included in understandings of what the
Jamette was as a kind of social space/population, and were certainly included
in a broad understanding of what the Jamette Carnival was, the use of the
term to designate a particular kind of individual is almost always applied to
women (that is, as I suggested earlier: a Jamette is generally never a man).
The Jamettes, then were a kind of metonymical extension of and perhaps a
distillation of a broader social category and its implications. This usage transcended the Jamette period and persists today:

> In present-day Trinidad, the word jamet [*sic*] no longer exists in popular usage
> to denote the un-gendered subaltern or "underworld" classes. Its feminized ver-
> sion continues in the popular vocabulary, however, and is part of a whole con-
> stellation of words used to describe women whose being or behavior is judged
> to be morally loose, sexually promiscuous, crude, or noisily quarrelsome. (de
> Freitas 1992, 15)

The Jamette class (men and women) did not encompass all laborers per se. The
upper classes of Victorian society were, especially in the colonies, generally
consistent in distinguishing between those who were productively employed
(and knew their station): the honest and often romanticized working classes;
and the un- and underemployed whose "idleness" was of their own making,
who were politically dangerous and morally corrupting. The key distinguishing characteristic between types of poor people, all else being equal within
a given population, was whether one labored or not. Interestingly, laboring
as a positive social activity was valued by both conservative and liberal/pro-
gressive ideologies alike. Those who occupied the lowest social order were
those who were poor and did not work, refused work, and/or were engaged in
morally dubious activities. Karl Marx calls these the lumpenproletariat in *The
Eighteenth Brumaire of Louis Napoleon* (1852) and says of them:

> Alongside decayed roués with dubious means of subsistence and of dubious
> origin, alongside ruined and adventurous offshoots of the bourgeoisie, were vaga-
> bonds, discharged soldiers, discharged jailbirds, escaped galley slaves, swindlers,
> mountebanks, Lazzaroni, pickpockets, tricksters, gamblers, maquereaux [pimps],
> brothel keepers, porters, literati, organ grinders, ragpickers, knife grinders,

tinkers, beggars—in short, the whole indefinite, disintegrated mass, thrown hither and thither, which the French call la bohème . . . (Marx 1852)[5]

A central characteristic (no less Victorian in the centrality of its importance) of this lumpenproletariat was the implied presence of contamination, filth, and disease. Indeed, implicitly it seems as though the lumpenproletariat are themselves epidemical with regard to the broader class struggle. Marx's delineation of this non-class of people seems very much in keeping with the writings of prominent reformers of the period, including Charles Kingsley's (see below) friend Henry Mayhew who, in describing English society, bemoaned what he called "the nomad" whom he distinguished from civilized members of society:

> By his repugnance to regular and continuous labour—by his want of providence in laying up store for the future . . . —by his passion for stupefying herbs and roots, and, when possible, for intoxicating fermented liquors . . . —by his love of libidinous dances . . . —by the looseness of his notion as to property—by the absence of chastity among his women, and his disregard of female honour—and lastly, by his vague sense of religion. (Mayhew 1861)

Thus, in late nineteenth-century England and consequently its colonies, there persisted an imbricated relationship between class, impurity, and danger to the social order which was further compounded by contemporary ideas of race and gender. The awareness these relationships and their public expression, already deeply entrenched and widely reproduced through the kinds of moral instructional literary production to be found in England, made its way into the colonial travel literature in the colonies. Here, the presence of "lower" races such as Africans, Indians, and Chinese, made the issue of social control even more precarious, but also a ready substitute target for the same kinds of moral opining that the upper classes directed at the white working classes in Europe.

No matter, however, what level of judgement was visited upon white European workers, "delicate"-featured "coolies," effeminate and pale "Frenchmen," or "humorless" Chinese in Trinidad, the deepest level of fascination and revulsion is reserved not simply for people of African descent, but for women of African descent: the Jamettes.[6]

The colonial regime of representation in the 1870s and 1880s in Trinidad was largely expressed through memoirs and travelogues meant for foreign consumption. Newspapers provide a local-colonial view of Jamette life, while official reports, legal documents, and other administrative sources provide yet another source. Charles Kingsley, whose work *At Last: A Christmas in the West Indies* provided much detail of life in Port of Spain in the 1870s and which is composed from the perspective of a visiting English man of letters, reflects that curious mix of Christian socialism, social reformer, racist, and romantic. His views of Trinidad are of interest here because of his perceptions of the urban population during the general era of the Canboulay riots. Notably, Kingsley's first impression of Port of Spain, as he tells it, is made upon arriving at "the low quay which has just been reclaimed from the mud of the gulf" where he sees "the multitude of people doing nothing. You will find them or their brown duplicates, in the same places to-morrow and next day" (Kingsley 1872, 86). Indeed, for Kingsley the most apt comparison he can find for the "idle" Trinidadians crowding the docks is the Lazzaroni of Naples. This is an intriguing comparison, for the Lazzaroni were not simply the mass of un- and underemployed street people of Naples, they occupied an important symbolic position in the kind of Victorian social and political taxonomy of labor. The Lazzaroni, by virtue of their lack of stability within the predictable universe of labor relations, were, certainly in the minds of authors like Marx and Engels, the very definition of the lumpenproletariat as noted above.

They were the antithesis of the revolutionary proletarians whose class-consciousness and organized resistance to oppression stood in stark contrast to the morally and politically dangerous "mobs" who were prone to act collectively in crowds and follow demagogues. I focus on Kingsley's comparison here, and contextualize it within the revolutionary discourse of the day primarily to highlight the persistence of the Victorian virtues of order and productivity within the political thought of Victorian liberals. The *disorderly* poor are the problem. For Marx, in fact, they most probably were permanently lost to the revolutionary struggle. Kingsley was no Marxist, but, like Mayhew, was instead an early pro-labor Christian Socialist.[7] He was fascinated, as many Victorians were, with the "tropics" (Thompson 2006) and he tended to focus on the relationships between race, education, order, and civilization, as did many of his contemporaries. His attention to such matters further betrays the kind of "middle class fantasies about the lumpenproletariat" (Stallybrass and White, 1986) that are more broadly captured in writings about the world of the Jamettes, their Carnival, and the role of women in that context. We should not be surprised, then, to see the kind of rhetoric surrounding the Jamette Carnival and Jamette women that we see. According to contemporary accounts, the Jamette Carnival was marked by the presence of "the usual ostentatious promenades of those ladies whose existence is usually ignored or accepted as a necessary evil" (Crowley 1996, 57). These types of observations, and there are many, are a fair indication of the general preoccupation

Victorian reformers had with class, notions of both physical pollution, ideas about desire and sexuality, and the precariousness of the social order.

By the 1860s, a new form of Carnival had emerged and was a touchstone for a general commentary on the state of the moral, economic and political state of the colony. Local newspapers, including the more conservative *Port of Spain Gazette*, were prolific in their description of the general collapse of the carnival and its appropriation by the lower classes. What is remarkable, however, about contemporary descriptions of the carnival from the late 1860s to the riots of 1881, is the amount of attention paid specifically to women masqueraders, and especially to black women. The "foreign" fascination with black women in Trinidad is a mainstay of works such as Kinglsey's and, even earlier, Charles William Day's (1852). Whereas "colored" middle- and upper-class women are almost universally praised for their beauty, exoticism, and colorful attire, black women are generally singled out as exemplars of the degeneracy and savagery of the lowest orders. Descriptions of black women in general tended to focus on their "coarseness" and "primitiveness," and over-all they seem to stand for the enduring challenge of the "civilizing mission" of the reform-minded colonial classes.[8] Indeed, "Jamette" as a term becomes synonymous with lower-class women whose social position reflects every kind of dangerous transgressive possibility: they are prostitutes, masculine in demeanor, violent, outspoken, loud, entrepreneurial, public, and in positions of power and authority in their communities. Even relatively more favorable descriptions such as Day's note: "Parties of negro ladies danced through the streets, each *clique* distinguished by boddices [*sic*] of the same colour" (Day 1852, 313). Indeed, the role of women in masquerade bands is increasingly noted in the 1860s and 1870s, especially in relation to the Canboulay celebrations.

As Peter Stallybrass and Allon White note, "The relation of social division and exclusion to the production of desire emerges with great clarity in the nineteenth century city" (Stallybrass and White 1986, 126). This observation is reflected in the idea and use of the term "Jamette" itself, which, by most accounts, is derived from the French term diamètre (literally "diameter"), meaning the line that cuts across the "circle" of society and divides low from high, rich from poor, black from white. The idea of a social dividing line is itself worth a brief exploration. As Andrew Pearse writes:

> In Trinidad the superstructure was by no means monolithic. There were persistent antagonisms between the British administration and the French landed gentry, and sharp collateral competition between the Catholic and Protestant religious institutions. But there was agreement as to public order, a hierarchical

status system grouped beneath the office of Governor, a recognised system of behaviour as between one class and another, and the existence of an effective and productive labour force, Christianisation and "civilisation" (Pearse 1988 [1956], 191).

Carnival itself, with its overriding themes of license, transgression, inversion, and disruption was a pushing point on the idea of a diameter that should not, or indeed, could not be crossed, but routinely was. By naming a whole class of people, their activities, cultural forms, ideas about gender, sexuality, race, and class *after* the very limits of their lives, there must have been more than a degree of consciousness about the relationships between their actions and their political condition. As Rosamond King says, "their political engagement was connected to their consciousness of the implications of their performance" (King 1999, 209). Women, in this political and economic class, were Jamette all year long, not simply during Carnival time. Carnival was a temporal space that allowed women to push against the conceptual framing that identified them *in general*. If, as Stallybrass and White have argued, Victorians mapped the hierarchies of the social world onto the body, the embodied rituals of reversal and transgression undertaken by the Jamette women of the nineteenth century were certainly political in nature and, I would argue, quite self-consciously so. The heightened political awareness of the Jamettes was not created by the events of 1881 and beyond. The coordinated mobilization of that political awareness in and around Carnival in response to attempts by the colonial police force to eliminate a vital space of cultural expression should certainly be seen as intentional. The goal of the Canboulay actions was protest and resistance; it was not a spontaneous and wanton "riot."

The Canboulay Riots of 1881

Canboulay was not beloved by the ruling elite. It was denounced and decried at every opportunity. Even after the events of the 1880s, the goal was not the faithful preservation of the Jamette carnival as a kind of cultural heritage. The end of the Jamette era, such as it was, was through reform, not repression. But starting in 1877, with the appointment of Captain Baker as inspector-commandant of police, the government took a turn at more draconian forms of control with the probable goal of destroying, if not Carnival itself, this version of it and all that it represented. In 1880, Baker had, as it were, taken the Canboulay revelers by surprise and successfully confiscated their torches, drums, and staves. No doubt Baker saw this as a victory and was intent on repeating this show of force the following year. What followed is remarkable in that a general truce amongst traditionally warring bands was negotiated and faithfully carried out. Furthermore, these now organized factions planned a resistance and carried it out. There was fighting and damage to property. Brereton notes that the fighting ended "inconclusively," but I do not think it was considered inconclusive in the minds of the protestors themselves. They had achieved a great victory, which was borne out by the arrival of Governor Freeling to address them and promise that their festivities would be allowed to continue. It is also worth noting that the representatives of the Borough Council who went to the governor to ask that he intervene described the "maskers" as "excited but not riotous" (Brereton 1979, 171).

The intrigue that surrounds the renewed disturbances two years later in 1883 are "juicy," in that the acts of violence that marred the celebrations that year were very much between bands, but more precisely between one band, the Newgates, and essentially all the other ones. It was widely reported that the defeated and humiliated Baker had enjoined the Newgate band to fight and perhaps even compensated them for their actions, all to discredit the Jamette Carnival. Indeed, it essentially worked. By 1884, the Canboulay was effectively abolished, and this opened the era of further, gradual, inexorable reform.

Conclusion

Given the social and political stakes, the overarching political character and quality of Jamette, public, creative forms of expression, and the intentional coordination of actors in the moment, the events leading up to Canboulay in 1881 might as well be renamed the Canboulay protests of 1881. Given that frequently the distinction between a "riot" and "protest" hinges on the legality of the actions involved, if not always the presence of violence, these distinctions must be nimbly reimagined in circumstances where virtually no form of "protest" is legal at all. Furthermore, although the events were violent, they were directed at a precise target of repression: the police themselves and, perhaps even more precisely, the figure of Captain Baker. In any event, the role of women was central to the success of the activities and, indeed, to the survival and perpetuation of expressive cultural forms that remain central to the *mas'* tradition in Trinidad.

Notes

1. It should be noted that there is a discrepancy in the historical record here, and that in the papers of Andrew Pearse, noted scholar of Trinidad Carnival, the account is preserved as the "eye-witness account of Frances Richard (not Edwards), 96, of 11 Rudin Street, Belmont." It was given to Trinidadian folklorist J. D. Elder on July 4, 1953. If the Pearse papers are correct, that would have made Frances Richard twenty-four years old at the time of the riots (Cowley 1996, 272).

2. Liberated Africans from Havana, Cuba, and elsewhere began arriving in Trinidad in significant but small numbers in the 1830s. Recruitment of labor from Africa was approved and began in earnest by the early 1840s, when nearly 14,000 liberated Africans were resettled in the Caribbean, including Trinidad (see Adderley 2006, 63–91).

3. I am focusing here on 1881 and the historical period surrounding it. I want to note that 1881 was not the first or last Carnival-related disturbance (there was another significant one in 1883, for example). I also do not have the space to cover the details of this period from a legislative point of view. For example, the catalogue of ordinances and other legal impediments imposed on the expression of African/Creole cultural forms are important to gaining a full picture of the events of this period.

4. These developments are well documented in excellent histories of Carnival, beginning, essentially, with the 1956 special double issue of the *Caribbean Quarterly* and continuing with Errol Hill's masterful 1972 *Trinidad Carnival* to the efflorescence of work in the 1990s, for example, that of Gordon Rohlehr (1990), Stephen Stuempfle (1995), John Crowley (1998), etc.

5. I am discussing Marx here not in the context of applying a Marxian analysis to the colonial Caribbean, but as an example of the pervasiveness of Victorian-era ideological assumptions that influenced observations and proposed reformations of the social order as seen from a European perspective. What strikes me is the similarity of the description and categorization of various social orders and the uniformity of the application of nascent nineteenth-century social science despite political ideological differences. It was these broadly shared ways of seeing the world, despite potential political differences among thinkers, that, in my view, shape the way the Caribbean is described by Europeans traveling to or residing in the Caribbean at this time. This applies, I believe, to Mayhew's observations about the English working classes as well.

6. These particular "sketches" of the diverse population of Port of Spain are glossed from Charles Kingsley's *At Last a Christmas in the West Indies*. This is one of the best-known late nineteenth-century popular works on Trinidad and was often cited in the travel literature to the West Indies into the early twentieth century.

7. Kingsley has a very curious passage in his chapter on Port of Spain, in which he defends the poor's right to be "idle": "If a poor man neither steals, begs, nor rebels (and these people do not do the two latter), has he not as much right to be idle as a rich man? To say that neither has a right to be idle is, of course, sheer socialism, and a heresy not to be tolerated" (Kingsley 1872, 86).

8. Kingsley's passage is worth quoting at length here: "I fear that a stranger would feel a shock—and that not a slight one—at the first sight of the average negro women of Port of Spain, especially the younger. Their masculine figures, their ungainly gestures, their loud and sudden laughter, even when walking alone, and their general coarseness, shocks, and must shock. It must be remembered that this is a seaport town; and one in which the license usual in such places on both sides of the Atlantic is aggravated by the superabundant animal vigour and the perfect independence of the younger women. It is a painful subject. I shall touch it in these pages as seldom and as lightly as I can. There is, I verily believe, a large class of Negresses in Port of Spain and in the country, both Catholic and Protestant, who try their best to be respectable, after their standard: but unfortunately, here, as elsewhere over the world, the scum rises naturally to the top, and intrudes itself on the eye" (Kingsley 1872, 87). As typically and casually racist as these types of "observations" are, they contain noteworthy bits of information. For example, Kingsley here identifies the "perfect independence," of young Creole women, a detail that is borne out in historical research.

Bibliography

Adderley, Roseanne Marion. *"New Negroes from Africa": Slave Trade Abolition and Free African Settlement in the Nineteenth-Century Caribbean.* Bloomington: Indiana University Press, 2006.

Allsopp, Richard. *Dictionary of Caribbean English Usage.* Oxford: Oxford University Press, 1996.

Barnes, Natasha. "Body Talk: Notes on Women and Spectacle in Contemporary Trinidad Carnival." *Small Axe* 7 (March 2000): 93–105.

Brereton, Bridget. *Race Relations in Colonial Trinidad, 1870–1900.* Cambridge: Cambridge University Press. 1979.

Carr, Andrew T., and Eugene Beard. "A Rada Community in Trinidad." *Caribbean Quarterly* 3 (1) (1953): 36–54.

Cowley, John. *Carnival Canboulay and Calypso: Traditions in the Making.* Cambridge: Cambridge University Press, 1996.

Crowley, Daniel J. "The Traditional Masques of Carnival." In *Trinidad Carnival: A Republication of the Caribbean Quarterly Trinidad Carnival Issue,* ed. Andrew Pearse, 42–90. Port of Spain: Paria Publishing, 1988 (1956).

Cummings, James Damian. *Barrack-yard Dwellers.* Kingston: University of the West Indies, School of Continuing Studies, 2004.

de Freitas, Patricia A. "Disrupting 'the Nation': Gender Transformations in the Trinidad Carnival." *New West Indian Guide* 73 (1/2) (1999): 5–34.

de Verteuil, Anthony. *The Years of Revolt: Trinidad, 1881–1888.* Port of Spain: Paria Publishing, 1984.

Elder, J. D. "Cannes Brulees." In "Trinidad and Tobago Carnival (Special Expanded Issue)." *Drama Review* 1.42 (3) (Fall 1998): 38–43.

Franco, Pamela R. "The 'Unruly Woman' in Nineteenth-Century Trinidad Carnival." *Small Axe* 7 (March 2000): 60–76.

Fraser, L. M. *History of Trinidad*. London: Routledge, 2014 (1891, 1892).

Green, Garth L., and Philip W. Scher. *Trinidad Carnival: The Cultural Politics of a Transnational Festival*. Bloomington: Indiana University Press, 2007.

Hall, Tony. "Lennox Pierre, an Interview with Tony Hall." In "Trinidad and Tobago Carnival (Special Expanded Issue)." *Drama Review* 1.42 (3) (Fall 1998): 41.

Joseph, E. L. *History of Trinidad*. Port of Spain: Columbus Publishers, 1837.

King, Rosamond S. "Jamette Women's Double Cross: Creating an Archive." *Women and Performance: A Journal of Feminist Theory*, no. 21 (11:1) (1999): 203–210.

Kingsley, Charles. *At Last: A Christmas in the West Indies*. London: Macmillan and Co., 1872.

Mavrogordato, Olga J. *Voices in the Street*. Port of Spain: Inprint Caribbean, 1979.

Noel, Samantha A. "De Jamette in We: Redefining Performance in Contemporary Trinidad Carnival." *Small Axe* 14, no. 31 (1) (March 2010): 60–78.

Pearse, Andrew. "Carnival in Nineteenth Century Trinidad." In *Trinidad Carnival: A Republication of the Caribbean Quarterly Trinidad Carnival Issue*, ed. Andrew Pearse, 4–41. Port of Spain: Paria Publishing, 1988 (1956).

Pearse, Andrew. "Mitto Sampson on Calypso Legends of the Nineteenth Century." In *Trinidad Carnival: A Republication of the Caribbean Quarterly Trinidad Carnival Issue*, ed. Andrew Pearse, 140–63. Port of Spain: Paria Publishing, 1988 (1956).

Powrie, Barbara E. "The Changing Attitude of the Coloured Middle Class Towards Carnival." In *Trinidad Carnival: A Republication of the Caribbean Quarterly Trinidad Carnival Issue*, ed. Andrew Pearse, 91–107. Port of Spain: Paria Publishing, 1988 (1956).

Reddock, Rhoda E. *Women, Labour, and Politics in Trinidad and Tobago: A History*. Kingston: Ian Randle Publishers, 1994.

Rohlehr, Gordon. *Calypso and Society in Pre-Independence Trinidad*. Port of Spain, Trinidad: 1990.

Scher, Philip W. *Carnival and the Formation of a Caribbean Transnation*. Gainesville: University of Florida Press, 2003.

Sookdeo, Neil A. *Freedom, Festivals and Caste in Trinidad After Slavery: A Society in Transition*. Xlibris, 2001.

Stallybrass, Peter, and Allon White. *The Politics and Poetics of Transgression*. Ithaca: Cornell University Press, 1986.

Trotman, David V. "Women and Crime in Late Nineteenth Century Trinidad." *Caribbean Quarterly* 30 (3/4) (September–December 1984): 60–72.

Trotman, David Vincent. *Crime in Trinidad: Conflict and Control in a Plantation Society, 1838–1900*. Knoxville: University of Tennessee Press, 1986.

Turner, Mary. "'The 11 O'Clock Flog': Women, Work and Labour Law in the British Caribbean." In *Working Slavery, Pricing Freedom: Perspectives from the Caribbean, Africa and the African Diaspora*, ed. Verene A. Shepherd, 249–72. Kingston: Ian Randle Publishers, 2002.

Winer, Lise. *Dictionary of the English/Creole of Trinidad and Tobago*. Montreal: McGill-Queen's University Press, 2008.

Chapter 4

Taking the Queen to the Streets: The Jaycees Carnival Queen Competition and the Pretty *Mas'* Aesthetic

—Samantha Noel

Trinidad Carnival experienced a number of shifts in the mid-twentieth century that would shape its evolution. The introduction of the Jaycees Carnival Queen competition into Trinidad Carnival was one of the most important steps that the authorities took to institutionalize the festival and suppress the various creative expressions of the masses. The Junior Chamber International, a worldwide association of young professionals, established the Trinidadian Jaycees division in 1949.[1] The Trinidad organization prided itself in community engagement, and the Trinidad Carnival Queen competition certainly offered the Jaycees one way of pursuing this goal.

Both the *Argos* and the *Trinidad Guardian*, the two major newspapers, promoted in different ways the continental model of Carnival during the early twentieth century in an effort to displace the popular Jametre Carnival of the late nineteenth century.[2] These developments occurred despite race riots and an emerging labor movement of the 1930s catalyzed by returning members of the British armed forces, who had experienced discrimination in Europe only to find a lack of employment and rights at home. In addition, the Seditious Publications Draft Bill was passed in 1920 to control political periodicals such as the UNIA's official organ, the *New World*.[3] A decade later similar controls began to affect Carnival through state censorship of calypsos, the voice of the masses.[4] By the advent of World War II, the American presence posed another challenge to traditional moral codes. Carnival went hand in hand with prostitution, crime, and gambling.[5] Eventually, the forces of suppression threatened the melodic yet treasonable strides of the steel bands.

The postwar governing bodies created by the newspapers hoped to regain aesthetic and performative control of Carnival, now with a potential international audience at stake.[6] One of them, the *Trinidad Guardian*'s Carnival Celebrations Committee, held the first Carnival Queen show in 1947.[7] By the late 1950s, the competition had developed into the Jaycees Carnival Queen Show.

The Jaycees Carnival Queen competition ritualized the celebration and idealization of women of European and mixed descent in the realm of Carnival. During colonialism and the first decades of independence, the competition influenced how gender and class were presented in Carnival and in society. The first beauty pageant of its kind in Trinidad and Tobago, the show was part of a greater tradition of beauty pageants in the colonial English-speaking Caribbean.[8] Colonial female subjects were expected to adhere to the models of beauty and femininity celebrated in the Jaycees Carnival Queen competition. The Jaycees Carnival Queen became a symbol of nationalism, representing the perfect beauty of the island nation. This "beauty queen" ideal still heavily influences contemporary women masqueraders.

In this chapter, I will examine how the Jaycees Carnival Queen competition upheld upper and middle-class mores in opposition to a largely black and working-class aesthetic, thereby creating a national tradition. By the 1940s, the competition became the focus of the annual festival. It eclipsed the Calypso King competition, the hub of creative, social, and political expression for the black masses. I will first present the aims of the Carnival Queen competition in order to understand how each queen's reign transcended the short Carnival season so that she became an eminent figure throughout the year in colonial Trinidad. Imagery of the competition in newspapers also helped to promote a Eurocentric archetype of the ideal woman, further imposing the ideologies of the elites to all.

Through an examination of how the reigning queen performed and publicized a Victorian femininity, I will explain how the competition celebrated the type of woman the female colonial subject was expected to become. A visit by Princess Margaret in 1955 further promulgated these ideals, since she represented an archetype of royalty to aspiring Carnival queens. By and large, the Carnival queen was the elite's systematic response to the ever-present Jamette figure who was closely associated with Carnival. The Jaycees Carnival Queen represented the antithesis of the working-class culture from which the Jamettes and the musical form calypso emerged. But, more importantly, under the auspices of the elite-run governing organizations of the festival, the founding of the queen competition was part of a larger scheme to change the face of Trinidad Carnival—the Jaycees Carnival Queen not only became the core of Carnival, but she also served as the visual marker of modernity many felt the festival needed.

While some scholars have claimed that the advent of the bikini *mas'* took place in the 1980s, I argue that this costume aesthetic existed in Trinidad Carnival as far back as the 1950s.[9] It was a key part of the grand costumes for the Jaycees Carnival Queen competition. The face and body of contestants had to be illuminated, contributing to the beauty pageant-style orientation of the competition. As a result of this tradition, costumes were increasingly utilized to accentuate women's figures in Carnival. The aesthetic of the costumes seen in the competition differed from those on the streets during Carnival. In fact, many of the designers who created pageant costumes later became notable Carnival costume designers and contributed to significant changes in costume design in the 1970s.

The designers' shift in orientation toward an emphasis on the body also changed how masqueraders and spectators perceived the Carnival costume aesthetic. Costume designs from the 1970s onward required less material and, thus, less creative execution. This meant that a new evaluation of creativity in the carnivalesque sphere was bound to occur. Structure, innovation, and greater color palettes were not emphasized as much. The bikini became the basis of the costume, embellished with beads, sequins, appliqués, headpieces, and occasionally feather plumes. Visually, the bikini *mas'* of this contemporary moment did what costumes never did before in Carnival: complement the masquerader's body. This new focus on physicality in costume design coincided with the masquerader's awareness of her body and its potential for creative expression. This new awareness of the body in Carnival inspired revelers to prepare their bodies in a way that paralleled the physical preparation of Jaycees Carnival Queen contestants. This caused changes in the masqueraders' actions. The presence and actions of these women masqueraders had a great impact on the festival.

History of the Carnival Queen Competition

In *Cultural Conundrums*, Natasha Barnes notes that, according to historical evidence, acquiescent white femininity ensured the maintenance and reproduction of the racial hierarchy of plantation society in the Caribbean.[10] Yet, these white women were never considered as symbolic of plantocratic power as white men. Barnes explains that women's invisibility in the public sphere changed by the twentieth century, and asks about this shift: "what ideological conditions in the twentieth century enabled white women to assume a visible constitutive presence in plantocratic cultural representation?"[11] While Barnes cites the social organization and cultural practice of cricket as the first site in the Anglophone Caribbean where this shift was apparent, I would argue that in Trinidad, Carnival was the domain in which white womanhood was first displayed and celebrated in public.

The pageantry of Trinidad Carnival assumed an especially stately demeanor by 1940 when the governor and his wife began officiating at the opening show of the Marine Square (now Independence Square) competition on Carnival Monday.[12] Before the end of World War II, middle-class white women often played *mas'* on lorries, although it was rare to see whites immersed in the merrymaking.[13] Lorries were still being used even after the war, as evidenced by a photograph of middle- and upper-class women masquerading in a lorry party at the 1949 Carnival (figure 1). Authorities not only ensured that the festival promoted and maintained the predominance of a Eurocentric aesthetic, but they also made certain that women of mostly European descent were exhibited and commemorated in protected spaces during Carnival.

Within this paradigm, the Carnival Queen competitions emerged. In an effort to raise funds for the "Guardian Neediest Case Fund," the *Trinidad Guardian* first organized one in the early 1920s.[14] The Calypso King competition of 1946 included a Carnival Queen competition. However, it would be the Carnival Celebrations Committee's presentation of the event in 1947 that offered the beauty pageant independently within the arena of Carnival.[15] Even this early in the competition's development, the stakes were high as both the winner and the runner-up won all expenses-paid trips to Barbados.[16] The next year, the competition was part of an agenda to offset the threat of a mostly Afro-Trinidadian Downtown Carnival competition.[17] The *Trinidad Guardian*, which backed the competition through the Carnival Celebrations Committee, referred to the winner as Miss Trinidad and, on its front pages, featured photographs of the contestants and the winner of the competition.[18]

The agencies of the colonialist ruling class employed the aforementioned measures to usurp a festival still dominated by the cultural practices of the black masses. Newspaper headlines about the event plastered in the *Trinidad Guardian* promoted what the elites saw as the new symbol for Trinidad Carnival—the Carnival Queen. The front page of an issue of *The Guardian* from 1949 is such an example. With the headline "Seven More Queens Join Savannah Contest," photographs of the seven recent arrivals are supplemented by a caption that includes descriptions like "21-year old blonde" and "17-year old brunette" for the contestants (figures 2A and 2B).[19]

For the organizers of the competition, it was imperative that the Carnival Queen competition emerge as the antithesis of the vulgarity and licentiousness (and thereby Africanity) that, in their view, had come to dominate Carnival. The violent steel band clashes, the defiant masquerading traditions, and the inappropriate "wining" of Jamettes all caused the white elite to feel threatened. These practices prompted campaigns to change what they saw as the "ugly" face of Carnival.[20] Earlier attempts to transform Carnival from "ugly" to "beautiful" only had a temporary impact on the festival in the early twentieth century. This time, in post-World War II Trinidad, the European aesthetic and ideological stamp would have to bear a more permanent impression. Through the continuation of the mandated "continental" model for Carnival costumes and behavior, in addition to the introduction of a beauty pageant, the elite reinstated the might of the British crown. The flashy pageantry that was Trinidad Carnival mirrored the royal processions and nationalist parades developed in Europe.[21] Trinidad Carnival would be manipulated to serve a similar purpose, with the Carnival Queen as monarch.

To insure this success, the Carnival Queen had to share the physical and racial traits of the European colonizer. Usually, contestants for the competition were selected from the communities and social circles of the committee members.[22] Social clubs and businesses also made bids to enter candidates into the competition, sometimes at the last minute.[23] Women of the middle and upper classes, with light complexions and straight hair, were often considered. Given the prevalence within the competition of foreign-born nationals from other British colonies in the Caribbean or from North America and Great Britain, many of the entrants were not even Trinidad-born. This complicated the paradigm of the Carnival Queen competition and how it was situated in the festival at this historical moment; conceivably, the Carnival Queen might not be a native of Trinidad, or even actively engaged in the inner workings of the festival. However, she would attain a level of prestige in Carnival that was unattainable to most.

Still, one had to meet certain criteria to be considered for the competition. Contestants who were not native Trinidadians had to be bona fide residents who had lived in the colony at least two years prior to the competition. Also, they had to be unmarried and not in school. Previous Carnival Queens were ineligible, and contestants had to be between the ages of seventeen and twenty-six. Those contestants under the age of twenty-one needed a parent's or guardian's written consent to enter the competition.[24] The next step would be to receive sponsorship from a business that would pay for the costume, evening gown, and, in most cases, the ballet-oriented training for the event.[25] The training usually lasted about six months and also included classes on speech, walking, and self-presentation on stage.[26]

There were two main portions of the competition: evening gowns and costumes. The contest tended to emphasize theatrical, whimsical, and fantasy-
oriented displays. The evening gowns were judged on theme, design, impact,
and dressmaking technique.[27] For the costumes, the judges focused on theme,
impact, originality of design, ingenuity in construction, ease of movement on
stage, and what was referred to as "the spirit of carnival."[28] Contestants had to
walk elegantly to the accompaniment of classical music. The costumes were
so large that small wheels were attached to their bases, providing support for
the contestant.[29] The program often included a cultural segment such as the
"Creole Review" of 1952, a three-act "historical" review of Afro-Trinidadian
music and dance traditions.[30] Having such a feature in the Carnival Queen
competition only attested to the depreciated level the cultural practices of the
black masses were relegated to when featured in this grandiose event.

The affiliation of the *Trinidad Guardian* with the competition ensured
continued publicity for the pageant. Extensive coverage featured numerous photographs of the contestants and the reigning queen enthroned with
crown and scepter. Her official reign over Carnival lasted only from the night
of Dimanche Gras to midnight on Carnival Tuesday. She was, however, also
expected in the course of a year to participate in regional and international
pageants. While her duties were few, her prizes were vast and included trips to
New York and London. By 1954, the value of the prizes for the Carnival Queen
exceeded those for all the other Carnival competitions combined.[31]

As Carnival Queen contestants, white women now entered the public
domain as cultural workers (serving as ambassadors of the colony's culture),
challenging their traditional status as leisured wives or daughters.[32] The winner of the competition, as the title of Queen implies, assumed all the accoutrements and regalia of royalty. This is evident in an image of Angela Graham,
the newly crowned Carnival Queen of 1955, who sits on a throne bejeweled
in a long and layered frock (figure 3). The stage design surrounding her emu-
lates the decor of royal palaces, further contributing to the perception of the
Carnival Queen as fantastic, unattainable, and prodigious in the eyes of the
ordinary colonial subject.

Apart from nineteenth-century practices of role reversal, when enslaved
Africans masqueraded as kings, queens, princes, and princesses, depictions of
royalty in Trinidad visual culture can be found most frequently in the institutionalized Carnival of the twentieth century.[33] One lorry entrant from the
1949 Carnival entitled "Miss America, Miss Trinidad, Miss England" includes
an elaborately designed structure meant to replicate a fort, with the words
"England Fort Read" on it (figure 4). Three women pose as these pageant
queens in formal wear, including sashes, and are positioned in front of flags

that represent the three countries. Apart from symbolizing the political, cultural, and economic ties of a powerful empire, a young and vibrant capitalist world power, and a British colony, the lorry also demonstrates how beauty pageants have nationalist identifications that are closely linked to race and power. Another example depicts Queen Elizabeth I with the costumes mimicking the royal attire of sixteenth-century England, and the masquerader portraying Elizabeth standing in the middle (figure 5). In another picture from 1949 Carnival, a blonde woman dressed in a costume entitled "Queen of Atlantis" crosses the Queen's Park Savannah stage with the assistance of six men, who may have been part of the same band (figure 6). Clearly, her costume demanded such help, but what is noteworthy about the image is that, juxtaposed with these men, she epitomized the privileged position of white women in Trinidadian society.

The emblematic nature of the Carnival Queen was made even more apparent in 1953 when, on June 2, the day of the coronation of Queen Elizabeth II, plans were made to have a Coronation Carnival on the streets of Port of Spain to coincide with the historic event. At the crowning in Westminster Abbey, many representatives from the Commonwealth were present to witness the occasion.[34] People in the United Kingdom and the colonies also watched the coronation via a live telecast.[35] Meanwhile, in Trinidad, Carnival participants masqueraded as sailors, wild Indians, and robbers, among others, all within the designated color scheme of red, blue, and white—the colors of the British flag.[36] The Wild Indian costumes featured headpieces fashioned in the shape of the royal coat of arms, while jerseys with coronation prints were popular costumes. By far, the highlight of the Coronation Carnival was the parade of the Carnival Queen of 1952, Rosemary Knaggs, through the streets in a golden coach (figure 7). Dressed in an ornate gown, with a cape, blue sash, and "crown of state," she was accompanied by a mounted escort of policemen dressed in white, red, and blue who marched behind her coach to the tune of "British Grenadiers."[37] A troop of Grenadier Guards fully attired in tall black velvet hats, scarlet coats, and black trousers also escorted Knaggs.[38] Upon her arrival at the Queen's Park Oval, local dignitaries, including the colonial secretary and his wife and the mayor of Port of Spain, formally greeted her.

Just like the sovereign states of Europe who linked formal and informal, official and unofficial, political and social inventions of tradition, the colonial authorities of Trinidad thought it important to replicate the coronation of Queen Elizabeth II through Carnival.[39] Through ritual and procession, Rosemary Knaggs became Trinidad's substitute for the "real" and "authentic" queen who was crowned at Westminster Abbey that day. As early as 1950, staff writers at the *Trinidad Guardian* referred to the winner of the Carnival Queen competition as "Her Majesty," reinforcing the British crown's social impact.[40] By 1953, the Carnival Queen was able to emulate the British monarch with considerable authenticity as the United Kingdom coronation designers of Elizabeth II's accoutrements also designed the Carnival Queen's crown and scepter.[41] Trinidad Carnival at this historical moment was thus much more than a period of mere revelry and enjoyment. It is clear that the Carnival Queen competition represented an important means by which the elite could shape Carnival according to their own ideas and interests, and reinforce the collective cohesion of loyal colonial subjects whose identities were bound to the British Crown. Carnival was therefore instrumental in focusing colonial reverence on everything British and elite.

Two years after the coronation of Queen Elizabeth II, her sister Princess Margaret visited Trinidad as part of a tour of the colonies in the West Indies.[42] In the weeks leading to her arrival in February, the *Trinidad Guardian* featured articles about the princess's life and favorite pastimes, including one titled "Princess Margaret Regards Dressing Beautifully As Part of Her Job," which gave a detailed account of her sense of fashion (figure 8).[43] "Princess Margaret," readers were told, "uses pink nail polish—never red." "Even after hours of reviewing troops in broiling sun, her nose is never shiny and her hair never disarranged." The underlying purpose of the article and others like it was to present the princess as a role model to young female colonial subjects.[44]

Meanwhile, reports in British newspapers criticized the formal nature of the princess's engagements, since she would meet "few people other than white people, and . . . the islanders would have insufficient opportunity of seeing her."[45] However, according to the colonial correspondent for the *Times of London*, the West Indian press collectively welcomed the princess's visit and suppressed any criticism of the tour colonial subjects may have expressed. On January 31, Trinidad was her first stop after leaving London. The princess was expected to make a speech, reply to addresses of welcome, and speak at other selected ceremonies in each territory.[46] When she arrived the next day, her every move was closely followed by the press, including her motorcade around the major sites on the island as well as introductions to various officials. Pictures of her being greeted by genuflecting figures of authority were splashed across the front pages of newspapers.[47]

The culmination of the visit was a state banquet held in the princess's honor by the governor general, the highlight being the official introduction of the princess in her gown (figure 9). "A Dream Walking" was the phrase chosen by the *Trinidad Guardian* to refer to Princess Margaret who, according to the newspaper, wore an Empress Josephine hairstyle, a diamond tiara, and a pure white silk-organza ball gown.[48] The fetishization of Princess Margaret bespoke the romantic veneration of the young Queen Elizabeth and her sister that parallels how, in the minds of many, white women were perceived in Trinidad. Thus, it would seem logical to continue the adoration of Trinidadian white women by bestowing upon them the honor of being Carnival Queens.

As a result of these two momentous occasions, other facets of Carnival were jostled to the sidelines in 1956 as the energies of the Carnival Celebrations Committee became more focused on the Carnival Queen competition. News came of unprecedented prizes in store for the winner. Apart from receiving two roundtrip tickets to New York plus a free five-night stay at the Waldorf Astoria, the Carnival Queen would also receive a refrigerator, a gas cooker, an automatic Singer sewing machine, clothing, jewelry, furniture, and luggage. The committee also insisted on giving the reigning queen a deluxe model five-seater Volkswagen donated by a car dealership, which it considered "particularly suitable as a gift to a girl because of its ease of operation."[49] Comparable increases in the prizes for other competitions like the Calypso King competition, the Band of the Year, and the Individual Masquerader of the Year were not considered by the committee. One irate member of the public wrote in a letter to the *Trinidad Guardian* about the disappointment he and other masqueraders felt of the insignificant prize, a $5 silver cup, given to the best individual masquerader for Carnival.[50] In response to these claims, the committee stated that the cups were worth more and that winning bands also received cash prizes ranging from $5 to $225. As far as the Carnival Queen prizes were concerned, the response emphatically stated that merchants donated those prizes.[51] One city councilor expressed his bewilderment with the Carnival Queen competition when he asked in his letter to the editor, "Why was it . . . that young girls of a certain racial group here were never selected as 'Beauty Queens' to represent the island, and were never sponsored?"[52] Despite attempts to defend the competition, it was only a matter of time before these discriminatory tactics eventually caught up with the administrators organizing Carnival. The contention between the black masses, who saw themselves as the true architects of the festival, and the Carnival Queen competition, the pet project of the elitist Carnival Celebrations Committee, would finally manifest itself during the next year's celebrations.

Tensions brewed high from the beginning of 1957's Carnival season, with the Carnival Bands Union demanding higher prize monies and later threatening to boycott the competition at the Queen's Park Savannah.[53] Trinidad's newly elected chief minister, Eric Williams, sought to remedy the obvious partiality in Carnival by establishing the government-led Carnival Development

Committee (CDC) to oversee Carnival proceedings.[54] Not only did this committee intend to build additional bleachers, costing $80,000, and to increase revenue for prizes, but they also improved the prizes for the Calypso King; this included a trip around the West Indies with organized singing engagements, a seven-tube Murphy radio, a cup from Angostura Bitters, $100 from Angos Gin, $100 from British Paints, and $75 from Williams himself.[55] Even so, better prizes, which still did not approach the value of prizes for the Carnival Queen competition, were not enough for two calypsonians. The night before the Calypso King competition, which was staged as merely a section of the Carnival Queen Show, the Mighty Sparrow and Lord Melody decided that they would not participate.[56] At the Young Brigade Tent, Sparrow performed the song "Carnival Boycott," in which he proclaimed this news.[57] Although it is not clear how many times Sparrow sang this song during the Carnival season, he campaigned in prose for a movement to boycott festival proceedings governed by the elitist administrative organization.[58] In the song he complains of the blunt inequities between what he sees as the elite's Carnival and the people's Carnival:

> *What really cause the upset*
> *Is the motor-car the Queen does get*
> *She does nothing for Carnival*
> *She only pretty and that is all*

The issue that plagued Sparrow and his colleagues the most is articulated in these lines: "She does nothing for Carnival / She only pretty and that is all." The fact that they did not see the queens as true cultural workers could not be said more bluntly.[59] As far as he was concerned, the steel pan players, the calypsonians, and the masqueraders of history and *Ju Ju*, all of them men, were intrinsic to the festival and not the privileged white women of the Carnival Queen competition. The calypso situated black men as hard-working and frugal creators of Trinidad's creolized cultural forms for which they should be commensurately rewarded, and expressed a desire to maintain a gender economy in which they would be paid more than the queens. More importantly, as mentioned in the first chapter, these black working-class male calypsonians were recognized as embodying the cultural contributions of the black masses in a festival already entrenched in patriarchy. Black men thus negotiated their position in the colonial power structure during Carnival, already a tradition oriented in patriarchy, through calypso, steel pan, and masquerade.

After such an unpredictable year in Carnival, it was more than happenstance that in 1958 an organization called the Junior Chamber of Commerce

(Jaycees) took over the running of the Carnival Queen competition.[60] While this change took the task of choosing the queen away from the elite-run yet public-oriented Carnival Improvement Committee, it placed the competition fully into the elite's cultural, social, and ideological domain. The Junior Chamber International, a worldwide association of young professionals, established the Trinidadian Jaycees division in 1949.[61] The Trinidad organization prided itself in doing "activities and programs that have the common goal of developing the individual and improving the community" through charitable events.[62] A beauty pageant certainly offered the Jaycees one way of pursuing this goal since, despite being an elaborate event, it did involve what some viewed as the personal development of young women as well as the continued legacy of raising money for charity. If nothing else, it allowed the elite to continue eulogizing white women and to successfully gain proprietorship over Carnival. It would be at least another decade until the competition was again challenged.

As the Carnival Queen competition grew in prominence, so too did the number of Jaycees branches in Trinidad and Tobago. Each branch organized a Carnival Queen competition for their respective regions, and the winner competed in the Port of Spain competition. Despite the harsh accusations made by calypsonians and interest groups alike, no one could deny the alluring effect the pageant had on the general population. Members of the public kept abreast of the annual competition through the press, debated which of their favorites would win, and celebrated the reigning queens with awe.[63] Eventually winners of the competition would represent Trinidad and Tobago at prestigious pageants such as Miss Universe.[64] Founded in 1952, the Miss Universe Pageant was an American-based competition in which contestants from mostly European, Asian, and South American countries participated. The traditional winner of the Carnival Queen competition would qualify for the international pageant, which seldom promoted contestants of African descent into the qualifying rounds. This would all change in 1962, when Miss Haiti, Evelyn Miot, became the first black woman to make it to the semifinals. This was a groundbreaking year in the world of beauty pageants, and for Trinidad as it marked independence from Great Britain.

In an effort to raise Carnival to the status of a national festival while heeding anti-colonialist call to celebrate Creole culture, the new government of 1962 established the Queen and King of Carnival competition. This contest decided the best costume among all the queens and kings of each costumed band in a clear attempt to remove the pageant connotation of these royal titles from the festival. Still, by this time, numerous queen shows had been launched throughout the island, most of them attempting to fill the void of pageants celebrating women of African and East Indian descent. Members of the public became more critical of the Jaycees Carnival Queen competition for not allowing young women of other ethnicities to win the coveted prize, a fact the Jaycees always vehemently denied.[65] As early as 1952, the Miss Caroni Queen competition came onto the scene with nine participants eager to capture the crown in the predominantly East Indian county.[66] In 1955, the Miss Port of Spain beauty pageant emerged and featured a wider representation of ethnicities (figure 10). The Queen of Industry Contest, which began in 1965, was essentially a public relations tool for local manufacturers, part of a scheme to diversify the economy. Contestants representing the factories where they worked were featured in large spreads in local newspapers that provided information on the different products their employers manufactured.[67] Unlike the major beauty pageants of this era, this competition, which appropriated these women for financial gain, featured working-class women who may not have otherwise entered a beauty pageant, but who nonetheless used this pageant as an opportunity to empower themselves. By the 1970s, the Miss East St. George Beauty Pageant, the Miss Ebony Pageant, the Miss Divali Queen Show, and the Miss Better Village Queen Show were among the plethora of beauty pageants held across the country.[68]

In the history of Trinidad, 1970 was a tumultuous year. This year, the stronghold of the Black Power movement confronted the hegemonic order and demanded equal opportunities and better working conditions for the working poor. However, the movement also changed the face of the Jaycees Carnival Queen, literally.[69] In 1971, Elicia Irish became the first woman of African descent to win the Jaycees Carnival Queen competition.[70] It is safe to conclude that this crowning was a strategic move on the part of the Junior Chamber of Commerce, given the changing sociopolitical climate in the country. While in former years the top three placements in the beauty pageant were women of mostly European descent, in 1971 both the winner and one of the runners-up were black, and the other runner-up was of mostly Chinese descent.

Yet, despite the apparent progress finally being made in the beauty pageant industry, there were many discrepancies that had been overlooked. That same year, the government established a Commission of Enquiry that investigated how these competitions were organized so that regulations and procedures could be established. In fact, the major impetus behind the formation of the commission was a controversy surrounding the winners of some beauty pageants not receiving prize monies.[71] The commission held hearings on the early stages of the industry's development in Trinidad, which entailed an investigation of the workings of the Carnival Queen competition. The president of the

Junior Chamber of Commerce (Jaycees) of Port of Spain was peppered with questions accusing the organization of exclusion and discrimination. In his response, however, the president emphatically stated that race was never an issue in the selection process, a statement he could have easily proven with the reigning queen.[72]

At the same time, the singularity of the Trinidad Carnival beauty pageant and the Jaycees Carnival Queen competition seemed to pervade popular visual culture and stimulated an implicit yet dynamic shift in the way women perceived themselves and were perceived within the sphere of Carnival. According to Pamela Franco, dressing up and looking good allowed Afro-Creole women to "stylistically reference [sic] another time and place, . . . construct new realities, . . . recover personal histories" and, most importantly, allowed them "to be visible" as architects of their Carnival performances.[73] Franco's assessment of black women's activities in Trinidad Carnival over time and the importance of their self-presentation through costuming and beauty aesthetics is correct and significant. Yet, by the 1960s, the legacy of beauty pageants encouraged women to beautify themselves for Carnival with a new discernment.

Now, with the racial exclusivity of the Carnival Queen finally challenged, the scope of women's participation and positioning in the festival was enlarged. In 1977, a milestone was accomplished when Trinidadian Janelle "Penny" Commissiong became the first woman of African descent to be crowned Miss Universe. Although by this time the Jaycees Carnival Queen competition had lost much of its prominence, Commissiong's win still represented a major milestone. The members of the elite used the competition to determine the aesthetic and moral precepts for the festival, and they greatly influenced how beauty was to be perceived in the popular imaginary. Undoubtedly, despite the contestation between the working-class black men, who fought for their right to proprietorship, and the Carnival Queens, who were symbolic of the power of Eurocentrism, the Jaycees Carnival Queen competition positioned women at the forefront of the festival.

The Queen and the Pretty *Mas'* Aesthetic

Although the Jaycees Carnival Queen competition diminished in the popular imaginary, its legacy remained important in Trinidad Carnival. One facet that subliminally remained within the creative scope of the festival is the competition's tradition of costume design. Since the 1950s, the swimsuit, and, in some cases, the bikini had been a major part of the costume aesthetic for the Jaycees

competition, often elaborately designed with embroidery and other embel-
lishments. Similar costumes were designed for other contestants that same
year and in years to come. The Jaycees Carnival Queen competition presented
women of European descent as prized spectacles in capricious and revealing
costumes. Yet, at the same time, this arena became the breeding ground for a
new aesthetic posturing and a new practice within Carnival that situated the
woman at the core of the performative space.

The costumes are of significance for how they differed completely from
those worn on the streets by costumed bands on Carnival Monday and Tuesday. Elaborately adorned with significantly less fabric than the men's costumes (which portrayed ancient Roman emperors and European royalty), the
Jaycees Carnival Queens' costumes were precedent-setting. During the late
1960s and 1970s, artist Carlyle Chang and designers Wayne Berkeley, Peter
Minshall, and Christopher Santos, all of whom became prominent Carnival
costume designers, created costumes and evening gowns for the competition.[74] The costumes they designed were intricate and much larger than the
costumes that were created for the competition up to the mid-1960s. In 1967,
for instance, Peter Minshall designed a costume called "Once Upon a Time"
for Ingrid Anderson, the Jaycees Carnival Queen that year, and it was characteristic in size, structure, and concept of this new creative sensibility.[75] The
leotard suit was bedazzled with sequins and other ornamentations, comple-
menting the remainder of the costume attached to Anderson with a girdle
and supported with wheels. This elaborate extension of the costume encap-
sulated the theme of fantasy, with its four-point stars, fairies, and birds all
interconnected with the transparent foliage.

The costume designers associated with this competition set a precedent
for the aesthetics they would establish as designers of Carnival bands. The
influence of their fantastic and capricious costumes influenced thousands of
women beyond the boundaries of the pageant and entered the public domain
during Carnival. Indeed, the plethora of beauty pageants that engrossed
the populace may have offered women a new mode to envisage themselves
within the glamour of the carnivalesque sphere. With the knowledge that
many of the designers gained from the Jaycees Carnival competition and
others like it, costumes could now be created to entice women masqueraders
of the 1970s. More than any of the other designers mentioned earlier, Wayne
Berkeley was cognizant of the possibilities of the Jaycees Carnival Queen
aesthetic tradition and incorporated it into his Carnival designs from the
beginning of his career.

In presentations such as "Secrets of the Sky" from 1973, which he designed
with Bobby Ammon, Berkeley began to experiment with what was to become

the fantasy *mas'* aesthetic. Although he utilized the conventional elements of costumes of the period, he incorporated the whimsical disposition inherent in the fantasy *mas'* aesthetic, using a pastel color palette for the headpiece and other attachments, along with a gold bikini for the body of the masquerader. He continued this tendency years later with "Heromyth" of 1989, and in 1991 with "Swan Lake," which was inspired by the ballet of the same name and for which he won Band of the Year.[76] In 1993, he borrowed from the stage again with his winning presentation "Strike up the Band," whose costumes capture the character also noticeable in costumes from the Jaycees Carnival Queen competitions. Other bandleaders tapped into this phenomenon.[77] In 1970, Edmund Hart produced "Inferno," a presentation that, although suggestive of hell, invites perceptions of what the word can symbolize sensorially and performatively. A decade later, Hart and his wife Thais created "Reflections of my Childhood Days," a whimsical and nostalgic production.[78]

Visual associations of these costumes can be made throughout the Americas especially with the Las Vegas showgirl, who has had a notable influence in Trinidad Carnival, a style that exists throughout the Americas. Carnival in Brazil today includes elaborate floats for samba schools on which women are sometimes dressed in scanty yet ornate costumes while dancing to rhythmic samba music. But there was a notable history of this aesthetic in pre-revolutionary Cuba where women, dressed in elaborate costumes, danced in glamorous productions in the casinos and nightspots of Havana. The type of entertainment that Americans experienced in Cuba was transported to Las Vegas where the transcultural tradition continues.[79] These examples are major influences in the costume aesthetic and self-presentation of female masqueraders in Trinidad Carnival.

The relatively new costumed band Tribe has captured the essence of the showgirl and the Jaycees competition's artistic legacy. Founded in 2005 by Dean Ackin after Tribe was a successful all-inclusive section in the costumed band Poison, Ackin felt impelled to form a new band out of a sense that *mas'* needed to be transformed.[80] Grateful for the opportunity to run his own section in Poison privately, Ackin keenly observed that the once-legendary band began splitting up into factions, which later contributed to its demise.[81]

Even before Tribe made its first presentation as a band, it had already gained a large and loyal following. Ackin and his staff chose to keep the name "Tribe," which had been the name of their section while it was a part of Poison. But the meaning of the word had additional significance for them: a group of people with one common purpose.[82] From its naissance, the band was groundbreaking, as it became the first all-inclusive band in Trinidad Carnival, "all-inclusive" being a term used in Carnival to describe a package a patron pays for that includes unlimited supplies of food, drink, and other amenities. However, the term "all-inclusive band" can be deceiving since, quite ironically, bands such as Tribe excluded a considerable number of people due to the expensive prices of costumes and offered amenities. Ackin did not stop there with his innovativeness. Like Headley, Ackin understands masqueraders as consumers who purchase more than a costume, and he believed that they should enjoy amenities that would make their masquerading experience as comfortable and memorable as possible. Tribe also offers a shuttle service for masqueraders who are unable to reach the starting point on time, paramedic services, and a cool zone, among other things.

However, beyond these innovative efforts to attract and maintain a niche clientele with unique services, an obviously crucial factor in appealing to masqueraders is the costume design. Keeping in mind the popular predilection for the bikini *mas'* aesthetic, Ackin knew he had to hire designers who could create costumes that suited the typical female masquerader, who, he says, wants to look sexy and feel good about herself. This intention is evident in a costume called "Autumn Sprite" from Tribe's 2008 presentation entitled "Myths and Magic." Using a color palette of bright orange and lime green, in addition to feather plumes, appliqués, beads, and sequins, the structure and overall aesthetic of the design recalls the costumes seen during the height of the Jaycees competition. In fact, this contemporary costume design and aesthetic mirror those of the Jaycees Carnival Queen costumes more than the Carnival costumes created since the 1970s by former designers of the competition.

The visual presentation of Tribe in the public eye is integral to the band's appeal. From the design of their website and promotional brochures to the stage design for the launch of the costumed band to the public, the marketing and overall packaging of every aspect of the band is insistent in its appeal that promises a "cream of the crop" product. In an interesting sense, Tribe has instigated a renaissance of the Jaycees Queen archetype in contemporary Carnival. With this in mind, one cannot totally disregard criticisms of Tribe as being elitist given its high prices and the use of mostly light-skinned and straight-haired models for its brochures. This, after all, goes hand in hand with Ackin's vision of his band offering its niche market the "Ultimate Carnival Experience," which was the slogan for Tribe.

It was not long before the media began to focus on the concerns many people had about Tribe's alleged elitism. Acclaimed journalist Terry Joseph reported in an article written in 2005 that a woman encountered discrimination at the Tribe *mas'* camp because of her size.[83] The reporter claimed:

Women with breasts bigger than 34C and whose waists exceed 34 inches are not being allowed in Tribe's "Nylon Pool" section, while the band's "Tale of Benguela" subdivision is refusing any female with a waistline bigger than 40 inches or bra-cup better than 36D; the organisation coming up with a lame excuse about using Swarovski rhinestones which, they said in a statement, "needed a rigid frame to be displayed."[84]

The reporter's findings augmented existing suspicions about an apparent exclusivity in the thriving band. Ackin, who was surprised and perplexed by the article, adamantly denies the charges and believes that it is a fabricated story, stating that the journalist and other critics eventually had a change of heart after "they came on the road and saw all ethnicities, ages and sizes."[85] Nevertheless, Tribe has five private sections whose designers work independently but ultimately answer to Ackin. Local fashion designers run these sections, which are known to cater to a select clientele. If nothing else, these facts evoke the boundaries and restrictions that were an intrinsic part of the Jaycees Carnival Queen competition, thus continuing this ethos in Trinidad Carnival today.

Even so, women are an undeniable component of the festival's present configuration, and the Jaycees Carnival Queen competition was influential in bringing this about. Emblematic of the bourgeoisie's never-ending influence over Carnival, this new model does not adhere to the nationalist celebrations of the folk. The folk in this sense meant black masculinity and how it was exhibited in traditional Carnival characters, calypso, and steel band, all of which no longer prevail in contemporary Carnival. In a drawing entitled "Bat Descending with Feathers" from the "Tropical Night Series," Trinidad artist Christopher Cozier interrogates this schism, which remains an issue today. A woman is both a contemporary masquerader and the traditional Carnival character called "Bat," appearing ethereal as she is captured in the piece as if in mid-flight. Her new hybrid identity, although ideologically conflicted, is nevertheless attainable as the bat wings attached to her forearms seem to synchronize visually with another aspect of her costume that also connotes flight—her feather-plumed headpiece. Certainly, the piece speaks to the fact that many of the celebrated designers of Carnival have been critical of the costume aesthetic prevalent today. Peter Minshall, for instance, considers many of these bands "indistinguishably bland fantasy," paying "homage to an immature glamour aesthetic that owes more to Las Vagas and Xena the Warrior Princess than to Port of Spain."[86] Despite the widespread criticism of an apparent lack of creativity in contemporary Trinidad Carnival, Cozier's artwork is an alternative commentary that recognizes the aesthetic stamp of women on contemporary costume aesthetic. "Bat Descending with Feathers" thus seems to canonize the bikini-clad woman masquerader as a traditional Carnival character.

The Jaycees Carnival Queen and the Performance of the Satiate Body

Without question, Jaycees Carnival Queen contestants created a legacy that epitomized an inevitable ideal for future women masqueraders. The competition, with its idealized femininity and celebration of white womanhood, represented a shift in the way women could be perceived when presenting themselves during Carnival. As a symbol of desire, the Jaycees Carnival Queen became emblematic of that which is unreachable in an increasingly consumerist society. Rebecca Schneider's ideas on the female body as insatiable commodity are apt here as she writes of how the female body has been scripted as an emblem of desire and property very much like commodities theatrically displayed and circulated in the marketplace.[87] In describing how gendered bodies maneuver through and interact within networks of power, she also argues:

> In seeking to possess her and her emblematic consumptiveness . . . he acquires not satisfaction but the social insignia of insatiability—inaccessibility itself. He "owns" or "controls" or is "wedded to" consumption itself, the inaccessible emblem, the driving force of market fever.[88]

When the idea of the insatiable woman, who is emblematic of consumption and property, is applied to Trinidad Carnival, one can discern how the insatiable desire of the Carnival Queen contestants prompted a new reading of women's bodies once the bikini *mas'* was transferred to the costumed bands. During the 1970s when this new bikini aesthetic became popular, it offered women an opportunity to show their bodies, as opposed to depending solely on the costume.

Such a concentration on the presentation of the body in public speaks to the reality of arousing the desire or envy of onlookers. Undoubtedly, the Jaycees Carnival Queen competition typified how women could transform their bodies using a strict exercise routine, wearing make-up and appealing hairstyles, and dressing in a revealing costume.[89] Carnival allows for rebellious carousing, but it also constructs a social framework where the woman masquerader's body is centrally positioned. In these costumed bands, women masqueraders wear revealing costumes while gyrating to soca music, while men—both masqueraders and onlookers—have the opportunity to consume them visually. Are women masqueraders' performances informed by a desire to be a fetishized commodity? If so, does this imply a lack of agency in these women?[90] These questions are in the discursive vein of Simone de Beauvoir, who explains that women are socialized to mark themselves with the visible trappings and performance of femininity within masculinist discourse.[91] In the bounds of the ongoing yet limiting performative process of being a woman, there is the possibility for the implications of these acts to be reassessed.[92] It is probable that some women masqueraders employ particular, strategic configurations of spectacle that "constitute an appropriation, perhaps more accurately a reappropriation of spectacle to the end of disrupting conventional discourses of gender and sexuality."[93] Such a desire to become a spectacle may also be informed by the tradition in Trinidad Carnival in which certain women were entitled to such idealization. Yet this desire to be a spectacle in turn provided contemporary women a vocabulary for parading, flaunting, and celebrating their bodies in public.

Since there is a focus on the body, some female masqueraders tend to have a desire to affirm their affinity to youth culture associated with Carnival. This is because Carnival in Trinidad now represents a body-beautiful culture where the objective is to make the figure conform to a standardized beauty ideal. Months in advance, people register at gyms so that they can work arduously at achieving a "perfect body" and, in turn, a perfect image that is certainly a legacy of the Jaycees competition. For this reason, the body of the masquerader has become the costume.[94] The Jaycees Carnival Queen is iconic for contemporary masqueraders as she has made an impact on how the female masquerader views her body and her self-presentation in contemporary Carnival, which in turn contributes to the masquerader's awareness of how integral her body is to the overall aesthetic of the costumed band. Along with the bathing suit that accentuated the contestant's body, the Jaycees Carnival Queen played a part in how the contemporary female masquerader influences the direction of the dominant costume aesthetic so that her body is most pronounced.

On the other hand, one must not discredit the impact of Janelle "Penny" Commissiong, Trinidad's first Miss Universe of 1977. Not only was she the first Trinidadian to win the international beauty pageant, but she was also the first black woman to gain that coveted title.[95] What made her feat even more fascinating was the fact that she had no association with the Jaycees Carnival Queen competition.[96] Her success was widely celebrated and heralded by the media, the government, and private corporations, and she was given countless gifts. Apart from receiving Trinidad and Tobago's highest national award, the Trinity Cross, calypsonians commemorated her in song during the 1978 Carnival season. The calypsonian Wellington praised her with the following lyrics:

> *No one could remember when*
> *They see such a specimen:*
> *Miss Trinidad and Tobago,*
> *Sweet Janelle Commissiong.*[97]

As a black woman, who won the title that was, and remains, recognized as the sign of the most beautiful woman in the world, Commissiong epitomized black female beauty in Trinidad. Furthermore, Commissiong, who played *mas'* in Peter Minshall's 1978 presentation of Zodiac, possibly contributed to the change in Carnival whereby women were more associated with the festival than men and were the desirable figures in the carnivalesque sphere.

Still, it would take a decade or so, with the introduction of the "Poison Girl," for the association of the desirable woman to Carnival to be made even more distinct. Named after the legendary band Poison, the "Poison Girl" was Trinidad Carnival's truest example of the insatiably desired woman whom every man wanted to see and every woman wanted to be: a young, attractive, and sometimes economically independent woman.[98] The media constantly fetishized her image as she came to emblematize what women's presence and involvement became in Trinidad Carnival. The clever marketing strategies of Poison's business-oriented bandleader along with the addition of all-inclusive sections contributed to the popularity of the band and the archetype that his female members became. Apart from publicizing the costumed band, Michael Headley would also hire popular soca artistes to perform with the costumed band during Carnival Monday and Tuesday.

However, unlike her predecessor, the Jaycees Carnival Queen, the "Poison Girl" was not only of European descent; she could also be of African, Asian, South Asian, and Arab descent, thereby representing the inclusion of all racial types into the idealized woman masquerader archetype. Poison's bandleader, Michael Headley, ensured the presence of women of varying sizes, skin complexions, and socioeconomic backgrounds. He designed affordable costumes that were adaptable to any body type, and employed an extensive color palette so that there would be costumes for as many skin tones as possible.[99]

Headley's insistence on abiding by these aesthetic guidelines certainly does not limit the vibrancy of women masqueraders' expressive bodily movements. The accoutrements of the costumes simply function as visible signifiers of women's bodies being performed while masquerading in Trinidad Carnival. Thus, the purposeful Jaycees-inspired self-marking that women are immersed in during Carnival could be seen as a type of hypersexuality, and there is an opportunity to perform this sexuality in such a way that it is rendered unfixed and even unknowable, so much so that performance becomes a site of resistance. Women's bodies function as the decisive tool with which this resistance is manifested. Although these women may collaborate in their own visual fetishization, woman masqueraders become their bodies, ultimately wearing them as costumes.[100]

Despite the fact that Carnival is no longer male-dominated in masquerade, a development that traditionalists often correlate with what they see as a drastic attenuation of creativity, the presence of men's bodies can still be felt within the performance space of Carnival. Men frequently comprise the majority of spectators along the streets during Carnival Monday and Tuesday. There is something to be said of the interrelations that exist between the masquerader and the spectator. Although male viewers often voyeuristically consume women masqueraders, these interrelations consist of an active performance on both parts. Within this exchange in which the man as the consumptive *beholder* is in the midst of possessing the woman masquerader's apparent emblematic consumptiveness, the male viewer engages in a performative response to her presence.[101] But this performative exchange is not predicated on a mere objectification of the woman masquerader; she is defiantly articulating her body during this commodifying encounter.

When investigating the exchange between artist and spectator in performance art, Kristine Stiles uses the term "commissure" to theorize a key feature of performance art—its function as a connector.[102] This concept is useful in thinking about the inevitable interrelations that occur during Carnival. Here, a masquerader can be a performer who partakes in a performative exchange with another masquerader. This can even be done with a viewer who, by virtue of his or her presence, becomes linked to the performer by mutual active viewing and sometimes movement. Since the boundary that separates performer and viewer is not clearly delineated in performance art, Stiles observes in another context that there is "both fluid action and interaction" between "performing and viewing subjects," and thus interdependence is cultivated, a connection is made.[103] These engaged encounters between performer and viewer are reminders of how influential the Jaycees Carnival Queen is in carnivalesque performance.

The Jaycees Carnival Queen was representative of the stake the European elite maintained in Carnival. A fabricated personage, she was almost a replica of the queen of England, clearly standing in direct opposition to the Jamette who never felt compelled to abide by pretentions of uprightness. Yet, while her image in the gown evoked royalty, her costume often exoticized and eroticized her, positioning her desirability at the center of the male imaginary. The Carnival Queen instigated a reassessment of how women could perceive their bodies and how they choose to present themselves in the public sphere, particularly through a noncompliant performance of hypersexuality. While the Carnival Queen competition ensured that a certain costume aesthetic appealed to a Eurocentric worldview, the queens' costumes also served to establish new possibilities in the continuing creative development of Carnival, leading to the birth of the costume aesthetic that prevails today.

Notes

1. Jaycees of Trinidad and Tobago, *Presenting the Jaycees of Trinidad and Tobago* (Port of Spain: Imprint, 1973), 1.

2. The term "Jametre" (from the French word "diametre") became the descriptor for a class of people. "Diametre" here refers to the imaginary line that divided society into two dichotomous fractions, namely, the respectable and the criminal. Since members of this underclass predominated among Carnival participants in the late nineteenth century, the festival soon became associated with them and, henceforth was referred to as the Jametre or Jamette Carnival.

3. "Who fear the Sedition Bill?" *The Guardian*, March 13, 1920. Marcus Garvey's United Negro Improvement Organization published the *New World*.

4. Gordon Rohlehr, *Calypso and Society in Pre-Independence Trinidad* (Port of Spain: Gordon Rohlehr Publishing, 1990), 125.

5. Hollis Liverpool, *Rituals of Power and Rebellion*, 383.

6. "Visitors Arriving Here for Carnival Frolies," *Trinidad Guardian*, March 2, 1946, 1.

7. Gordon Rohlehr, *Calypso & Society*, 407.

8. Natasha Barnes, "Face of the Nation: Nationalisms and Identities in Jamaican Beauty Pageants," in *The Gender and Consumer Culture Reader*, ed. Jennifer Scanlon (New York: New York University Press, 2000), 287.

9. See Natasha Barnes, "Body Talk: Notes on Women and Spectacle in Contemporary Trinidad Carnival," *Small Axe 7* (March 2000): 93–105. Also Daniel Miller, "Absolute Freedom in Trinidad," *Man* 1.26, no. 2 (June 1991): 323–41.

10. Natasha Barnes, *Cultural Conundrums: Gender, Race, Nation and the Making of Caribbean Cultural Politics* (Ann Arbor: University of Michigan Press, 2006), 52.

11. Ibid.

12. "Governor Attends Contest," *Trinidad Guardian*, February 6, 1940, 1.

13. Barbara E. Powrie, "The Changing Attitude of the Coloured Middle Class Towards Carnival." *Carnival Quarterly* 14, nos. 3–4 (1956): 224–32.

14. "Trinidad and Tobago Commission of Enquiry into Miss Trinidad and Tobago Beauty Contest 1971," *Report of the Commission of Enquiry into I—Miss Trinidad and Tobago*

Beauty Contests, 1971 II—The Organization of Such Contests and Competitions in Trinidad and Tobago III—Regulations and Procedures Recommended (Port of Spain, Trinidad: Government Printery, 1973), 1.

15. Gordon Rohlehr, *Calypso and Society*, 407.

16. "Acting Governor to Attend Celebrations in San Fernando," *Sunday Guardian*, February 16, 1947, 2.

17. The Downtown Carnival competition ("Downtown" referring to eastern Port of Spain) comprised of black working-class participants who lived in this part of the capital.

18. "King Carnival Starts 1948 Reign Tomorrow," *Sunday Guardian*, February 8, 1948, 2.

19. "Seven More Queens Join Savannah Contest," *Trinidad Guardian*, February 24, 1949, 1.

20. "Carnival Fun Ends; Lenten Season Begins," *Trinidad Guardian*, February 20, 1947, 1; "Court to Take Strong View of Clashing During Celebrations," *Trinidad Guardian*, Thursday February 16, 1950, 3.

21. Eric Hobsbawm explains that the invention of tradition was essential to the maintenance of the Republic and acknowledges the invention of public ceremonies as one of these major innovations. See Eric Hobsbawm, "Mass-Producing Traditions: Europe, 1870–1914," in *The Invention of Tradition*, eds. Eric Hobsbawm and Terence Ranger (Cambridge: Cambridge University Press, 1992), 263–307.

22. *Commission of Enquiry*, 5.

23. "Firms Rush To Send Candidates for 'Carnival Queen' Contest," *Trinidad Guardian*, February 26, 1949, 1.

24. "Wanted—Queens To Sponsor," *Sunday Guardian*, January 8, 1956, 1.

25. Personal communication with Ursula Steiger-Herrera, February 3, 2006.

26. Ibid.

27. *Commission of Enquiry*, 1.

28. Ibid.

29. Ibid.

30. "Many New Features Expected to Appear for Carnival Weekend," *Evening News*, February 22, 1952, 6.

31. Gordon Rohlehr, *Calypso and Society*, 419.

32. For more on the concept of the queen as cultural worker, see Natasha Barnes, *Cultural Conundrums*, 55–56.

33. See John Cowley, *Carnival, Canboulay and Calypso: Traditions in the Making* (Cambridge: Cambridge University Press, 1996), 16–17, and Judith Bettelheim, "Jonkonnu and Other Christmas Masquerades," in *Caribbean Festival Arts: Each and Every Bit of Difference*, eds. John W. Nunley and Judith Bettelheim (Seattle: University of Washington Press, 1988), 39–83.

34. "The Queen Crowned at Westminster," *London Times*, June 3, 1953, 12.

35. Ibid.

36. "Queen Rides in State," *Sunday Guardian*, June 7, 1953, 1.

37. Ibid.

38. Ibid.

39. Eric Hobsbawm, "Mass-Producing Traditions: Europe, 1870–1914," 264.

40. "18 Year-Old Typist Crowned Carnival Queen," *Trinidad Guardian*, February 21, 1950.

41. Gordon Rohlehr, *Calypso and Society*, 424.

42. "Princess's Tour of the Caribbean," *London Times*, January 22, 1955; "Court Circular." *London Times*, February 1, 1955.

43. *Trinidad Guardian*, January 2, 1955.

44. Ibid.

45. *London Times*, January 22, 1955.

46. Ibid.

47. *Trinidad Guardian*, February 2, 1955.

48. "Diamond Tiara at Banquet," *Trinidad Guardian*, February 4, 1955. The reference to Princess Margaret sporting an "Empress Josephine hairstyle" would have none-too-subtly associated her with perhaps the Caribbean's most famous female monarch: Napoleon Bonaparte's Martiniquan wife, Empress Josephine (1763–1814).

49. "Volkswagen, Big Prize For Queen," *Sunday Guardian*, January 8, 1956.

50. "Plea For Attractive Prizes For Individual Masqueraders," *Trinidad Guardian*, February 2, 1956.

51. Ibid.

52. "Councillor Asks Some Questions About Carnival Competitions," *Trinidad Guardian*, February 15, 1956.

53. Gordon Rohlehr, *Calypso and Society*, 448–49.

54. *Sunday Guardian*, March 3, 1957.

55. Michael Anthony, *Parade of the Carnivals of Trinidad, 1839–1989* (Port of Spain: Circle Press, 1989), 260; *Trinidad Guardian*, March 2, 1957.

56. "Sparrow and Melody 'Strike,'" *Trinidad Chronicle*, March 3, 1957.

57. Ibid.

58. Gordon Rohlehr explains that Sparrow also may have become so captivated by the spirit of protest and felt so compelled to sustain the rebellious stance that he boycotted at the last minute, even after the late compromise came with the formation of the CDC and the modest increase in the Calypso King prize. He also speculates that "Carnival Boycott" may have been a "bomb" tune that was purposely released at the last moment before Carnival. See *Calypso and Society*, 450–51.

59. See Natasha Barnes, *Cultural Conundrums*, 61 for a further exploration of this point.

60. *Commission of Enquiry*, 1.

61. Jaycees of Trinidad and Tobago, *Presenting the Jaycees of Trinidad and Tobago* (Port of Spain: Imprint, 1973), 1.

62. Ibid.

63. Michael Anthony, *Parade of the Carnivals*, 238; Gordon Rohlehr, *Calypso and Society*, 447.

64. *Commission of Enquiry*, 1.

65. Ibid.

66. "9 Compete for Caroni Queen Title." *Evening News*, February 23, 1952.

67. *Trinidad Guardian*, September 9, 1965, 3.

68. *Commission of Enquiry*, 6.

69. For a comprehensive examination of the social, cultural, and political factors that led to the Black Power movement, see Selwyn Ryan, *Race and Nationalism in Trinidad and Tobago: A Study of Decolonization in a Multiracial Society* (Toronto: University of Toronto Press, 1972), 343–69.

70. *Trinidad Carnival & Calypso 1972*, 23.

71. *Commission of Enquiry*, 6.

72. Ibid., 5.

73. Pamela R. Franco. "'Dressing Up and Looking Good': Afro-Creole Female Maskers in Trinidad Carnival," *African Arts* 31, no. 2, special issue: "Women's Masquerades in Africa and the Diaspora" (Spring 1998): 62–67.

74. Ibid.

75. *Trinidad Carnival & Calypso 1968*.

76. "Berkeley Hat Trick," *Trinidad Guardian*, February 14, 1991.

77. "Berkeley Wins Band of the Year," *Trinidad Guardian*, February 15, 1993.

78. *Trinidad Carnival Magazine 1980*, 51.

79. For more on the cultural cross-fertilization between the United States and Latin America, see John Storm Roberts, *The Latin Tinge: The Impact of Latin American Music on the United States* (New York: Oxford University Press, 1999).

80. In an all-inclusive section or Band, masqueraders pay for a costume, unlimited drinks, unlimited food, and other accoutrements.

81. Personal communication with Dean Ackin, August 3, 2007.

82. Ibid.

83. "Trouble in the Tribe," *Trinidad Express*, October 7, 2005. A *mas'* camp is the headquarters of a costumed band.

84. Ibid.

85. Personal communication with Dean Ackin.

86. From Peter Minshall's presentation at the "Second Annual Conference on Sustainable Tourism," presented by the Caribbean Tourism Organization and TIDCO, May 15–18, 1998.

87. Rebecca Schneider, *The Explicit Body in Performance* (London: Routledge, 1997), 88.

88. Ibid., 52.

89. Schneider says that the "object in display plays on the sensuousness of the (dislocated) viewer, beckoning the viewer to enter (purchase) the object presented." See *The Explicit Body in Performance*, 88–89.

90. In "A Bit Much: Spectacle as Discursive Resistance," *Feminist Media Studies* 5, no. 1 (2005): 65–81, Helene A. Shugart and Catherine Egley Waggoner explain that many feminist film theorists identify ways in which specifically gendered discourses are inscribed upon the woman as cinematic spectacle who has no agency: Theresa De Lauretis, *Alice Doesn't: Feminism, Semiotics, Cinema* (Bloomington: Indiana University Press, 1984); Mary Ann Doane, *The Desire to Desire: The Woman's Film of the 1940s* (Bloomington: Indiana University Press, 1987); Mary Russo, "Female Grotesques: Carnival and Theory," in *Feminist Studies/Critical Studies*, ed. T. De Lauretis (Bloomington: Indiana University Press, 1986), 213–29.

91. Simone de Beauvoir, *The Second Sex*, trans. and ed., H. M. Parshley (New York: Alfred A. Knopf, 1993).

92. Judith Butler, *Gender Trouble: Feminism and the Subversion of Identity* (New York: Routledge, 1990), 43.

93. Helene A. Shugart and Catherine Egley Waggoner, "A Bit Much: Spectacle as Discursive Resistance."

94. I borrow the concept "body as costume" from Clare Lewis and Steve Pile's essay "Woman, Body, Space: Rio Carnival and the Politics of Performance." *Gender, Place and Culture* 3, no. 1 (1996): 23–41.

95. In 1986, Giselle LaRonde became Trinidad's first Miss World, and Wendy Fitzwilliam became Trinidad's second Miss Universe in 1998.

96. *Trinidad Guardian*, July 18, 1977, 1.

97. *Trinidad Carnival Magazine*, 1978.

98. Philip Scher examines their sociopolitical impact on the festival. See Philip W. Scher, "Copyright Heritage: Preservation, Carnival and the State in Carnival," *Anthropological Quarterly* 75, no. 3 (Summer 2002): 453–84.

99. Personal communication with Michael Headley, June 8, 2007.

100. Clare Lewis and Steve Pile, "Woman, Body, Space."

101. Schneider, 52.

102. Kristine Stiles, "Performance," in *Critical Terms for Art History*, eds. Robert S. Nelson and Richard Schiff, 2nd edition (Chicago: University of Chicago Press, 2003), 77.

103. Ibid.

Bibliography

"Acting Governor to Attend Celebrations in San Fernando." *Sunday Guardian*, February 16, 1947, 2.

Anthony, Michael. *Parade of the Carnivals Michael Anthony, Parade of the Carnivals of Trinidad, 1839–1989* (Port of Spain: Circle Press, 1989).

Barnes, Natasha. "Face of the Nation: Nationalisms and Identities in Jamaican Beauty Pageants." In *The Gender and Consumer Culture Reader*, ed. Jennifer Scanlon, 287. New York: New York University Press, 2000).

Butler, Judith. *Gender Trouble: Feminism and the Subversion of Identity*. New York: Routledge, 1990.

"Carnival Fun Ends; Lenten Season Begins." *Trinidad Guardian*, February 20, 1947, 1.

"Councillor Asks Some Questions About Carnival Competitions." *Trinidad Guardian*, February 15, 1956.

"Court Circular." *London Times*, February 1, 1955.

"Court to Take Strong View of Clashing During Celebrations." *Trinidad Guardian*, February 16, 1950, 3.

"Diamond Tiara at Banquet." *Trinidad Guardian*, February 4, 1955.

Doane, Mary Ann. *The Desire to Desire: The Woman's Film of the 1940s*. Bloomington: Indiana University Press, 1987.

de Beauvoir, Simone. *The Second Sex*. Trans. and ed. H. M. Parshley. New York: Alfred A. Knopf, 1993.

De Lauretis, Theresa. *Alice Doesn't: Feminism, Semiotics, Cinema*. Bloomington: Indiana University Press, 1984.

Edmondson, Belinda. "Public Spectacles: Caribbean Women and the Politics of Public Performance." *Small Axe* 13 (2003): 1–16.

"18 Year-Old Typist Crowned Carnival Queen." *Trinidad Guardian*, February 21, 1950.

"Firms Rush to Send Candidates for 'Carnival Queen' Contest." *Trinidad Guardian*, February 26, 1949, 1.

Franco, Pamela R. 1998. "'Dressing Up and Looking Good': Afro-Creole Female Maskers in Trinidad Carnival." *African Arts* 31 (2), special issue: "Women's Masquerades in Africa and the Diaspora": 62–67.

"Governor Attends Contest." *Trinidad Guardian*, February 6, 1940.

Hobsbawm, Eric. "Mass-Producing Traditions: Europe, 1870–1914." In *The Invention of Tradition*, eds. Eric Hobsbawm and Terence Ranger, 263–307. Cambridge: Cambridge University Press, 1992.

Jaycees of Trinidad and Tobago. "Presenting the Jaycees of Trinidad and Tobago." Port of Spain: Imprint, 1973.

"King Carnival Starts 1948 Reign Tomorrow." *Sunday Guardian*, February 8, 1948, 2.

"Many New Features Expected to Appear for Carnival Weekend." *Evening News*, February, 1952, 6.

"9 Compete for Caroni Queen Title." *Evening News*, February 23, 1952.

"Plea for Attractive Prizes for Individual Masqueraders." *Trinidad Guardian*, February 2, 1956.

"Princess Margaret Regards Dressing Beautifully as a Part of Her Job." *Trinidad Guardian*, January 2, 1953

"Princess's Tour of the Caribbean." *London Times*, January 22, 1955.

"The Queen Crowned at Westminster." *London Times*, June 3, 1953, 12.

"Queen Rides in State." *Sunday Guardian*, June 7, 1953, 1.

Rohlehr, Gordon. *Calypso and Society in Pre-Independence Trinidad*. Port of Spain: Gordon Rohlehr Publishing, 1990.

Russo, Mary. "Female Grotesques: Carnival and Theory." In *Feminist Studies/Critical Studies*, ed. T. De Lauretis (Bloomington: Indiana University Press, 1986).

Scher, Philip W. "Copyright Heritage: Preservation, Carnival and the State in Carnival." *Anthropological Quarterly* 75 (3) (2002): 453–84.

Schneider, Rebecca. *The Explicit Body in Performance*. London: Routledge, 1997.

"Seven More Queens Join Savannah Contest." *Trinidad Guardian*, February 24, 1949, 1.

Shane, Lilac. "Who Wants Mas?—Watch the Girls!" *Evening News*, February 3, 1967, 7.

Shugart, Helene A., and Catherine Egley Waggoner. "A Bit Much: Spectacle as Discursive Resistance." *Feminist Media Studies* 5 (1) (2005): 65–81.

"Sparrow and Melody 'Strike.'" *Trinidad Chronicle*, March 3, 1957.

Stiles, Kristine. "Performance." In *Critical Terms for Art History*, 2nd edition, eds. Robert S. Nelson and Richard Schiff, 77. Chicago: University of Chicago Press, 2003.

"Trinidad and Tobago Commission of Enquiry into Miss Trinidad and Tobago Beauty Contest. 1973." *Report of the Commission of Enquiry into I—Miss Trinidad and Tobago Beauty Contests, 1971 II—The Organization of Such Contests and Competitions in Trinidad and Tobago III—Regulations and Procedures Recommended.* Port of Spain, Trinidad: Government Printery.

Trinidad Carnival & Calypso. Government magazine, 1972.

Trinidad Carnival Magazine. Government magazine 1973, 23.

Trinidad Guardian, February 2, 1955.

Trinidad Guardian, September 9, 1965, 3.

Trinidad Guardian, July 18, 1977, 1.

"Visitors Arriving Here for Carnival Frolies." *Trinidad Guardian*, March 2, 1946, 1.

"Who fear the Sedition Bill?" *The Guardian*, March 13, 1920.

Chapter 5

Practicing Jametteness: The Transmission of "Bad Behavior" as a Strategy of Survival

—Adanna Kai Jones

Show it off gyal and let di world see.
(Roll it gyal, roll it gyal)
—"Roll it Gyal"[1]

Someone once asked me, "I mean, all they're really doing is just shaking their butts! So what's the big deal?" With a knee-jerk response, I could not help but be offended. As a Trinidad-born, US-raised avid "it" roller, there is always a certain pride that overcomes me every time *I roooooollllllll, roll it gyal, roll it gyal*. I grew up rolling my "it" and even taught my younger brother how to roll his "it" at the tender age of five. Growing up in a decidedly Trinidadian household, there were often direct and indirect discussions about how and when to roll our "its," why we do or do not roll our "its," the problems with rolling one's "it," the gendered importance of protecting one's "it," the difference between rolling one's "it" around family and rolling one's "it" around others (including those of other nationalities or races), the difference between adults rolling their "its" and children rolling their "its," and, of course, the difference between males and females rolling their "its." Even if your family avoided addressing the topic of "its," if you listened to soca music or dancehall reggae, indulged in the revelry of Carnival, or went to Trini limes (hangouts) and fetes (parties), at some point, it would be almost impossible to avoid dealing with the overwhelming pervasiveness of the rolling "it."

Caribbean bodies are sexually marked and recognized by their renowned abilities to roll their "its"—a skill informally learned at a very young age. This movement includes, at the very least, dexterous and vigorous rolls, gyrations, thrusts, and shakes of the hip, pelvis, and buttocks. It is colloquially known as "winin'" (or the wine) in Trinidad, Guyana, and Jamaica, "wukkin'-up" in Barbados, "despelote" in Cuba, "perreando" (or el perreo) in the Dominican Republic and Puerto Rico, and "gouye" (or the gouyad) in Haiti (just to name a few). The rolling "it" is often associated with festive spaces—such as dance-hall, Carnival, and parties—as well as with popular music genres like soca, dancehall-reggae, reguetón, and kompa. The rolling "it" is sometimes recognized as a dance in and of itself (e.g., the dutty wine, from the dancehalls of Jamaica, or the bicycle wine, created and promoted by Trinidadian soca artist Denise "Saucy WOW" Belfon); or it can be a movement within a larger dance complex (e.g., the rumbas of Cuba). As a result, the dancer retains the option to make their rolling "it" the sole focus of their dancing, or to use "it" as a subsidiary movement of a larger dance phrase.

Furthermore, the Caribbean rolling "it" has both public and private connotations due to its associations with spaces such as Trinidadian-style Carnivals[3] and private family gatherings, including weddings. And within the Caribbean, winin' has and continues to be practiced by persons of various ethnicities, races, genders, and classes. Yet in spite of this fact, the rolling "it" remains overwhelmingly normalized as always already linked to black/African histories and female/feminized bodies. This is especially due to the legacy of the transatlantic slave trade and the historical pathologizing of Afro-women's and Afro-slaves' body parts (Dixon-Gottschild 2003; Sheller 2003; Hartman 1997).

Tracing the Roots and Routes of the Winin' Trinidadian "It"

The roots and routes of the Caribbean rolling "it" are quite expansive. In other words, there is no single narrative for the wine's pathway into its current iteration; rather, any semblance of a narrative is at best a labyrinth that has no definite beginning and promises no finite conclusions. Within Trinidad alone, antecedents of the wine can be located within the sacred and secular dances of the Yoruba and Igbo peoples from West Africa as well as of the Bantu peoples of the Congo region (Warner-Lewis 1991). For example, the dances and especially the movements associated with the rituals of the Orisha religion are often comprised of a gyrating or vigorously thrusting "it." For example, in one of the dances for Shango—the Yoruban deity of fire, thunder, lightning, masculinity, and virility—the dancer's hands must slice up into the air, as if to take lightning from the sky, and then bring it back down towards their crotch, whilst vigorously thrusting their hips forward.[4] On the other hand, the dances of Oshun—the Yoruban deity of fresh waters, femininity, fecundity, and love—emphasizes a billowing "it" that moves in circles and figure eights, which can symbolize the act of cleansing or preparing oneself for love or giving birth.[5]

Other roots of the Trinidadian wine are also linked to private Hindu festivities, such as the dances performed during matikor.[6] Additional influential ties include the movements associated with belly dancing, which were retained by Trinidad's small Syrian and Lebanese populations. Moreover, many of the Trinidadian Afro-Creole[7] dances, such as the bele (or bel aire), also emphasize swaying and rolling one's "it" to the pulsating rhythms of drums. Lastly, the coupling of dancers (specifically the pairing of men and women as they wine) was strongly influenced by the European court dances practiced by plantation slave owners, including the French quadrille and the Spanish dances associated with pasillo and castillian music (Hill 1972, 40, 72). In effect, the winin' body is a hybrid, diasporic body that is both marked and unmarked by multiple histories and traditions, all of which offer winers a plethora of ways in which their "its" can be used, performed, and understood.

Case in point, some of my Trinidadian informants,[8] who I have unofficially deemed *wine connoisseurs*, proclaim to have the ability to identify someone based on how they wine, or at the very least identify where or how that person learned to wine. In casual conversation, many have argued that one's winin' skills can reveal the winer as masculine, feminine, heterosexual, homosexual,[9] black, white, or Chinese,[10] East Indian, American, Latino, African, Jamaican, Bajan (Caribbean terminology for Barbadian), and/or Trini (Caribbean terminology for Trinidadian). For instance, a few of my informants from Trinidad stated that there is a difference between the ways Indo- and Afro-Trinidadians wined. As one older male stated, "[East] Indians seem to have like an off-timing *ting tuh di side*, and we [of African descent] have a smooth roll."[11] Another Trinidadian male living in Brooklyn said,

> I can tell where West Indian women are from. I mean, I know how Trini girls does wine, easy. Bajans do more of a wukkin'-up, and Grenadian women have like a kinda jab-jab wine, like a jukkin' jukkin' kinda ting. Jamaican women wine a bit more . . . raunchy. And the smaller island countries, like St. Nevis or St. Kitts, can REL wine. Like di party could jus' start and dey already sweatin', yuh know.[12]

Whether or not these observations are accurate is not particularly important here. What is important is how one rolls their "it" is deeply connected to the conceptualization of particular places, spaces, and lived identities.

In harping further on this point of view, Susan Harewood reports that Bajans also "mark wukking-up as an area of cultural distinctiveness" (2006, 182). She quotes a longtime Bajan columnist, Al Gilkes, as stating,

> [Wukking-up] is a talent which I am convinced is uniquely Bajan. Trinis sing about wining and that's exactly what they do. They wind their hips and backsides but they cannot wuk up like a Bajan. Nor can Jamaicans, Americans, Europeans, Japanese, Chinese, Russians, Indians or anybody else on the face of the earth. Africans come close but what they do is more like choreographed movements than the natural, free and innovative rhythmic wuk-up of the Bajan. (Ibid.)

Noting these three examples, it is clear that rolling one's "it" not only plays a critical role in upholding the evolving iterations of Caribbean identities, but it also helps many Caribbean men and women ascertain an overall sense of self, especially in relation to other bodies who do or do not roll their "its." According to these wine connoisseurs, a winer's very identity is written into their wine, so much so that how they roll their "its" can be used as a gauge for deciphering where that person is from or not from, who they are, and what their intentions might be.

In further tracing the roots and routes of the winin' Trinidadian "it," many scholars of the Trinidadian Carnival regularly argue that the corporeal legacies of Trinidad's Jametre figure and their "scandalous" participation in the nineteenth-century carnivals have been passed down to today's winin' Trini/ Caribbean[13] Carnival revelers as part of their "birthrights" (Noel 2010, 60). For example, Maude Dikobe encourages researchers to situate the winin' of today's female soca artists within the local discourses of Trinidad. In addition to calling attention to the importance of the woman's bottom in Afro-Trinidadian culture, she historically situates winin' performances within the politico-historical lineage of the Jamette. In so doing, she argues, one can better recognize "the importance of the ways these women are challenging traditional forms of repression, be it racial, gender, or otherwise" (Dikobe 2004).

Daniel Miller observes, "Obscenity is one of the oldest accusations to be made against the Trinidadian Carnival, and the pissenlit ("wet the bed") [masquerade] of the nineteenth century, with their rags of menstrual blood, caused as much of a stir in their time as does wining [*sic*] today; moreover women were also central to the construction of this 'Jamette Carnival.' Wining [*sic*], then, is related to a tradition of Carnival [. . .]" (1991, 327). Furthermore, Carnival historian Samantha Noel stresses that the bikini costuming and Carnival winin' of today's Trinidadian Carnival is a clear embodiment of Jametteness, which she defines as "a performativity that asserts both a creative and subversive impact on the festival [i.e., Carnival]" (2010, 61). She states, "The pelvic oscillations, gyrations, and wining [sic] that 'plagued' the festivities [the first half of the twentieth century] symbolized the social, artistic, economic, and sexual independence and freedom of these [Jamette] women" (2010, 76). Evidently, for scholars like Miller, Dikobe, and Noel, the Jamette's legacy of using their "its" to push back against the deplorable conditions they had to endure is not only a precursor for today's winin', but this legacy also remains intricately linked to the Carnival space itself.

The Jamette Figure and her Embodied Legacies

Jametres (unisex) were a subculture of mostly Afro-Creole ex-slaves, especially associated with the post-emancipation (post-1938) Trinidadian Carnival. Derived from the French term "diametre"—meaning "diameter"—the creolized term, "Jametre," referred to the "imaginary line that [divided] society into two sectors, the respectable and the criminal" (Noel 2010, 62). During that time, Port of Spain, the colony's capital and a decidedly white/elite space, was "infiltrated" by ex-slaves and poor immigrants looking for work, who then had to endure oppressive and deplorable living conditions, such as overcrowded and unsanitary barracks. Consequently, any attempt to circumnavigate, resist, subvert, or simply highlight such living conditions was quickly defined as Jametre behavior and thus heavily policed and/or criminalized, for example, via the passing of anti-vagrancy, anti-squatting, and anti-obscenity laws.

The fact remains that post-emancipated Trinidad had failed to provide any mechanism to support the transition of the formerly enslaved into full citizenship. As a result, low-classed Afro-Creole men and women found themselves struggling to obtain "legitimate" ways of surviving the sociopolitical structures of the island. The promise of full citizenship, namely, "upward economic mobility and control of one's [own] body, labor, and relationships" (King 2011, 215), was never realized by the colonial state. In reality, "freedom" was comprised of "inadequate and limited employment and education and was further restricted by the laws and ordinances passed to control black [and low-classed] bodies and behavior" (King 2011, 215). Even their participation in the Trinidadian Carnival itself was heavily policed. Those most often accused of being Jametres were the Afro-Creoles who participated in the annual Carnival as stick fighters, singers, dancers, and drummers (Brereton 2002, ix). Moreover, because the condition of being marked as a Jametre was inextricably linked to any type of consciousness and embodied logic that existed

below or outside of the limits of white/Victorian respectability, poor immigrant women from East India and Venezuela (Trotman 1984, 70) prostitutes,
madames, and practitioners of East Indian religions or obeah[14] were also stigmatized under these anti-Jametre policies (Cowley 1996, 72).

Within the Trinidadian context, gyrating "its," and specifically Jamette
(female) behavior, maintain a long history of being controlled and policed
by derogatory name-calling, for instance. In turn, the image of the Jametre
figure remained overwhelmingly stigmatized as a low-class, black, dancing (read: vulgar and uncontrollable), female body. Due to the longstanding
belief that Africans and their descendants were primitive and savage, and
that their abnormal "its" caused them to be inherently deviant (e.g., Saartjie
"Sara" Baartman, who was misnamed the Hottentot Venus),[15] the conflation
between African-derived practices and beliefs, female bodies, poverty, and
unruliness (i.e., any behavior considered illegal, criminal, or disreputable)
was easily supported throughout the colony by the ruling class. This is further
reflected in the evolution of the terms "Jametre," a derogatory name predominantly imposed on formerly enslaved Afro-Creole men and women, into the
modern term "Jammit," a slanderous description of any female, but usually of
African descent, assumed to be of the lowest class, who exhibits obscene and
unruly behavior, including prostitution.[16] Thus, it has become almost impossible to overlook how the various uses of the term "Jamette" both undermine
and "feminize the cultural practices of" masqueraders from the nineteenth-
century Jametre Carnival through to today's Trinidadian-style Carnivals,
especially when considering the ways in which Afro-women's sexuality is
both policed and scrutinized (Noel 2010, 62).

This stigmatic image was then further solidified through violent and inva-
sive legal and social practices. For example, in his article "Women and Crime
in Late Nineteenth Century Trinidad," David Trotman states "members of the
elite, including the already free black and colored middle class, opposed the
entry of women into the [legitimate sectors of the] workforce" (1986, 247–52).
To make matters worse, the Contagious Diseases Ordinance, first mandated
by the United Kingdom parliament in 1864, was vigorously enforced in the
late nineteenth century. In particular, Trotman states, "The Act required
women accused of common prostitution to register and to be periodically
examined for venereal disease and, if diseased, to be incarcerated in a certified
hospital ward. [...] In the hands of the police the ordinance became a tool to
harass not only prostitutes, but all lower-class women" (1984, 70). Noel adds,
"Because of the subjugated social standing of the Jametre women, the police
constantly scrutinized them, following them on a regular basis and, in some
cases, extorting sexual favors. Those who did not comply might be sent to the

courts to be registered as common prostitutes, a marker that made them even more vulnerable to official harassment" (2010, 64).

In an effort to interrupt these skewed power structures, the Jametres inserted their "its," their feminized "its" in particular, into the Carnival space. Scandalous masquerades included the Dame Lorraine (fashionable lady with her oversized buttocks), the Baby Doll (who was in constant search of her child's father), and the pissenlit (the bed-wetter), as well as its variations, including the chie-en-lit (the bed-shitter) and pisse-du-sangre (the menstruater). These costumes not only spectacularized the embodied injustices endured by Jamettes (women), but, as a performance, these masquerades also politicized the ways in which the ruling class were always already implicated in the violent impositions against Afro-Creole women and their "its," both by and through the state. For example, the pissenlit masquerade utilized prolific gyrations of one's "it" as political strategy of resistance. Said to be "a modification of a Martinican masquerade called chie-en-lit" (Noel 2010, 64), the Trinidadian iteration of the pissenlit ranged from men and women wearing chemises to nightgowns to oversized diapers. The cloth covering their "its" would have stains simulating menstruation, diarrhea, and/or urination. Moreover, according to newspaper reports, they often smelled like their assumed characters (Cowley 1996, 46). The vulgar exaggeration of their constituent "it" parts and its many functions of waste were further exaggerated by their dancing, which generally consisted of a rapid shifting of their "its" from side-to-side, as well as backwards and forwards, all whilst singing obscene songs (Brereton 1975, 48).

With regards to men's performances of the pissenlit, Rosamond King comments on their performance, asserting that some versions of this masquerade "revealed black men's bodies, complete, at times, with an exaggerated penis,[17] an exaggerated physical representation of black masculinity that was then very much feared" (2011, 217). Pamela Franco further elaborates that the pissenlit masquerade "allowed [men] to introduce a sexualized hobbyhorse performance (2000, 63),"[18] which often simulated "sexual horseplay with the poui sticks" (Côté ci Côté la 2012, 238)." Although the jamet's (male) depiction of the pissenlit called attention to the stigmatization of the black/African male "its" as a site and citation of fear and sexual violence, especially against white/elite women (King 2011, 218), the Jamette's (female) depiction of this character was often singled out as deplorably scandalous, more so than the men.[19] Franco explains, "In the topsy-turvy world of Carnival, *jamet* [*sic*] women were probably 'playing' with the term *pisser* [meaning to pee or urinate], as a way to linguistically foreground menstruation. [In effect, the] linguistic play, coupled with the menstrual cloth, highlights the distinctly female character" of this masquerade (2000, 63).

Moreover, historian and anthropologist Philip Scher elucidates "that *pis-senlit* is also the French word for 'dandelion' [. . .]" (2007, 115). Seeing that most of the Jametre masqueraders spoke, or at the very least understood, the French patois that was commonly used throughout the island, Scher specu-lates "that, as with so much else in Carnival, a double entendre was at work: the pissenlit was a soiled flower, or possibly a maiden deflowered" (2007, 115), or, to be explicit, raped. Thusly, this masquerade also called attention to the particular abuses the Jamette (female) body endured, especially through its use of female nightgowns and signs of menstruation, or violated "its." In fact, Trotman's research on women and crime in nineteenth-century Trinidad corroborates Franco's findings. He documents a significant increase in the number of reported rape cases by Afro-Creole women during the Jametre Carnival (1986, 247–52). It was also common for Jamettes (women) to be bat-tered or sexually humiliated in public by other Jamets (men) (Mohammed 2003, 138).[20] Ultimately, the pissenlit masquerade was a clear commentary on the sexually violent plight of the Jamette (female) in general.

Ultimately, the dances associated with these masquerades specifically magnified the public yet intimate stigmas the Jamettes often encountered by, at the very least, forcing the viewer to acknowledge the corporeality of their "its" as their own. Although much of the written descriptions of that time, especially by the newspapers, dismissed the pissenlit's dancing as "disgust-ing gestures" (Cowley 1996, 128) or "dancing in the lewdest manner" (Cowley 1996, 110), the grotesque, unruliness associated with the pissenlit masquerade further promoted the use of the "it" as both a site of resistance and a citation of both state-induced and gendered violence. Evidently, the Jametre man and woman donned the colonized black female image and her associated "it" as a strategy for challenging the negative stigmatizations that haunted the corpo-real black female body.

Applying Mimi Sheller's theoretical framing of erotic and vulgar perfor-mances of citizenship, it is clear that for the Jamette, the "bodily politics of freedom [extended] both below and beyond the state" (2012, Location 587) on two levels: 1) at the level of the body, especially seeing that the act of roll-ing one's "it" literally emphasizes one's lower realm, and 2) at the level of society, such that the positionality of the Jametre was to live below the line of legitimate citizenship. In effect, each thrusting taunt of the Jamette's "its" performatively reclaimed her body and her "its" as her own property, to be used for her own needs and desires. As Noel states, "When jamettes violated the conservative rules of etiquette in everyday life and during Carnival, they prompted a reevaluation in Trinidadian society of the ways in which women appeared and behaved in public, thereby challenging society's control of their bodies" (2010, 60). Even still, by the turn of the twentieth century, authorities, through legal ramifications, had succeeded in keeping the Jametres out of the Carnival festivities. Thereafter, Jamette behavior—specifically any vulgar, cantankerous, or unruly behavior performed by *women*—was further socialized *out* of Trinidad's *public* spaces.

Recuperating The Legacy of Her Bad Behavior
(A Story-Tale/Tail[21] About Jamette-ness)

Within the logic of today's Trinidadian-style Carnival, the link between the female body, winin', and "bad behavior" is undeniable. In fact, the terms "winin'" and "bad behavior" are often used interchangeably during the carnival season. Therefore, in an attempt to fully comprehend the embodied legacy of the Jamette figure, I now bring into focus modern-day performances of "bad behavior." Influenced by the Afro-Trinidadian feminist writer Marlene Nourbese Philip and dance scholar Susan Foster, I turn to the materiality of the winin' body itself. In *Choreographing History*, Foster argues that the material body should be read as "a bodily writing," whose actions, or lack thereof, are derived from specific histories and traditions that perpetually work to construct corporeal meaning (1995, 3). In turn, because the winin' body is a hybrid, diasporic body, its bodily writings are constantly being read and misread by spectators whilst simultaneously re-presenting corporeal meanings about itself and the other bodies it encounters. In order to decipher these layered readings and writings, I then turn to Philip's essay on the experience of African-Caribbean women and the silenced histories they are made to carry. Here, she positions the material body as a space, a site that is both impacted by, and which impacts, the outer world (1994, 288). And only by remaining rooted within this place—the bodily space—can one best decipher *"the effect of this space [the body] on the outer space—'place'"* (1994, 288). In effect, what is to come next requires me to stay attentive to the lived experience of the winin' body itself, as well as its bodily writings, all while calling attention to the complex ways the winin' body itself is written upon.

During the fall of 2009, I began my ethnographic research on the small Caribbean community within the Los Angeles area. At that time, my only connection to this community was through my cousin, who introduced me to a particular Trinidadian family that seemed to be at the center of the Los Angeles soca scene. Then, I had a very particular kind of access into this family, one that was based on the assumed fact that because I was born in Trinidad, I should be privy to all things Trinbagonian, or Caribbean to say the least.

However, being that I was a newcomer to the Los Angeles area, I struggled to ascertain close ties with any of the family members; hence, I found myself very much outside the private, intimate, and interpersonal connections that they had forged over the years. In turn, my intervention into the lives of this particular Trinidadian family further circumvented my unstable positionality as that of a "native" ethnographer.

As a precursor, it is important to note that I spent the entire morning before the LA Carnival at the home of that same "particular Trinidadian family." There, we ate together, prepared our costumes together, laughed together, and even had a few warm-up winin' sessions as we listened to soca. These were the micropolitics that then played out on the road. These intimate, private moments of bonding became the building blocks upon which our winin' antics and scenes were produced and developed. Through our winin' acts, we masqueraders publically staged our complex, private, and intimate micropolitical relationships. Moreover, the spectators, who were mostly of Caribbean heritage, or at the very least Carnival enthusiasts, supported the revelry with love and awe; some even stole a few wines from the masqueraders. *On di road,*[22] there seemed to be an unspoken alliance between us all. Whether well-established or only created in the moment of winin', these alliances—fostered by the belief that we were all rooted in the same ideologies of the Trinidadian-style Carnival community—provided a feeling of comfort and safety, which also supported our use of excessive winery, without shame, in that public, *foreign* place.

*"**And just so my journey began!**" Upon arriving to the LA Carnival that year, I spent the first 15 minutes searching for the parade route*[23] *and the band I had signed up to play mas"*[24] *with (the Joyce Producschun mas' band*[25]*). Along the way, I, along with a few other "lost" Carnival revelers decided to take a quick jump-up*[26] *with the TriniFetters band.*[27] *Soon thereafter, with our flags waving high and whistles blowing to the beat of the soca, we continued to move through their band in search of our own. When we had finally reached our truck, we were so excited that we all began rolling our "its" and vigorously waving our rags and flags in the air. Although the parading of the bands had not officially started, everyone had already begun to revel in the excitement of Carnival (read: partake in drinking and dancing in the streets). And as I readied myself, I overheard masqueraders all around saying things like:*

"Make bacchanal in di roooaaad!"[28]
"Madness ah tell yuh, MADNESS!"
"All'yuh, we goh get on rel bad today."
"I see yuh come to free-up yuhself!"
"Leh we sho' dem how it's really done."

In the name of Carib[being]ness, we were ready to "behave like we had no behavior," whether or not the streets of LA were ready for us is another story. Then, almost simultaneously with this pre-Carnival banter, I thought to myself,

Wait! How bad is bad? What kind of bacchanal and madness are we actually going to bring? And what if our "freein'-up" just looks like commesse to dem American spectators? What exactly are we representing, and to whom? Oh gosh, I wonder if I'll have to be more of an observer than a participant today? Hmmm, I hope I get tuh wine-up on Joel today; he is just too cute. But wait nah, I wonder who will end up winin' on me? Well yes, what have I gotten myself into? . . .,

And before I could run like hell away from the parade route, Carnival had begun. The truck moved forward, the music blasted through the air, my thoughts immediately stopped, and I lent myself to the lyrical commands of Iwer George:

Raise dem flags!

Raise yuh Fla-a-ags, Let me see-ee-e dem.

Raise dem flags!

Raise yuh Fla-a-ags, Let me see-ee-e dem.[29]

The truck then turned the corner and our energy jumped from zero to 60 in what felt like seconds. Any conventional rules of morality, respectability, manners of conduct, or public display of sexuality were immediately footnoted and at times tossed to the side. The winin' marathon had begun!

In order to translate the above ethnographic scene, I want first to underscore the "talk" of winin', specifically the ways Trini/Caribbean winers talk about winin' amongst themselves. My intention here is not to privilege the word over the moving body, but rather to identify the intricate negotiations, subjectivities, and positionalities winers occupy. In other words, I am focused on the particular ways their discourses on winin' are embodied and performed. Gender studies scholar Michelle Rowley suggests that talk can be "the means by which we can explore experience [itself], [. . .] specifically the performance [. . .], content, and intertextuality of talk" (2002, 28). Following Rowley's framing, the talk that accompanies winin', in tandem with the bodily writings of my winin' informants, lays bare the complex, often contradictory discourses that both construct and deconstruct winers' subjectivities.

From "madness" to "bacchanal," to "freein'-up" and "bad behavior," the cryptic ways we Trini/Caribbean winers talked about our revelry on that particular day, at that particular Trinidadian-style Carnival provides another important point of entry for deciphering the performative work that goes into these moments of excitement. Similar to the lyrics of the soca tunes featured above, these words, commonly used to describe the festive scenes associated with the Trinidadian-style Carnival, further point to the residual retentions of the colonial encounter between Trinidad's white/Victorian ruling class and the "unruly" post-emancipation masquerades of the late nineteenth-century Jamettes. In other words, the lived, praxis of *getting on bad* not only highlights the historical *mis*readings by Trinidad's colonizing class of the nineteenth-century Jamettes'[30] rebellious dancing and masquerading, but it also points to the rambunctious ways these historically invisibilized women used the performative labor of "misbehaving" to gain some semblance or feeling of "freedom."

> *"**Back to di road!**" About an hour had passed when the deep, heavy voice of soca artiste Denise "Saucy WOW" Belfon blasted across the big truck's large speakers—"Yuh watchin' meh move my wais' boy, **Jamm-It!**"—I quickly jumped onto my two feet and swung my "it" to the right in rhyme with the words "**Jamm-It.**" Belfon continued—"Look meh in meh eye when yuh wan' come **Ram-It!**"—and I sharply swung my "it" to the left. It was at that point I felt someone else's "it" roll in rhythm with mine. The music continued—"Doh make di movement make yuh **PANIC! PANIC! PANIC! PANIC!**"—and as my rolling "it" moved in relation to this new-found rolling "it," we found ourselves making back-half circles to the right, to the left, to the right, and again to the left. As the song continued, I raised my hands in the air and started rolling my "it" in quick circles, accenting the downbeat each time I rolled to the back. Then, as quickly as we had come together, we abruptly separated our "its" and continued to chip forward with the rest of the band. Although I only briefly turned around at one point to see who was behind me, I never took the time to find out who he was exactly. But so it goes during Carnival; sometimes, getting a wine is more important than worrying about with whom it is yuh winin'.*

In recalling this fleeting encounter with someone else's "it," it is important that I further clarify the bodily writings of that particular wine. At best, my "it" barely grazed his "it," which sent him the message that I was *not* looking to sexually entice him. Moreover, his choice to respect my intimate space sent me the message that he too was *not* looking for sexual enticement. Because dancing masqueraders instantaneously negotiate how they present themselves by using their winery to relate to and engage with other winin' and/or non-winin' masqueraders and spectators, these subtleties, negotiated through the dancing itself, can more quickly send a clear message to one's dance partner than words ever could. Now, I hesitate to make generalized statements such as, when a man and a woman wine fast and rough with each other it usually means they want to sleep with each other, or that they know each other well. That is just not always the case. In other words, it is always important to take into account the particular context that is allowing the couple to interact

in that particular way. With regards to the above scene, our actively winin',
dancing bodies offered a more nuanced filter for understanding our intentions and desires. In fact, because we did not engage with each other solely on
a sexual level, our winery worked to complicate the expectations of sex and
hypersexuality often etched into our black dancing bodies.

My intention here is to call attention to the always-unfolding saga of the
tempestuous hate/love or shame/pride relationship many Caribbeans maintain with the wine. In contextualizing how his informants conceptualized
their own winery, Miller explained, "Caribbean societies have commonly
been characterized by a cultural dualism abstractly conceived as a structure
of opposition between what Wilson (1973) calls 'reputation and respectability'
and Abrahams (1983) 'rude and serious'" (Miller 1991, 327). In diving deeper
into these moments of ambiguity, the multiple sensory and censorings that
get negotiated both on and off the dance floor reveal Jamette-like behavior—
namely, a playful, tricky, and multifaceted relationship that winin' revelers
maintain with their particular "its" (e.g., using their rolling "its" as a citation and not an actualization of sex). In addition to being described as "bad
behavior," as discussed above, winin' can also be marked as "good behavior."
In fact, the wine is seen as simultaneously sweet and sour, nice and nasty, or
desirable and detested, so much so that these meanings often slip in and out
of each other. For example, "sweet"—in the colloquial Caribbean sense—can
describe something that is beautiful, attractive, well presented, coveted, highly
apt, skillful, sensual,[31] and/or "respectably" provocative (another common
synonym: juicy). Conversely, "bad"—again, in the same sense—can describe
something that is spectacularly skillful and desirable yet crass, transgressive,
and/or hypersexual (other common synonyms: nasty, stink, wotles, wassy,
slack, rude).

The word "wine" itself is a triple entendre that opens up a performative
space for flexible circumvention. The playful interaction between wine (the
gyration of one's "it"), wine (the alcoholic beverage), and whine (the sound
made when complaining) creates yet more liminal spaces within which winers find room to wiggle in and out of stilting definitions, which also imbues
care and visibility to the intricate complexities associated with their rolling
"its." The descriptors compound these complexities when describing what
the "it" actually does during each roll and gyration. Some descriptors include
"cock 'it,'" which characterizes the arching of the lower back that occurs when
the butt rolls towards the back (one can cock back or up); "bubble 'it,'" which
references the bouncing of the butt that happens during faster wines as well
as the slow deliberate circling of the hips;[32] "tic-toc 'it,'" which explains the
stop-and-go action of the hips as they rotate in a circle, similar to a ticking

clock; "snake 'it,'" which details the rippling or wave-like undulations of the hips that can be performed to the front, the back, or to either side (similar to the movement of a snake); "jam 'it'"—or, as they say during Carnival, "jam on a bumpa"—which means to throw your hips into another's "it" (it is expected that a man would jam his "it" onto the rear-end of the winin' woman); and "jukk 'it,'" which literally translates into poke "it" and describes the forward thrusting of one's "it."

These terms, like the word "wine," can then be used in various ways, including ways that express erotic playfulness and (hetero-)sexual tensions. For instance, the term "cock" also means to ready a gun for firing, describes a male chicken, and is a slang term for "penis." Similar to the cock in search of a hen to mate with, the male winer can use his superb winin' skills to "wine as if he's cocky" to attract a viable winin' (female) partner, which could then lead to bedroom activities, if both dancers are willing. With regards to the gun metaphor, "cockin' 'it'" refers to the act of readying one's "it" for "destroying" its "target." Here, the goal is to bewilder someone with a spectacular wine. On the other hand, a female cockin' her "it" can be interpreted as either readying herself to destroy the competition (i.e., other winers) with her exceptional winery, or readying herself for a partner to wine *on* or *with* her. Such *tails/ tales*, which remain written into each roll of one's wine, help to forge the dialectic between those who are winin' and their potential or current winin' partners. As exemplified above, the winin' subject embodies flattery and slander, in addition to gendered, racial, and transnational identifications, with every gyrating jiggle, bump, and roll of their "it."

Let us further consider the various names of the rolling "it" mentioned in the first paragraph of the introduction: "despelote," which means all over the place or mess; "perreando," which refers to doing *it* (read: winin' or sex) doggie-style; "gouye," which means to grind; and "wukkin'-up" (aka "hard-wuk" or "wukkin'"), which literally means "working-up." Here, "work" refers to both the often tiresome labor that goes into dancing and rolling one's "it," as well as the physical work associated with the bedroom (in other words, to take or give wuk). With regards to the sexual tensions played out in the above ethnographic scene, it is important to also consider the overall cultural importance of sex and sexual behavior. This points to the heart of the sexual tensions that permeate the experience of winin' itself. For instance, because the interpersonal exchanges that privately inform winers' bodily writings vary from lusting after their first memorable winin' partner to participating in private winin' contests as a child with their cousins and/or siblings, many of my informants insist that winin' is not about sex,[33] whilst others would quietly admit that, yes, sexual tensions do get played out as they wine. Such apparent contradictions, however, provide my informants with the multiple scripts necessary for them to both comprehend and perform various modes of winin'.

Effectively, because of the work Jamettes put into the space of Carnival, today's winers rely on the layered ambiguities of the wine itself in order to embody the slipperiness necessary for navigating in and out of colonization (e.g., a body seized and organized by white/Victorian constructs of gender and racism) and decolonization (e.g., a body in the process of reclaiming itself via the complex ambiguities of winin'). To borrow from Caribbean feminist Kamala Kempadoo, the Trini/Caribbean winer remains, at once, bounded and in flux—rooted in "elements of geography, history, politics, and culture, yet somewhat fuzzy and amorphous at the edges" (2004, 7). *On di road*, the Trini/Caribbean rolling "it," is not only informed by the bold masquerades and gyrations of the nineteenth-century Jamette figure, but also by each winer's interpersonal genealogies and their own shifting relationships to other winers. As the evidence has shown, the ambiguous micro-politics of the rolling "it" itself remain rooted within the ever-evolving, multivalent cultural traditions of the Caribbean region itself. In effect, the act of winin' must be interpreted as expansive and polyvalent. Winin', therefore, allows the winer to experience his/her identity as flexible and negotiated in the moment. For, as Stuart Hall has continually argued, Caribbean people are always already delineated as enigmas, as problems, and as open questions, especially unto themselves (1995, 8), and winers throughout the diaspora are no different.

Notes

1. Layne, Benjamin, and Hinds. "Roll It Gyal." Lyrics transcribed by author from YouTube, https://www.youtube.com/watch?v=GL-fdbp4yJM.

2. In using quotes to set "it" apart in potentially ambiguous syntactic settings where the word it would commonly function as a pronoun, I playfully envisage the "it" as a common noun with multifaceted connotations. At the corporeal level, the "it" is comprised of one's hip, buttocks, and genitalia, which further indicate a major point of intersection within the body. Without our "its," it would be impossible to dance, let alone sit, stand, walk, run, bend down, pass gas, urinate, defecate, orgasm, and procreate. We are conceived because of copulating "its," then birthed through an "it," and soon thereafter, we are marked and identified because of our "its" (i.e., boy "its" versus girl "its"). Yet, in spite of the ubiquity of "it"—in that every human is imagined as having an "it" as part of their bodily composition—how we come to know and relate to our own particular "its" remains organized by the uneven politics of race, gender, sexuality, class, and nationhood, which are further complicated by the personal discourses, traditions, and histories that circumscribe each winer's particular writhing "it."

3. Here I am specifically referring to Carnivals throughout the world that are heavily influenced by and/or modeled after the Trinidadian Carnival, such as the Carnivals held in Toronto, Notting Hill, Miami, Brooklyn, and Hollywood.

4. I learned this dance whilst taking Afro-Cuban classes in Los Angeles with Kati Hernandez from 2009 through 2014. Whilst taking an Afro-Caribbean class in Trinidad, under the instruction of Christopher Walker, I also learned that Shango dances differ slightly throughout the Caribbean. Redman, the drummer, informed me that in Trinidad, although the "it" still gyrates, much of the emphasis is on stomping one's feet and shifting one's balance from side to side. Redman, casual conversation with author at the New Waves! Institute 2015/Dancing While Black Performance Lab in Port of Spain, Trinidad, July 22–31, 2015.

5. I also learned this dance whilst taking Afro-Cuban classes in Los Angeles with Kati Hernandez from 2009 through 2014. This dance is practiced similarly in Trinidad.

6. Matikor is an all-female, Hindu, pre-wedding fertility ceremony that showcases dances that emphasize their rolling "its" (Mahabir and Pirbhai 2012; Mehta 2004).

7. Here the term "Creole" means born in the New World.

8. The research methodology for this chapter is rooted in the multi-sited ethnographic fieldwork I did for my dissertation project, from 2009 to 2014. My dissertation sought to encapsulate the complex relationships forged by predominantly Trinidadian and Barbadian informants, living both in the US and the Caribbean itself. Other informants represent Jamaica, Haiti, Belize, and St. Vincent, whilst others maintain simultaneous blood ties to multiple Caribbean nations. In terms of ethnicity, they include Indo-Creole (i.e., of East Indian descent), Spanish-Creole, and Afro-Creole mixtures and lineages; with regards to class, they range from low/working class to upper middle class. Although my informants live in the Los Angeles and New York City areas, as well as parts of New Jersey, many of them maintain deep connections to other Caribbean communities within the US and beyond. In fact, during my fieldwork, from 2009 through 2014, they were, and still are, involved in the Trinidadian-style Carnivals of New York City, Los Angeles, Hollywood, Miami, Atlanta, Toronto, Notting Hill, Jamaica, and Barbados, in addition to Trinidad itself (either as DJs, party promoters, costume makers/designers, and/or masqueraders). However, as my ethnographic relationship with them developed, I was only able to follow them and participate in the Carnivals of Brooklyn, Los Angeles, Hollywood, Jersey City, Barbados, and Trinidad. With regards to interviews, most of my data was received through casual conversation with the participants and producers of these Trinidadian-style Carnivals. I only formally interviewed eleven of them.

9. There is a "heteronormative" way of winin', especially with regards to male winers. For example, if a man's winin' accentuates his rear end more than his genitals, then he can be interpreted as homosexual. Even local Trinidadian terms, such as the offensive term "batty-man," associates the butt (aka "the batty") with being a homosexual male.

10. According to many of my Trinidadian and Anglophone-Caribbean informants, white and Chinese people were imagined as having no rhythm and thus were conceptualized as being unable to wine or, at the very least, to keep the rhythmic timing of each roll.

11. Anonymous informant (family friend), casual conversation with author and her family, August 2009.

12. Anonymous Trinidadian male (Carnival masquerader living in Brooklyn), informal interview over the phone with author, July 16, 2013.

13. The "Trini/Caribbean" shorthand is my attempt at acknowledging the performative slipperiness of Trinidadian and Caribbean identities within the diaspora. I specifically privilege the "Trini/" prefix, as opposed to "pan-," due to the central role Trinidadian-style Carnivals play in the lives of my winin' Caribbean informants who all participated in Trinidadian-style Carnivals. In effect, I identify my winin' subjects as "Trini/Caribbeans" so as to address the multifarious ways in which these particular winin' bodies weave in and out of particular modes of belonging to their own particular nations whilst indirectly representing Trinidadian*ness* via their participation in these Trinidadian-style Carnivals. Moreover, this is my subtle way of acknowledging the various ways we Trini/Caribbeans slip in and out of connection to our homeland(s), as some of my informants have parentage from multiple islands. Their slippery connections to their national roots and to family are further complicated by social media (e.g., Facebook, Instagram, or Twitter) and free instant-messaging application programs (e.g., Skype, WhatsApp, or Google Hangouts). Effectively, my informants often remain active members of multiple communities through these virtual connections. In the end, I want to keep visible the ways in which winin' bodies evidently weave in and out of particular modes of belonging to both the Caribbean and the US.

14. Obeah men/women are said to be masters of occult powers and practices, believed to have derived from several secret African traditions and beliefs. They are often associated with herbology, magic, mysticism, sorcery, and religious practices—although obeah is not considered a religion in and of itself.

15. Saartjie "Sara" Baartman was a Khoi Khoi woman from South Africa who was presented throughout Europe as a "sideshow freak" and scientific anomaly during the early 1800s.

16. It is also important to note that during Carnival season, the term "jammit" can also refer to the spectacular/vulgar winin' and revelry of both men and women.

17. Often, Jametres would use a bois, which is the name of the stick used for stick fighting, as these penile exaggerations. The bois was usually made out of the yellow bark of the poui tree; for this reason, it is sometimes called a poui stick.

18. Franco explains that men's participation increased after 1884. Due to a ban on sticks and stick fighting, stick fighters ingeniously used masquerades as a way to sneak around their poui sticks onto the streets (Franco 2000, 63 fn12).

19. Citing various newspaper reports, Franco argues that men were rarely singled out, if ever (Franco 2000, 62–63).

20. It is important to note that there were also Jamettes who were infamously known to beat and publically humiliate men, especially ex-lovers.

21. I use the shorthand "tale/tail" throughout this chapter to simultaneously mean tales, as in story tales, and tails, as in the corporeal "it" (namely, one's hip and butt area). I do this to acknowledge that one's body is capable of "telling" stories, as well as to indicate that I too am working to translate the stories "told," or rather practiced, by the dancing, corporeal "it."

22. Trinidadian/Carnival colloquialism for the Carnival parade route.

23. The parading of the bands for the Los Angeles Carnival occurred along Manchester Avenue near the LAX airport. The starting point was one block up from where Manchester

Avenue and Sepulveda Boulevard intersected. The ending point was at Westchester Park, where Manchester Avenue and Lincoln Boulevard intersected.

24. "*Mas'*" is a Trinidadian-Creole term for the word "masquerade."

25. That year I played *mas'* with Joyce Producshun's band. It was a T-shirt section—meaning our "costume" was wearing matching T-shirts—and the name of our section was "We are All One Under the Sun." This slogan was used to include all the countries being represented, including Trinidad, Barbados, Grenada, Japan and the US. It expresses a sentiment of connectivity through the love of soca music and dancing, namely, winin'.

26. Like the phrases "free-up" and "get-on," the phrase "jump-up" can be used to describe the overall jumping, winin', waving, and dancing that occur during Carnival. In other words, this phrase does not necessarily mean that all you are doing is jumping up and down.

27. The current Trini-style Carnival is made up of *mas'* bands, which are organizations that one pays to play *mas'* with. In addition to costumes, they also provide the music and entertainment, which often includes a big truck (where the DJ and sound system resides), food, and drinks. In general, masquerading men and women dance and parade through the streets, behind a big truck.

28. Here, someone was singing the lyrics to Destra Garcia's hit soca tune for the 2009 Trinidadian Carnival season; lyrics transcribed by author. YouTube, February 16, 2009, https://www.youtube.com/watch?v=tzMhI8m8MeE.

29. Lyrics from "Ready," by Iwer George, transcribed by author. YouTube, December 22, 2008, https://www.youtube.com/watch?v=iuVVXMCMe08.

30. Jametres (unisex) were a subculture of mostly Afro-Creole ex-slaves, especially associated with the Carnival of post-emancipation Trinidad in the late nineteenth century. Today, the words "Jamet" (male), "Jamette" (female), and "Jametre" are each pronounced "jam-it" or "jam-eht."

31. Alicia Arrizón explains the subtleties between sensuality vs. sexuality: "While sexuality is characterized by sex, sexual activity and sexual orientation, to be sensual is to be aware of and to explore feelings and sensations of beauty, luxury, joy and pleasure. [. . .] Sexuality and sensuality are different, and yet overlapping, concepts that shape, influence, and inspire one another. While sexuality may be expressed in ones' sensuality, a subject's sensuality stimulates her/his sexuality. Usually, one can perform sensuality in music, clothing, fragrance, and accessories, or while walking, singing and dancing" (Arrizón 2008, 192–93).

32. I was told by two Caribbean dancer/choreographers, Chris Walker (Jamaica) and Makeda Thomas (Trinidad), that you have to imagine hot soup or porridge that is so thick, that it takes more energy for the bubble to break its surface; in effect, you must roll your hips at the extreme edges of a full hip rotation. Makeda Thomas and Chris Walker, casual conversation with author, November 16, 2013.

33. This positioning falls in line with what Miller terms autosexuality. He explains, winin' "may therefore be understood as the repudiation of sexuality as an act of exchange. Autosexuality then transcends questions of sexuality and becomes tantamount to a rejection of sociality, or a momentary escape from [or denial of] that act of exchange which binds one to the world and its relationships, and in particular, to what women may increasingly be regarding as oppressive relationships" (Miller 1991, 334).

Bibliography

Arrizón, Alicia. "Latina Subjectivity, Sexuality and Sensuality." *Women & Performance: A Journal of Feminist Theory* 18, no. 3 (2008).

Brereton, Bridget. *Race Relations in Colonial Trinidad, 1870–1900*. New York: Cambridge University Press, 2002.

Brereton, Bridget. "The Trinidad Carnival: 1870–1900." *Savacou: A Journal of the Caribbean Artists Movement* 11–12 (1975).

Cowley, John. *Carnival, Canboulay, and Calypso: Traditions in the Making*. New York: Cambridge University Press, 1996.

Dikobe, Maude. "Bottom in de Road: Gender and Sexuality in Calypso." *PROUDFLESH: A New Afrikan Journal of Culture, Politics & Consciousness* 3 (2004). http://www.africare-source.com/proudflesh /issue3/dikobe.htm.

Dixon-Gottschild, Brenda. *The Black Dancing Body: A Geography from Coon to Cool*. New York: Palgrave Macmillan, 2003.

Harewood, Susan J. *Calypso, Masquerade Performance and Post National Identities*. Doctoral dissertation, University of Illinois at Urbana-Champaign, 2006.

Hall, Stuart. "Negotiating Caribbean Identities." *New Left Review* 209 (1995).

Hartman, Saidiya. *Scenes of Subjection: Terror, Slavery, and Self-Making in Nineteenth-Century America*. New York: Oxford University Press, 1997.

Hill, Errol. *The Trinidad Carnival: Mandate for a National Theatre*. Austin: University of Texas Press, 1972.

Foster, Susan, ed. "Choreographing History." In *Choreographing History*. Bloomington: Indiana University Press, 1995.

Franco, Pamela. "The 'Unruly Woman' in Nineteenth-Century Trinidad Carnival." *Small Axe* 7 (2000).

Kempadoo, Kamala. *Sexing The Caribbean*. New York: Routledge, 2004.

King, Rosamond S. "New Citizens, New Sexualities: Nineteenth Century *Jamettes*." In *Sex and the Citizen: Interrogating the Caribbean*, ed. Faith Smith. Charlottesville: University of Virginia Press, 2011.

Mahabir, Joy, and Mariam Pirbhai, eds. *Critical Perspectives on Indo-Caribbean Women's Literature*. New York: Routledge, 2012.

Mehta, Brinda J. *Diasporic Dis(Locations): Indo-Caribbean Women Writers Negotiate the Kala Pani*. Kingston, Jamaica: University of the West Indies Press, 2004.

Miller, Daniel. "Absolute Freedom in Trinidad." *Man, New Series* 4, no. 2 (1991).

Mohammed, Patricia. "A Blueprint for Gender in Creole Trinidad: Exploring Gender Mythology through Calypsos of the 1920s and 1930s." In *The Culture of Gender and Sexuality in the Caribbean*, ed. Linden Lewis. Gainesville: University Press of Florida, 2003.

Noel, Samantha A. "De Jamette in We: Redefining Performance in Contemporary Trinidad Carnival." *Small Axe* 14, no. 1 (2010).

Philip, Marlene Nourbese. "Dis Place the Space Between." In *Feminist Measures: Soundings in Poetry and Theory*, eds. Lynn Keller and Cristanne Miller. Ann Arbor: University of Michigan Press, 1994.

"PISSENLIT (Wet the Bed)." *Côté ci Côté la: Trinidad and Tobago Dictionary, The Signature Edition*, ed. John Mendes. Port of Spain, Trinidad and Tobago: Zenith Services, 2012.

Rowley, Michelle. "Reconceptualizing Voice: The Role of Matrifocality in Shaping Theories and Caribbean Voices." In *Gendered Realities: Essays in Caribbean Feminist Thought*, ed. Patricia Mohammed. Kingston, Jamaica: University of the West Indies Press, 2002.

Scher, Philip W. "The Devil and the Bed-Wetter: Carnival, Memory, National Culture, and Post-Colonial Consciousness in Trinidad." *Western Folklore* 66, nos. 1–2 (2007).

Sheller, Mimi. *Citizenship from Below: Erotic Agency and Caribbean Freedom*. Durham: Duke University Press, 2012.

Sheller, Mimi. *Consuming the Caribbean: From Arawaks to Zombies*. New York: Routledge, 2003.

Trotman, David. *Crime in Trinidad: Conflict and Control in a Plantation Society, 1838–1900*. Knoxville: University of Tennessee Press, 1986.

Trotman, David. "Women and Crime in Late Nineteenth Century Trinidad." *Caribbean Quarterly* 30, nos. 3–4 (1984).

Warner-Lewis, Maureen. *Guinea's Other Suns: The African Dynamic in Trinidad Culture*. Dover, MA: Majority Press, 1991.

Chapter 6

"Thirty Gyal to One Man": Women's Prolific
Presence in the Trinidad Carnival

—Asha St. Bernard

In 2015, following several band launches to commence a new Carnival season, a Facebook user expressed her frustration in a post: "Carnival costume photoshoots: where the black people at doh? #aesthetics? one of the reasons why I am adamant about buying my niece black dolls. #smh@society." This blogger's vexed response to photographs of models displaying brand-new Carnival costume designs incited many similar responses. One person's brief but interesting comment below the post read, "Almost all advertising in Trinidad," in a display of her agreement with the issue brought up by the blogger—namely, that a lack of racial/skin-color diversity in Carnival costume advertising is a common practice in Trinidad.

Like those Facebook users and many others who pay attention to trends in advertising, I cannot ignore some glaring signs by marketers who privilege some racial and ethnic groups over others, especially on the basis of skin complexion and other physical attributes, like hair. This has become a prominent issue particularly with high levels of competitiveness among Carnival businesses, whose organizers in turn, rely on cultural prejudices to stand out in the competition by highlighting valued notions of beauty to endorse their brand. Despite these blatant practices, businesses manage to thrive and continue to attract growing numbers of participants each year. This points to the level of dominance and consent that has taken over the Carnival celebrations and which perpetuate inequality in representation.

The problem, therefore, is that many popular contemporary Carnival organizers use limited indicators of representation to market and sell their products. My aim in this chapter is to analyze the very nuanced ways race, class, and gender are used in the process, by paying particular attention to their media output—namely, various texts on some of these organizers' websites, and their promotional material—while in some instances, juxtaposing and/ or comparing them to other Carnival texts. Due to the popularity of some of these businesses, their authority is inevitable and as such, they have a huge impact on how locals and foreigners understand and experience Carnival. I argue that together they contribute to, and magnify, the disunity and disenfranchisement steadily becoming more apparent in Trinidad Carnival.

This work is largely inspired by past inquiries into Carnival, such as the writings of anthropologist John Stewart (1986), who wrote engagingly about the growing business of Carnival and its effects on the masses. Regarding patrons' reactions to the alterations in Carnival, he notes, "Recent withdrawal has less to do with religion than with a feeling of encroaching emptiness in the festival." Stewart attributes this "feeling of encroaching emptiness," to "increased politicization of the festival" (291). Although not discussed in detail in this chapter, his work was seminal.

The Body

The deliberate disassociation of the middle class with Carnival post-emancipation, following the abolition of slavery in Trinidad in 1834, and the years that followed nearing the turn of the century, was an effect of colonial influence. The desire for hegemonic acceptance, particularly by those in the middle stratum to uphold dignity and maintain respectability,[1] was born from those early colonial relations. The concept of respectability is further explained by Samantha Noel (2014), who draws attention to the role of the Jamette—lower-class black women who were looked down upon as they used their bodies in dance, as a form of rebellion against the rigid hierarchal system (65). She states, "These more rebellious women were aware of how the body could be used as a form of protest" (66). Consequently, they posed a threat to the hierarchal order that was trying to be upheld and were therefore seen as inappropriate and taboo. Members of the middle class, then, saw Carnival as vulgar and oppositional, and therefore, unbecoming of someone with class. This juxtaposition of appropriate and inappropriate is explored here because the Carnival still remains significantly regulated by groups that have substantial cultural impact on the island. The regulation and management have brought about economic benefits, as they have assisted in crafting a perfectly packaged and desirable Carnival. However, one is left to wonder: who does this really benefit?

Ironically, the meaning of certain behaviors associated with Carnival were altered, appropriating some formerly taboo actions, such as the "vulgar" dancing of the Jamette, especially once performed by "respectable" members of society. Hence, certain aspects of the festival became more desirable once members of the middle and upper middle classes started doing it themselves.

Trinidad Carnival has since influenced the Carnivals in other Caribbean islands, and has been exported to the United States of America, Canada, and England by Caribbean immigrants. The Carnival saw enormous growth during the oil boom in Trinidad in the 1970s. Attire continued to evolve from more traditional costuming,[2] to what is now called "pretty *mas*,"[3] created by "formerly educated middle-class artists [who] changed aesthetic standards through their use of new materials . . ." (Green and Scher 2007, 15). The change in aesthetic can also be attributed to the commercialization of the festival. This type of masquerade is most prevalent in the Caribbean, and in Carnivals celebrated in the Caribbean diaspora nowadays.

Today, when people talk about "pretty *mas*'" for women, what comes to mind are showgirl-type costumes. These costumes are playfully and sometimes mockingly referred to as "bikini-and-beads" costumes since many of them are literally bikinis decorated with sequins, feathers, and beads that dangle and shake as the wearers dance energetically to Carnival songs. The disdain some people have for this new, popular type of costuming comes from the belief that the authentic creativity of past costume designers is now replaced by generic designs. Even Peter Minshall, one of the original pioneers of pretty *mas*', whose work is held in high regard for its extraordinary level of creativity and the theatrical performances it inspired, has shown his contempt for this new style of *mas*'. He is quoted as describing pretty *mas*' as "merely a handful of sequins and beads," and his dissatisfaction is seen clearly as he implies that there is a reduced level of creative value in contemporary Carnival costuming (*One on One*).

The modern-day Carnival celebrated in Trinidad is a period of festivity open to the public. There is something for everyone to get involved in. However, the majority of activities, as well as the best events and experiences, are restricted for those who can afford, sometimes exorbitantly, to be part of the fun. This is especially seen in the party events/fêtes that lead up to the street parade, and have become a crucial part of the overall Carnival experience. It is also evident in the street parade, where members basically pay for free reign of the streets, while non-paying participants or onlookers are restricted to the sidelines during these processions, sometimes violently, if they intrude.

Within a predominantly patriarchal, heteronormative space, and with the common perception that "sex sells," it is no great shock that the European aesthetic "ideal" female body has come to symbolize Trinidad Carnival. Likewise, with the increasing popularity of Carnival, it is unsurprising that Carnival and a display of sexuality are intimately interwoven. Linden Lewis (2003) firmly declares, "There is a strong correlation between sexuality and popular culture in the Caribbean" (7). Lewis does not give a distinct reason for this correlation, but rather insinuates that it is a cultural practice rooted in misogynistic, hyper-masculine tendencies. A connection between Carnival, sexuality, and the female body is evident in almost every element of Carnival, whether it is the music, masquerade, other social events, and especially through its promotional material.

Crucial to this discussion is the knowledge of the concept of the Carnival body. I define the Carnival body as belonging primarily to young, skinny, and predominantly light-skinned women. For women, it is an almost unattainable beauty "ideal" in accordance with mainstream heteronormative beauty expectations. Although men and women both sport a chiseled Carnival body, women are the ones whose bodies are more scrutinized through the blatant media emphasis on highly sexualized and objectified females during Carnival. Furthermore, the female Carnival body most advertised and popularized in Trinidad is light-skinned and mixed race. Denean Sharpley-Whiting's (2007) description of the women typically seen in hip-hop music videos is applicable to the women primarily used by popular Carnival businesses to promote their brand, and by extension, to represent Trinidad Carnival. Sharpley-Whiting writes:

> The majority of these women represent what historian Tiffany Patterson calls 'ascriptive mulattas,' that is, those whose physical beauty transcends characteristics such as darker hues, full lips, and the like, historically prefigured as less than ideal (non-European) (27).

The constant overrepresentation of the female Carnival body, often excessively sexualized, has many implications. Not only does this practice support patriarchy, as well as the objectification and misogynistic treatment of women, but also it persuasively affirms Trinidad as a sensualized, sexualized paradise, as these women's bodies implicitly invite people to Trinidad (for Carnival). Moreover, by highlighting a particular type of Caribbean woman, the people who have power to control discourse on the island assist in promulgating a narrow view of beauty, by denying the value of blackness/African features. This chapter addresses the overt sexualization present in modern Trinidad Carnival media through the practice of using female bodies to market Carnival, particularly the masquerade. Furthermore, I analyze the transposing of the Caribbean body to the Carnival body, an archetype that celebrates a North American and European ideal. The effect of this socialization is that Caribbean women are subjected to a hegemonic pressure to conform and celebrate an aesthetic that is unlikely for the vast majority of women.

Women in Trinidad have become indisputably representative of Carnival. In their work on women in Rio de Janeiro Carnival, Brazil, Lewis, and Pile (1996) write, "Carnival is profoundly gendered" (25); the same can be said about the Trinidad Carnival. While Carnival can be a time to challenge social norms or as Bakhtin (1965) popularly described it as a period of role reversal, in Trinidad, the Carnival is just another season to live out and even emphasize norms, including the different gender roles of men and women.

Women are, time and time again, used by the bandleaders for their personal economic gain. It is an all too familiar sight: the strategic placement of female sex symbols in an advertisement for a product unrelated to sex. Despite many of the women in these advertisements being educated and/or assertive, they are stripped of those qualities and sexually objectified to attract buyers. Hence, men are encouraged to be seen as active and in control of the circumstance whereas women are traditionally socialized and portrayed as passive objects to be desired by men.

Perhaps most important is the type of woman that is most valued by these advertisements, further adding to the inequality and discrimination found in media representations of Trinidad Carnival. While similar images are widely used across several Carnival bands, I discuss these issues by examining the still photographs from the 2015 Carnival offerings by Tribe and Bliss. My observations are based on a non-random quantitative content analysis. The sample is a convenience and judgmental one in that I looked at (n=50) images selected and maintained by the bandleaders and marketers who use the models and the ideal images as an advertising tool to attract women to sign up for a costume.

In her book, *Sexing the Caribbean: Gender, Race and Sexual Labor*, which focuses on sex work in the Caribbean, Kamala Kempadoo (2004) uses the term "heteropatriarchal" to help contextualize the Caribbean region. "Heteropatriarchal," she writes,

> denote[s] a structuring principle in Caribbean societies that privileges heterosexual, promiscuous masculinity and subordinates feminine sexuality, normalizing relations of power that are intolerant of and oppressive toward sexual desires and practices that are outside of or oppose the dominant sexual and gender regimes. This structuring principle privileges men's experiences, definitions, and perceptions of sexuality, whereby not only are appreciations of female (hetero) sexuality obscured, but homoeroticism and same-gender sexual relations are denied legitimacy. (9)

Kempadoo's description is especially helpful in that it elucidates a key part of my argument about female representation in media portrayals of popular Carnival bands, namely, the recognition of a hegemonic system that influences and normalizes social behaviors, including gender expectations.

While male promiscuity is commonly expected and naturalized, the same cannot be said about female sexual behaviour. Hence, the power relation is evident; women are still in many ways oppressed, even if informally. As is the case in patriarchal societies, men are the sex who generally have greater control over and advantage of resources (Watson 2003). If we take hegemonic masculinity into account, it becomes clear why representations of women outnumber those of men in organizations' efforts to sell Carnival, and more specifically, their products and services. Furthermore, the concept of "machismo," used to describe aggressive, hyper-sexed male, a well-known stereotypical characteristic of Caribbean men, can be used to explain the practice of treating women like objects to be controlled and consumed by men, and can be applied to the disproportionate exposure and exploitation of women's bodies in media. Hence, there is an obvious incongruity in the way female sexuality is treated; while the culture systematically subdues female sexuality, it shamelessly exposes the female body.

The Carnival Model

The incessant use of female bodies by Carnival band organizers to promote their bands and events is significant to the image of Trinidad Carnival. Plastered on websites and on other promotional materials, women's faces and bodies are often the first visual indicators of the festival. In fact, a simple Google image search of Trinidad Carnival conclusively demonstrates that the bejeweled woman is the key archetypical representative of Trinidad Carnival.

In the history of Carnival, females have only recently dominated the street parade (Franco 2007), the phenomenon of increased female participation is remarkable as it directly reflects the growing independence of Caribbean women and their desire not only to do things on their own, but also to be a part of and occupy traditionally male spaces. At the same time, however, it reflects society's hold on women. While women are stepping out more into the public domain with their increasing involvement in Carnival activities, many Carnival businesses focus on exploiting the female body and heteronormative femininity.

Compounded by Carnival's rapidly growing commerciality, businesses have not shied away from sexualizing women's bodies as a means of attracting a heterosexual male audience, and getting a female audience to identify. The sexy images of young, attractive women striking poses and modeling revealing costumes reflect normalized beauty ideals which both men and women are socialized to desire. Whereas men generally are supposed to want the women who have this prescribed look, women have a tendency to want to be like those women. This is problematic because we are already overwhelmed with similar images by the mainstream media, which is daily offering products and services for sale. The Trinidad Carnival, something culturally indigenous to Trinidad, has dissolved into another space that enforces these limiting standards of beauty and acceptance, threatening authentic creativity, longstanding traditions, individual self-expression, and self-value. What is being created is a generic, culturally non-specific look, void of any Caribbean detail.

Spotlight on Sexuality

Using models to advertise Carnival costumes and events is now a common practice. Observing the trend of Carnival models, one can deduce that the people of Trinidad and Tobago are all good-looking, sexually appealing, and fit—and none more so than the women. Along with a handful of young, muscular men, they exemplify the ideal Trinidadian bodies. These representations of the "ideal" body are not only informed by popular, dominant ideologies of the human body, and in particular women's bodies, but are also responsible for producing beliefs and fostering certain behaviors about which body types are valued, and which are not. Below are online images from Carnival bands: Tribe and Bliss. They present a relatively unvaried representation of ethnicity and body types in Trinidad and Tobago, whilst quite literally situating female sexuality under a magnifying glass.

These photographic images all have something in common—namely, the intentional allure of the female "ideal" model to sell the costume to potential masqueraders. These models, however, do not represent the vast majority of women who participate in Carnival, nor do they represent the men who also pay for costumes and parade the streets on Carnival Monday and Tuesday. As such, advertisements are part of the whole context within which we attempt to understand and define our own gender relations. They are part of the process by which we learn about gender (Jhally 1990). Apart from the minor details such as the heavy make-up, the models are slim and fit, women who, because of their "ideal" size, are considered sexy and attractive by many whose ideas of beauty have been informed by the media. It is also important to address how these women are portrayed and what types of women are used as representative of the "ideal" Carnival body.

Sexualization and Objectification

Regardless of the style and grandeur of the costumes, using models is a seemingly irreversible trend to attract potential customers and peddle costumes. Due to the competitiveness of the Carnival industry in Trinidad, many Carnival bands put serious efforts into these annual presentations. Therefore, it is not unusual that they host screenings where potential models are asked to show up wearing swimwear so their bodies can be more thoroughly inspected for blemishes and physical deformities.

This process, though perhaps reassuring to those whose bodies "make the cut" or pass the test, is potentially rather crippling to the self-esteem of other men and women who do not meet the recommended beauty standards, and also to some of those who will later see these models wearing costumes they too would like to wear. It is a practice that boldly reinforces the beauty myth sanctioned by the international fashion industry, which is largely unattainable. The common practice of choosing the models, as described above, is already a form of objectification. Models are chosen or discarded based strictly on their representation of an idealized body aesthetic.

Lewis and Pile (1996) address an important topic regarding the modification of Carnival costuming over the years. They make reference to the "uncostuming" of masqueraders, a phenomenon that is also being experienced in the Trinidad Carnival. Participants are less likely to be topless in the Trinidad Carnival than in the Carnival in Rio, but there has been a definite reduction in the amount of material used in the costumes for women in Trinidad Carnival bands (Barnes 2000). This skimpy costume trend is prominent in the images from the various popular Carnival band websites in 2015. These portrayals of scantily clad women appeal to the male sexual fantasy but also the false consciousness of women who have come to accept these skimpy costumes as the only way to appear as an attractive and "sexy" Carnival reveler on the main stage or the parade route.

The two images included in this chapter show some of the ways women are portrayed in popular Carnival media representations. Though women are more visible in popular Carnival media representations, I see it as less of an advantage on their part, in the sense of sexual affirmation, and more of a practice that establishes and maintains male sexual hegemony where sexualized female bodies are subordinate and constantly scrutinized. The "male

2015 Costume "Luxe" by Tribe for Trinidad Carnival.

2015 Costume "Ring of Fire" by Bliss for Trinidad Carnival.

gaze" (Mulvey 1975) is applicable to the still image as the ways the women are positioned and styled emphasize their erogenous body parts, lending them a greater sexual appeal to a heterosexual audience.

In the images above, it is apparent that the models cater primarily to the male gaze and can be seen contorting their bodies to appear sexier by elongating their spines and projecting their hips. Across carnival websites models are sometimes seen touching themselves—something Goffman (1976) refers to as the "feminine touch." In both images, the female models are shown in ways that a male model would not be expected to pose, maintaining a notion of heteronormativity, in which female subordination is normalized. Obviously these women have a function, and that is to show-off the costume. This is the denotative function. The connotative function is to sell Carnival through the promise of uninhibited sex. Hence, it makes sense that the bandleaders would showcase these images and highlight the "idealized" body type that has become the aesthetic of Carnival in Trinidad.

These representations naturalize the ideal body types in Trinidadian society while at the same time diminish other body norms of the vast majority of women. Who is shown by the media, and which features are highlighted, often come to represent what are typically valued as "ideal," desirable, and attractive. Advertisers want to ensure that they are encouraging women to have lower self-esteem about their body because this allows them to sell more products to women as a bridge to achieve the "ideals" in our culture.

The majority of Trinidadian people—young, middle, and older age—are not slim, athletically built, or light-skinned. Yet they are the ones advertised. Due to the popularity of these large Carnival bands—many of which sell out every year, and the number of young people they attract, seen masquerading in their costumes on the streets—this type of portrayal of the Carnival has become naturalized. Natasha Barnes (2000) asserts that:

> When cable television networks make images of Carnival revellers available to global audiences, what is delivered in these screens, devoid of history and context are parades of scantily clad, gyrating women that appear to market the island and its culture as a destination for sex tourism. (96)

Barnes's critique of a decontextualized Carnival, in which the history is lost in the artificiality and erotic displays showed via several media outlets, is noteworthy. It pushes the argument that not enough is being done to cultivate a Carnival that is free from these limiting portrayals that unashamedly deny other aspects of Trinidadian identity. Carnival visuals have become a central identifier of Trinidadian culture. By marketing the sexual characteristics of its people and showing them as exotic, men continue to be represented as hypersexual and promiscuous. The women, especially being synonymous with Carnival, simultaneously bear the burden of symbolizing the nation in a sexual manner. Hence, it should come as no surprise that foreigners, particularly males, come to Trinidad during Carnival looking for and *expecting* sexual pleasures from women.

The Era of the Carnival Body

Even when darker-skinned Afro-Trinidadian and Indo-Trinidadian women are featured in the advertising world, these women tend to have features more akin to the "ascriptive mulattas"—narrow noses and thinner lips. One must ask: where is the diversity in the media representations from a country that proudly promotes its rich racial diversity?

An equally noteworthy observation about the "ideal" Carnival body is the emphasis placed upon light-skinned women. Light-skinned women in the Caribbean have a long history of being regarded as "more attractive" than dark-skinned women, and this form of color stratification has its origins in the Caribbean's colonial history (Hunte 2005). Brown-skinned women, on the other hand, are colored enough to be perceived as exotic and sexual but still light enough to be thought of as respectable (Edmondson 2009).

As seen in the two images that I have provided, these longstanding traditions and perceptions are still common practice. Both images show models with different skin complexions, but with very similar appearances. Interestingly, each has long bouncy hair and slender features. When popular Carnival bands make these images part of their website or use them in other publications, the effect is that the images come to legitimize certain looks over others. The idea of a Carnival body is well known on the island. Trendy articles and blogs talk about the Carnival and often give readers tips and steps to follow to attain this look.

Conclusion

Trinidad Carnival continues to attract attention around the world as a festival worth attending. Its success has motivated many to get involved in the Carnival business, and the female body and her sexuality have become key to the marketing strategies involved. While men and people of all ages and races enjoy Carnival, the most frequently seen model, or representative of the Carnival, is a slim, light-skinned, sexy young woman. The constant use of this type of female has created a standard of beauty that unfairly represents Trinidadians. The models used in advertisements fit a very specific look, and this fantasy look is presented as the norm, as the quintessential Trinidadian woman. This woman, or the Carnival body that these businesses use as the representative of Carnival, is laden with cultural values and perceptions of beauty that are biased. Carnival has become yet another mechanism to maintain unrealistic heteronormative gender expectations. The very act of continuously promoting lighter-skinned women with more European features over darker-skinned women in a country like Trinidad—where the population is made up predominantly of Afro and Indo-Trinidadians—reflects the continuing importance of its postcolonial history in which "whiteness" is privileged over "blackness."

Notes

1. Respectability is the notion of being decent and proper, in keeping with the colonial authority and its ideological standards of attitudes and behaviors.

2. "Traditional costuming" refers to traditional Carnival characters that individuals usually made themselves and portrayed year after year. Each year a new costume was made and the masquerader would perform for money and/or sometimes scare and taunt the audience.

3. "Pretty *mas*'" ("*mas*'" is short for "masquerade" and will be used throughout this chapter) refers to the sexier, bikini-like (female) or board shorts (male) costumes that have been increasingly appearing in the street parade and especially sought after by younger masqueraders (though people of all ages purchase these costumes).

Bibliography

Barnes, Natasha. "Body Talk: Notes on Women and Spectacle in Contemporary Trinidad Carnival." *Small Axe* 4, no. 1 (2000): 93–105.

Bakhtin, Mikhail. *Rabelais and His World*. Cambridge, MA: MIT Press, 1965.

Edmondson, Belinda. *Caribbean Middlebrow: Leisure Culture and the Middle Class*. Ithaca: Cornell University Press, 2009.

Franco, Pamela. "The Invention of Traditional Mas and the Politics of Gender." In *Trinidad Carnival: The Cultural Politics of a Transnational Festival*, eds. Garth L. Green and Philip Scher. Bloomington: Indiana University Press, 2007.

Goffman, Erving. *Gender Advertisements*. New York: Harper and Row, 1976.

Goffman, Erving. *The Presentation of Self in Everyday Life*. New York: Anchor Books, 1959.

Green, Garth L., and Philip W. Scher. *Trinidad Carnival: The Cultural Politics of a Transnational Festival*. Bloomington: Indiana University Press, 2007.

Hunte, Margaret. *Race, Gender, and the Politics of Skin Tone.* Routledge: New York, 2005.

Island People Mas. Island People Mas, September 15, 2014.

Jhally, Sut. *Codes of Advertising.* New York: Routledge, 1990.

Kempadoo, Kamala. *Sexing The Caribbean: Gender, Race and Sexual Labour.* New York: Routledge, 2004.

Lewis, Clare, and Steve Pile. "Women, Body, Space: Rio Carnival and the Politics of Performance." *Gender, Place and Culture* 3, no. 1 (1996): 23–41.

Lewis, Linden. *The Culture of Gender and Sexuality in the Caribbean.* Gainesville: University Press of Florida, 2003.

Mulvey, Laura. "Visual Pleasure and Narrative Cinema." *Screen* 16, no. 3 (1975): 6–18.

Noel, Samantha. "De Jamette in We: Redefining Performing in Contemporary Trinidad Carnival." *Small Axe* 31, no. 14.1 (2010): 60–78.

"One on One with Vernon Ramesar—Peter Minshall." YouTube, September 9, 2014.

Sharpley-Whiting, Denean. *Pimps Up, Ho's Down: Hip Hop's Hold on Young Black Women.* New York: New York University Press, 2007.

Stewart, John. "Patronage and Control in Trinidad Carnival." In *The Anthropology of Experience*, eds. Victor W. Turner and Edward W. Burner. Chicago: University of Illinois Press, 1986.

Chapter 7

From Devi to Diva: Indo-Caribbean Women Rising in Trinidad's Chutney Soca

—Darrell Gerohn Baksh

This chapter explores the conflicts and complexities of Indo-Caribbean femininity at a moment when the Indo-Caribbean woman is breaking away from embodiments of devi, traditional models of female representation strongly tied to religious patriarchy, to diva, a contemporary persona publicly expressed in the realm of chutney soca, a popular form of Indo-Caribbean music that has absorbed the Carnival aesthetic in Trinidad. In this chapter, I trace the rise of Indo-Caribbean women to multiple historical influences and templates of female performance in the public spaces of Trinidad Carnival derived from several Afro-Caribbean archetypes: nineteenth-century Jamettes, twentieth-century calypsonians, and twenty-first century "soca divas." I also consider the impact of South Asian culture—specifically, female folk performance in private Indo-Caribbean spaces and the Hindi cinema "item girl"—on this emergence. I further propose how such agency is a transgressive act that breaks traditionally held ideologies ascribed to the societal roles and behaviors of Indo-Caribbean women and how, by taking charge of their own bodies, they are asserting their femininity and disrupting patriarchal hegemonies. In this way, I plot the movement of Indo-Caribbean women from the confines of the private and domestic to the occupation of the popular and the public, while also troubling the notion that, although Caribbean women are forging their own emancipatory spaces in Carnival, they are still playing into constructs of patriarchal authority and the masculine gaze. As such, my objective is to indicate how the public emergence of the Indo-Caribbean woman signals her control over (re)defining her own feminine identity, itself entangled within the constant tensions and symbolic negotiations between the vestiges of tradition and the prospects of modernity. I therefore contend that Indo-Caribbean women are, by shifting from devi to diva, *re-mixing*—that is, recasting, reclaiming, revising, and re-visioning—sociocultural expressions of themselves.

Historical Overview of Femininity in Trinidad

I want to begin my analysis by considering the importance of women to this investigation and asking why do they even count? First, within the contexts of Indo-Caribbean popular culture, women matter because surviving female folk performance traditions of the indentured experience bear heavily on the evolution of song and dance practices that are now identified as chutney soca. This chutney soca pulse, in joining Trinidad's Carnival phenomenon, further reinforces the fact that "Carnival Is Woman," as musician Rukshun proclaimed in soca tempo in 1995: that increased gendered visibility has become a primary driving force of a festival where women matter because they embody the licentious energy that powers the Carnival bacchanal in a transgressive enactment of liberation, though this escape is never complete because such agency does not immobilize female objectification and exploitation by masculine authority. This heteropatriarchal arrangement leads to, and allows for, further critical study into why women matter in terms of restructuring feminine identity formation because the woman, as a colonized body, has traditionally occupied a position of subservience in Trinidadian ideology—ethnic, religious, and sociocultural—which she has contested at different historical moments; for the Indo-Caribbean woman in popular Carnival culture, the complicated blend of multiple feminine influences creating the diva in chutney soca reinforces and widens constructs of identity as multivalent in the public and national spaces of Trinidad.

Within these spaces, the framework for gender norms is driven by colonial ideology that privileges Victorian "morality." As a subject of the British empire, the colonized Caribbean woman was expected to sustain culture within a social hierarchy that, at its core, pointed to ideas of "respectability"—what was and was not considered "respectable" behavior—which worked to uphold patriarchal dominance and restrict female independence. This respectability is defined as the "inside" of culture (Munro 2016), the domestic spaces of home and the public institutions of Christian churches, government, and private schools where self-restraint, industry, education, and respect for social hierarchies was exercised and the conservative values of British colonialism was cultivated (11). The "outside" of culture, in contrast, "corresponds with the street and rum shop" (11) and, with the abolition of enslavement in the nineteenth century, freed Afro-Caribbean bodies took to that "outside" in celebration and abandon in what would evolve into contemporary Carnival. It is within this festive space that a "forum for gender emancipation" (51) arose, challenging the "morality" that colonial oppression was so keen to control.

Jametteness: Women in Nineteenth-Century Carnival

Colonial indoctrination demanded that women "be Christian, modest dressers, dedicated mothers, and loyal wives relegated to the home" (Noel 2010, 66). To forsake these "moral" responsibilities and openly descend to the streets at Carnival was, therefore, "unbecoming" of the colonized woman and signified a public retaliation of those gender norms. As such, the Afro-Caribbean woman who resisted gender conformity and "violated the conservative rules of etiquette" (60) earned the reputation of Jamette, called by that name because her behavior was beyond the "diameter" or diameter of "respectability," especially with her performances that emphasized sexual corporeal exposure.

Heavily scrutinized by the authorities for indecency, this figure came to be identified with Afro-Caribbean working-class women who "behaved licentiously, dressed in a provocative manner, and often worked as [prostitutes]" (Noel 2009). Because of this perception, "Jamette" has survived in the vernacular speech of Trinidad to describe "women whose being or behavior is judged to be morally loose, sexually promiscuous, crude, or noisily quarrelsome" (De Freitas 1999, 15). By refusing to be censored and muted, the Jamette therefore threatened the colonial regime's restriction and silencing of women.

Motherhood versus Womanhood

At work, then, is a gender(ed) discourse that pits motherhood against womanhood. Colonial conditioning pushed the construction of femininity as maternal, associating it with "marriage, family, child-rearing . . . [and] caregiving" (16), rather than sexual. This denial of feminine pleasure worked to suppress the independence of the Caribbean woman. Those who rebelled against the hierarchy and participated in public spheres, like Carnival and calypso—historical and traditional performance domains of men—were socially condemned as "immoral" and "disrespectable."

How Calypso Queens Birth Soca Divas

The triumph of Calypso Rose (McCartha Lewis) in the calypso arena in the late 1970s marks a significant moment for Afro-Caribbean women. In the trailer of her biographical documentary, *Calypso Rose: The Lioness of the Jungle*, calypsonian Gypsy (Winston Peters) styles her the "mother of calypso" (lorraine1606 2011), a title that downplays Rose's defiant feats of winning the 1977 Road March, the most-played song of Carnival, *and* becoming Trinidad's first calypso queen the following year, by winning the Calypso King competition and forcing its name change to Calypso Monarch. Rose herself continues the de-emphasis when, in a promotional video on her official YouTube channel for the release of her 2016 album, *Far From Home*, she explains that her stage name was given to her because "rose is the mother of all flowers" (Calypso Rose 2016).

Shortly after, an interesting reversal occurs when a glimpse of the rebellious Jamette appears: an old performance clip of Rose dancing suggestively, with her legs open, knees bent and flapping, fanning her costume between her legs—in, what I suggest, is an effort to signal that her provocative movements are so "hot" that she needs to "cool" them down—while her back and, more importantly, her *backside* face the live audience. While age is a valid consideration, Rose still highlights the conflict of negotiating between motherhood and womanhood, "respectability" and "slackness." Even the use of "lioness" in the documentary title draws attention to this fact, as the image of a lioness can symbolize daring strength but also embody more nurturing and regal qualities. Rose endorses the latter in "Calypso Queen," a track from her 2016 album:

> Everywhere ah reign supreme
> The one and only calypso queen,
> No man alive or dead
> Coulda come and take the crown off meh head.

And, while no one is trying to rob Rose of her accolades, her monumental achievements paved the way for future generations of Afro-Caribbean women, not just in calypso but in calypso's party offspring, soca.

Soca Divas Take Over

The rise of women in soca can be attributed to their incorporation in soca bands, managed and led by men, at a time when more women were actively participating in the Carnival space. Popular bands of the 1980s and 1990s, including Charlie's Roots, Second Imij, and Taxi, all featured women as background vocalists who sometimes took to the frontline. The mid-to-late 1990s marked a significant period where a younger generation of women began to reposition their visibility in the soca scene, culminating in the production of the "soca diva."

What is meant by this label, one that has been frequently used in Trinidadian media to describe the women of soca but never actually defined? Munro (2016) titles an entire chapter of her monograph after the soca diva and, while never directly stating what it is, she *does* offer a frame of reference: expressions of "strong and independent women, in control of the microphone, the stage, and their self-representation" (133) who "place strong emphasis on fashion and glamour" (141). An article in the *Trinidad Newsday* reported that these women are "jazzing up their outfits, from the usual jeans and tanks to funky spandex and space-age accents . . . [with] a strong trend towards the 'Hollywood look'" (Matroo March 6, 2011).

This idea of a "Hollywood look" can be tied to the historic presence of American military in Trinidad during World War II that, in turn, contributed to a cultural colonization of sorts that has primarily included the rapid importation of American film, music, and television in recent years and, with it, has bombarded and enchanted Trinidadian women with the fashions of American actresses and pop-soul vocalists, including Beyonce, Jennifer Lopez, and Nicki Minaj. Through imitation and idolization, soca divas find inspiration to become their own "fashionistas" on the Carnival stage. Building on these notions, I propose that the soca diva is not just an image and a style but also a sound, an attitude, an energy, a movement—in the way that she moves her body and dances—a *mobilization* that, like the Jamette before her, challenges the politics of female identity and respectability. As Jamettes offended elite European ideologies of femininity, soca divas similarly scandalize and authorize a more sexual femininity.

Alison Hinds became popular when the Bajan Invasion—soca music and acts originating out of Barbados—hit Trinidad in the mid-to-late 1990s. The sole female member of the band Square One, Hinds quickly became known for her songs of erotic empowerment and independence, including tunes with sexual metaphors like "DJ Ride"—where she voices her desire for the man (deejay) to "bring that needle" (penis) and "ride [her] riddim" (Square One 1998)—in which she occupied a position of dominance. Like "needle," "iron" is also a phallic reference and, in "Iron Bazodee," Hinds is the wife who finds herself "in a J'ouvert band, with a sexy Moruga [village in deep southern Trinidad] man" who causes her to forget her husband's name because his "iron have [her] so *bazodee*" (Square One 1999) that it causes her to behave out of control with nonstop wining and grinding. The soca diva is in control when she behaves out of control.

Hinds may be best recognized for rolling her bumper on stage *and* for the feminist anthems she recorded when she departed Square One for a solo career. "Roll It," from her debut album, was a call for independent and strong women to "set de pace" and liberate themselves from the bondage of patriarchy. Hinds's recommendation is to "show it off, gyal, and let de world see" before breaking out into a chorus of "Roooooooll, roll it gyal, roll it gyal" (Hinds 2007), a rally cry encouraging women to flaunt the female sexuality that they had been publicly and historically denied.

Hinds stoked the feminist fire that other Trinidadian women of Afro-Caribbean descent would join. In 1999, Sanell Dempster, as the female lead of the band Blue Ventures, became the first woman since Calypso Rose's back-to-back victories of 1977 and 1978 to win the coveted Road March title with "De River." Another song with obvious sexual overtones that commanded men to "paddle in, paddle out, push yuh paddle [penis] all about," Dempster is in command of her sexuality, warning that "if yuh cyah take it, yuh better move out de way, boy" (Blue Ventures 1999). In 2005, she administers full control by instructing women, as "winer girl[s] in town," to "cock back yuh bottom and wine" because "you got de sweetness" (Dempster 2005).

Following in those footsteps, Destra Garcia emerged in 2001 as a member of the Roy Cape All Stars, drawing a tremendous following over the next decade. Now stylizing herself the Queen of Bacchanal, a personification of the festively female sexual energy that soca divas exude, she has had a string of hits that animate the domain that women of Carnival are seeking to conquer. In a 2011 recording, "Proppa," Garcia appealed to de "gyal wit' de bumper bling," a backside that I interpret as anything from sexy and fat to round and firm, who could "bounce de t'ing" (jiggle the buttocks), and designates them "captains 'pon de wuk-up train" (2011a), in a display of empowerment. The following year, she encouraged "attitude and a big bag o' wine" where the woman continued to be the "queen of the pack . . . just rude and slack" (2012). Her monster hit "Lucy" (2015) presents an autobiographical narrative that reinforces how the soca diva's public acts of defiance generate discord:

> I grew up as a real good girl, always home, doh go nowhere,
> As soon as I was introduced to Carnival dey say I loose,
> All down on de ground, wukkin-wukkin' up mih bottom,
> And it draggin-draggin' all over town, and dey say I "loosay" (Lucy). (Destra 2015)

It may be Denise Belfon, however, who earns soca diva supremacy. Taking Carnival 1995 by storm with a "rude posse" chant to "lay lay yuh bam-bam" (Belfon 1995), she became the self-proclaimed wining specialist who invoked the "Jamette" in 2002, eager to "bring out de Jamette inna me," which she described as "sexy," "hottie," and "saucy," a reference to her "Saucy Wow" epithet, so given because of her impressive array of flexible wining skills. At the end of the song, she cackles ecstatically and asks "how yuh like dat?" as she seeks praise for her power to "bring out" the latent Jamette energy that is the "real me" (Belfon 2002). The soca diva persona, then, facilitates female repositioning that has taken cues from Calypso Rose and revitalizes and revamps the historical Jamette in a contemporary context that places her in a leadership role where she is in charge of her own sexuality.

While her agency marks an effort in disrupting patriarchal control, the soca diva is also not without her own feminine anxieties. I return to the motherhood-womanhood gender dynamic I laid out earlier in order to ask what we can make of the *pregnant* soca diva, a seemingly incompatible image. An article in the *Trinidad Express* reported that a six-months pregnant Alison Hinds did not pass up the chance to demonstrate that "child-bearing status hadn't robbed her of ability to show [how she could wine], meanwhile inducing anxiety by prancing in high-heeled shoes . . . albeit in an outfit patently inappropriate for [her expectant] condition" (Joseph 2004). It was Fay Ann Lyons-Alvarez, however, who faced heavy criticism from the public when, during Carnival 2009, she found herself defending the choice to continue performing at fêtes and participating in competitions even though she was an expectant mother. She ended up taking three titles that year—Groovy Soca Monarch, Power Soca Monarch, and Road March—showing that a woman could simultaneously be a mother *and* a soca diva. Motherhood does not negate the womanhood that the soca diva is so keen to showcase.

Other soca divas found themselves pregnant the following Carnival: Nadia Batson (who miscarried) and Destra Garcia. However, in a move that worked to uphold the gender ideology soca divas had been troubling, both artists refrained from participation in the festival. Destra would make her return for Carnival 2011, tempting audiences with sassy lyrics in "Welcome Back":

Everybody know I's de mash-up gyal,
Yes, ah takin' over de Carnival,
Dey want more bacchanal so dey call me . . .
If yuh want to see me get on slack, welcome me back. (2011b)

Enter the Indo-Caribbean Woman

Having provided an historical context for the colonized female body of African descent in Trinidad, I want to insert the Indo-Caribbean woman into my analysis by asking where and how does she fit into this matrix? To start, some context of the Indian presence in the Caribbean is required. In brief, following the abolition of slavery in the 1830s, plantation owners petitioned the British for another source of labor as land was still arable in several islands for sugar cane cultivation. South Asians, predominantly from the very small Bhojpuri-speaking regions of Uttar Pradesh and Bihar in northern India, were eventually introduced to Trinidad under indentured labor contracts between 1845 and 1917, with the initial allure of financial riches and free return passage to India after five years. Most never returned, opting to resettle in their new surroundings; this decision marked the birth of the Indo-Caribbean community. Their addition to Caribbean society has been one marked by processes of cultural re-adaptation, integration, and negotiation that attaches new layers of meaning to the Caribbean experience which, in turn, yield a unique set of circumstances and conflicts. In an Indo-Caribbean framework, the reconstitution of Hindu—and to a lesser extent, Islamic—religious ideologies exacerbated existing prescriptions of femininity as purists sought to reform and control the Indo-Caribbean woman. It is this complication in which I am most interested.

Jahajins, the indentured women from India, were special in that they were recruited in far smaller numbers than men in the early period of indentureship and, as such, enjoyed a certain level of social and sexual autonomy because they were already independent and seeking a new life free from patriarchal control (Reddock 1985). While these women fell under the same Victorian guidelines of female respectability imposed by colonial authorities upon Afro-Caribbean bodies, it is their independence that posed further problems to an Indo-Caribbean patriarchy seeking to re-establish its supremacy over its women. Comprised predominantly of Hindu purists, men who occupied the upper echelons of Indo-Caribbean society, this patriarchy equated female independence to sexual immorality, casting jahajins as prostitutes—and, indeed, a percentage of them were—who needed to be controlled. This control manifested in a physically violent way by the late nineteenth century in the form of "wife murders" (see Reddock 1985; Mohapatra 1995) as Indo-Caribbean women were increasingly seen as violating their "expected" domestic commitments because they had taken command over their own sexuality. Wife murders, then, were a response to the transgressive actions of independent Indo-Caribbean women that endangered the integrity of

Indo-Caribbean men who sought not only to restore their patriarchal authority but to also reconstruct Indian cultural value systems in the Caribbean that rested heavily on the power of Hindu mythology to instruct, control, and "safeguard the continuity and unity of Indian culture" (Mohammed 1998, 394) in the Caribbean.

The "Ramayana," a sung religious text cherished among Caribbean Hindus, became the primary tool through which this project was executed using its hero, Ram, and heroine-wife, Sita, as models of social behavior. In the tale, Sita, an incarnation of the sacred feminine, devi, is depicted as "respectable," the submissive woman who is ever faithful to her husband and exemplifies motherhood, because the goddess figure embodies maternal qualities. As such, future generations of Indo-Caribbean women were raised to emulate devi and act like Sita. They were taught to conform to positions of social subservience that worked to protect Indo-Caribbean patriarchal hegemonies. Not surprisingly, the only sphere in which women *were* allowed authority was in the home, a position parallel to the one that Afro-Caribbean women were urged to adopt. As Indo-Caribbean women became more socialized, however, this oppression became harder to control.

Defying Devi: The Drupatee Dilemma

As soca became the public rage, surpassing its parent, calypso, as the music of choice for Carnival revelry in the 1980s, a flirtation with the Bhojpuri folk music flavors maintained by the Indo-Caribbean community became popular with male calypsonians, including De Mighty Trini (Robert Elias). "Curry Tabanca" was his 1987 hit, an ode to the heartbreak suffered by the singer-cum-narrator over the departure of his Indo-Caribbean lover whose body he yearnfully describes via Indo-Caribbean foods: "her sweet pholourie, daal and kutchela, baiganee, kalounjee, saffron, masala" (De Mighty Trini 1987). Food becomes the avenue through which the Indo-Caribbean woman— and, by extension, Indo-Caribbean culture—is celebrated and exoticized by non-Indo-Caribbean communities. Further adding to this process of "othering" that marks Indo-Caribbeanness as different is the high-pitched, embellished, and nasal vocal delivery—stereotypically "Indian"—of the young Drupatee Ramgoonai, who appears on the record's background vocals. That she is situated in the background is indicative of the "traditional" subservient positioning of the Indo-Caribbean woman, and indeed the colonized female body in the Caribbean that patriarchal constructs strive to enforce and reinforce.

Remarkably, in that same year, Drupatee stepped into the spotlight, coining "chutney soca" in song for the first time in "Chatnee Soca," the title track on her solo debut album of the same name that signaled the beginning of the public blend between Bhojpuri folk and soca music. From the onset of the narrative, Drupatee positions herself in the foreground, behaving defiantly when she states that her maternal grandmother, "naanee" in Bhojpuri-Hindi, tells her not to "party in Arima," a northeastern borough of Trinidad, but she "decided not to listen to her." Drupatee hails from Penal, a village in deep southern Trinidad that has traditionally and historically been an Indo-Caribbean space. To fête in Arima and "dance some soca" is to enact a significant and symbolic transgression of geo-cultural boundaries. And, while she admits she does not know about "kaiso"—owing to her Indo-Caribbean heritage—she "bunks up [meets] with Sankar" who will teach her a "different kind of soca," presented here as a recipe that mixes "some tassa with some conga, throw in some paratha, a little congo pepper, mango, then you have the answer" (Ramgoonai 1987). Chutney soca, in taking on a music-as-food metaphor, becomes this symbolic mixture of Indo-Caribbean and Afro-Caribbean sounds and tastes, familiar to those respective communities.

Interestingly, this song was recorded alongside a version in Bhojpuri-Hindi. In it, Drupatee describes a similar party scene but draws attention to a girl ("eyk lardkee") by the stage with a face like the moon ("jaisay chaand say mukhraa"). The gathered crowd ask themselves who she is ("kaun hay voh aapas may sab yay poochay hay") and Drupatee calls her "soca queen" ("soca raanee yay hay") (1987). That title coincidentally foreshadows her solo success in the soca arena the following year when "Mr. Bissessar" becomes a runaway hit, prominently featuring the tassa where "Chatnee Soca" ironically did not.

Introduced as a "soca tassa jam," the song advances the descriptive narrative of Indo-Caribbean partiers in a public space ("Aranguez savannah," a large outdoor area in northern Trinidad) but, this time, they are "jammin' de soca" music, not chutney soca. The narrative provides a sense of the complex blend that characterizes the Indo-Caribbean experience in public, popular spaces. Drupatee, as narrator, adopts a position of power and control: she commands the drummer, Mr. Bissessar, to "roll up de tassa"; she boldly declares that she "can't miss dis fête next year" (Ramgoonai 1988) and, on stage, she won the hearts of national audiences—the Afro-Caribbean community, in particular—for the ways in which she exposed and gyrated her body. Never before had an Indo-Caribbean woman dared to sing and swing (her waist) on a public stage. In setting this precedence, Drupatee's emergence is, thus, a defining moment that follows the thread of female agency I have been chronicling, encouraged by the following: the victory of Calypso Rose on the calypso stage, the increased participation of Afro-Caribbean women in Carnival, and the inclusion of women in soca bands.

Nevertheless, the increased visibility of the Indo-Caribbean woman in the public sphere was not celebrated in all quarters, and Drupatee testified to the heavy criticism she drew from the conservative Indo-Caribbean community in a documentary interview:

> When I first came out, it had some critics, being an Indian woman in singing calypso, being there on stage. They didn't like that at all; being an Indian, I not supposed to be . . . singing for a large audience . . . in the calypso arena. And I shouldn't be doing those things . . . they supposed to stay home. That is what they think of the Indian woman. (*Chutney* 1996)

Both a politics of race *and* gender are at play here. Drupatee stresses the conflict of "being Indian" as a factor in cultural production and public participation in Trinidad; to be of Indian descent and sing and dance on the "black"—i.e., Afro-Caribbean or Creole—stages of calypso and soca are incompatible and offensive. Indeed, Mahabir Maharaj, writing for the Hindu journal *Sandesh* at the time, protested in an article on February 19, 1988: "For an Indian girl to throw her upbringing and culture to mix with vulgar music, sex, and alcohol in Carnival tents tells me that something is radically wrong with her psyche. Drupatee Ramgoonai has chosen to worship the God of sex, wine and easy money" (Niranjana 2006, 113). Hence, Drupatee is cast as an Indo-Caribbean Jamette: she abandons her Indian tradition—one that stresses a life in emulation of devi—for the pursuit of "blackness."

Sat(narayan) Maharaj, the general secretary of the Sanatan Dharma Maha Sabha, the orthodox Hindu organization in Trinidad, affirms this notion in the same documentary when he refers to the rise of Indo-Caribbean popular music:

> Chutney has now become public. Now, we have absolutely no objection to chutney being accepted at the national level. But, what we have reservation about, is the obscenity that goes with it. Because you know in Trinidad, you have what you call the chutney dancers. And some of these dances are regarded as obscene. (*Chutney* 1996)

Sat Maharaj may claim no objections to chutney soca but he continues to be one of its worst, most outspoken, and controversial critics, claiming to represent the voice of the conservative (that is, purist) Hindu patriarchy. His comments were filmed—deliberately, I contend—in a Hindu temple as he sat, piously, flanked by sacred iconography. When contrasted to the images of Drupatee gyrating on stage, the juxtaposition asserts a "purity" that Drupatee—and, by extension, chutney soca—contaminates and degrades.

For Drupatee to sing and wine in public was to adopt and appropriate Afro-Caribbeanness—a "blackness" and a "Jammetteness"—that Sat calls obscene but that is also "vulgar, promiscuous, loud, and disruptive" (Niranjana 2006, 82) and, therefore, counterproductive to an Indo-Caribbean value system. It raises the politics of wining and, yet again, respectability: that is, what certain bodies are able—and *not* able—to do. Drupatee, however, is drawing on a much older female tradition, which Sat does not mention, brought with the jahajins to Trinidad: the matikoor, a Bhojpuri folk ritual performed by Indian women several days before a Hindu wedding ceremony.

"Matikoor Night Is For Ladies To Get Away"

An "Indian bridal shower" that involved an element of bacchanal and Carnival festivity where women harassed and taunted the prospective bride, the matikoor was a private space where men were prohibited. There, women asserted control over themselves and their bodies, while being able to voice their own perspectives on their femininity and sexuality. With no men around, women behaved candidly, joking, laughing, and singing fast folk songs with amusing and sometimes abusive texts (Myers 1998, 162). Considered the primary antecedents of chutney music, these songs offered women an expressive medium through which they found pleasure and freedom in a relaxed environment free from the restraints of the everyday domestic roles imposed upon them by their male counterparts.

An integral aspect of matikoor is dance, and women wined, gyrated, and "misbehaved" to the rhythms of tassa drumming. Tassa becomes a transgressive platform through which empowering feminine expression takes place. The rhythms drive women to dance and exercise control being out of control. It is this "lewd" energy, power, and enjoyment that Drupatee draws on when she brought "Mr. Bissessar" to public audiences. The hit remained relevant to the Indo-Caribbean female narrative when it was later remixed two decades later in 2009, during a period of chutney soca popularity amongst mainstream Afro-Caribbean media outlets and audiences. Resurrected, re-recorded, and refreshed by Big Rich (Zaheer Khan), the leading chutney soca producer of the late 2000s, he added soca diva Alison Hinds to the revamp.

The Breakout of Indo-Caribbean Women

Drupatee's vilification by the conservative voices did not impede her career. Encouraged by her pioneering action, "chutney posses" of Indo-Caribbean women would move away from dancing in the secret Hindu spaces of matikoor to dance and party in large public venues and nightclubs where chutney fêtes, attended mainly by the Indo-Caribbean community, soon became the rage (Manuel 2007, 420). By the 1990s, these "chutney posses" following in Drupatee's footsteps—or gyrations, as the case may be—sprung up across Trinidad. In the later part of the decade, Heeralal Rampartap would describe them in "Chutney Posse," how "dem young gyul, dey winin' to de ground" (1997) while Sonny Mann observed, in his hit "Everybody Dancing," how "Sherry jumpin' high-high an' winin' up she waist" (1995). Both narratives touted chutney soca as this new public dance craze, with women as its leading instruments.

Yet the debate over Indo-Caribbean women's involvement in public spaces would not end, as they took to the Chutney Soca Monarch stage to compete for the title of best chutney soca artist when the competition was introduced as part of official Carnival festivities in 1996. In those early years of the competition, the popularity of trained dancers like Michelle Bedassie flourished as they featured prominently in the live presentations of mostly male competitors wearing scantily clad outfits. In a year plagued with anxieties over the start of a new millennium, the Y2K bug, and aspirations toward futures that were progressive and ultra-modern, Bedassie appeared on stage with Rampartap as he sang about "Y2K Dulari" in the final round of Chutney Soca Monarch 2000.

Portrayed by Bedassie, Dulari, a stereotypical jahajin name, is first introduced to the audience in coy Bollywood style: the image of the devi clad in strategically draped saree material. Moments later, she sheds her cloth to reveal emerald-green shimmery tassels worn as a makeshift skirt over a pair of emerald-green, skin-tight "pum-pum" shorts, paired with a gold bikini embellished with hanging gold tassels that seem to move, fly, and shake in time to her fluid movements as she wines to the music. This symbolic public stripping, to the delight of the many male spectators, highlights the politics of respectability that afflict the Indo-Caribbean woman. Rampartap builds a narrative around tradition and modernity as he explains: "Cookin' in a *choolha*, washin' by de river: dat is all ah feel dis gyul could do" because "she born in de country [understood as rural southern Trinidad where many Indians still reside], come from a poor family; never take de time out to go an' party." Despite this, "in front ah everybody, she really surprise me" because he "never see she dance chutney." In the chorus, Rampartap eggs her on by chanting, "wine Dulari, wine for we." There is a very clear sense, then, that these public gyrations are evidence that she is "Y2K-ready for de twenty-first century," particularly as "dis new chutney style," which Rampartap is so eager for her to display, climaxes in a tassa interlude that represents the ultimate defiance against respectability. Bedassie wines without restraint and "trembles," in an almost epileptic shaking of the bottom, for the crowd, deliberately facing her backside towards them (*Chutney Soca* 2000). The removal of the saree signifies the discarding of patriarchal tradition and the shedding of Indo-Caribbean gender norms, while the costume reveal functions as a public symbol of female empowerment and emancipation.

"If Yuh See Dis Indian Gyal"

In 2014, Afro-Caribbean soca artist Olatunji Yearwood recorded "Wining Good," a song that praised this public sexual liberation and femininity of the Indo-Caribbean woman, whom he refers to as the "Indian gyal" in the recording. Yearwood sang, "she wining good, she wining rude, she talking that smut, she conduct loose, she want de wuk 'til it bruise." Her desire is not just for a dance from her male admirer but endless rough sex. The popularity of the song with Carnival audiences prompted a music video that starred model Anita "La Tigresa" Ramroop as the "Indian gyal" (FOX FUSE 2014). Her portrayal subverted patriarchal constructions of the Indo-Caribbean woman, as she is depicted in different roles: as a seductress in her crop top and pum-pum shorts; as a sex kitten in lingerie and fishnet stockings; as an active participant of Trinidad Carnival, wearing a frontline pretty *mas'* costume, a bikini bejeweled with shiny sequins and feathers; and as the demure devi wearing an ornate saree, paying homage to her Indian ancestry.

In the vein of Drupatee and Bedassie, Ramroop challenges patriarchal prescriptions by donning a Carnival costume, in which she displays and gyrates her body, for the salacious gaze of her Afro-Caribbean amour. It is this unbridled access and desire that is still a societal taboo and offends the Indo-Caribbean patriarchy. Interestingly, a sense of the constant negotiation between that patriarchal tradition and empowering modernity is gathered through a visual concept of detachment in the music video. In her saree, Ramroop is placed at a distance from Yearwood; they never come into physical contact with one another because, constructed as devi, she is untouchable to a non-Indian. This notion contrasts with the pretty *mas'* and bedroom scenes where there is ample physical and sexually implied contact that summons the Jamette spirit.

Thus, as Calypso Rose did for future Afro-Caribbean women in calypso and soca, so Drupatee does for future Indo-Caribbean women in chutney soca. And this newer generation of female singers are important because they continue to influence Indo-Caribbean women to break free from patriarchal Indian tradition and participate in Carnival while, in turn, widening the boundaries of Carnival by bringing Indo-Caribbean components into play. I call these Indo-Caribbean singers "chutney soca divas."

From Devi to Diva

The chutney soca diva arises out of the complex milieu of feminine templates I have discussed—the nineteenth-century Jamette and the Afro-Caribbean soca diva—but I propose that she is further complicated by the phenomenon of the Bollywood "item girl." Hindi cinema remains an important source of Indian popular culture for Indo-Caribbean communities. The consumption of film songs is important because they construct a sense of Indian identity that revolves around dance. The "item" number—"item" being a popular actress, like Aishwarya Rai, or Sunny Leone, a former porn star, with sex appeal—is important for Indo-Caribbean women, already familiar with matikoor song and dance, as a dazzling female sequence intended to "provide musical entertainment of a more sexually explicit nature" (Sen 2005, 221). I contend that the "item girl" is another figure that does not conform to the tenets of respectability, in that she is not the naïve, lovestruck, or heartbroken female lead of the film. As such, she provides further inspiration to chutney soca divas who are also drawing from the glamourized fashion senses of soca divas, themselves inspired by the dress of American superstars. Within this younger generation of female performers, Sally Sagram and Artie Butkoon are two important Indo-Caribbean women who are synergizing elements from these multiple templates to produce the chutney soca diva.

Sagram made her public debut with chutney soca band Spread Pal Crew in the mid-2000s as its sole female vocalist. She remained mainly in the background until she left the band to pursue a solo career before headlining her own band, Xtreme, in 2009. In 2012, instructing a man to "Put Some Love" on her, she places herself in a position of authority to self-demand those sexual desires:

Ah doh want yuh put no diamond ring on meh finger,
Ah doh want yuh put meh in no house with no maid and butler . . .
What I want from you boy, listen carefully,
Is every day and every night, just put some love on me. (2012).

The following year, she acknowledged that "yuh want to wine on meh, yuh want to grind on meh, doh think yuh could handle my sexy body" (2013), calling herself "Miss Hot and Spicy" when she graced the stage.

Artie Butkoon also made her public debut in the mid-2000s, singing "Who de hell is Pussoongi" (2005), an assertive response to a cheating lover and an avowal that she, as a woman, was in control of her situation and refused to stand for any misconduct. A vocalist with the Melobugz chutney soca band, she subsequently developed her own stage personality. If Destra Garcia was the Queen of Bacchanal, Butkoon became the Goddess of Chutney, a cheeky jab at the concept of devi as Hindu goddess that is transformed into *diva* through female domination of the chutney soca stage that transgresses and disrupts patriarchal expectations. In 2012, Butkoon established her transgressive intentions when she crooned: "When ah come out to party and ah rollin' mih booty [bottom], yuh know ah in de fête to get on dutty [dirty, vulgar]" (2012). Two years later, she further reinforced this image in "Chutney Seduction":

> . . . yes, come and take a taste,
> You cannot resist when I shake my sexy waist,
> People just going wild, every creed and race,
> When dey see de Goddess mashin' up de place [performing extremely well]. (2014)

Butkoon has since rebranded herself as RT and is now leader of the Venom band. Aside from taking cues from Drupatee, I argue that the rise of chutney soca divas headlining their own bands has been adopted from soca divas who have done the same: Alison Hinds formed the Alison Hinds Show in the late 2000s; Destra formed Bakanal in 2013; and Nadia Batson formed the first, and presently only, all-female band SASS in 2011.

Indeed, the ways in which chutney soca divas assemble and reassemble the various fragmented feminine influences that have come to bear on their agency as Indo-Caribbean women who sing and wine in the public, popular spaces of the nation have created new opportunities and possibilities for the contemporary self-expression of the Indo-Caribbean woman, even as I am aware that the enactment of this patriarchal resistance still perpetuates their objectification by men, as "oppositional behavior is inscribed within an ideological and festival space that is still largely controlled and defined by men" (De Freitas 1999, 29). As I have shown with Afro-Caribbean women, the colonized and patriarchal framework of Caribbean gender discourse pits motherhood against womanhood with the former suggesting "respectability, religiosity, sacrifice, and permanent commitment, the other playfulness, promiscuity, fickleness, and transience" (21). For the Indo-Caribbean woman, there is a double jeopardy because she reshapes a form of imposed femininity that attempts to desexualize her, through Hindu ideals, in the private sphere, while her agency in public spaces is defamed as both sexual *and* "black" because it invites the Afro-Caribbean masculine gaze *and* jeopardizes the Indo-Caribbean patriarchy by promoting its destabilization. Indeed, this is the crux of the matter concerning Indo-Caribbean women in chutney soca: that the patriarchal purists are at pains to control the feminine expressions of Indian sexuality hidden by the trappings of Sita, devi-incarnate, that women are publicly shedding as they seek to recast themselves as chutney soca divas, modifying their feminine cultural and sexual expressions to claim and reclaim space.

In this chapter, I have explored how chutney soca has acted as a platform for the breakout of Indo-Caribbean women from the patriarchal confines of devi to the more expressive chutney soca diva. I have connected the development of the chutney soca diva to the larger narratives of other significant Afro-Caribbean female archetypes in the Caribbean because they impact Indo-Caribbean women and the ways in which they express their femininity and sexuality in their transition from private to public arenas. I have posited that their femininity is widened with access to those multiple templates, creating the multilayered persona that I term the chutney soca diva. I have considered how this figure, like other Afro-Caribbean figures that have preceded her, publicly defies gender norms of patriarchal ideologies that have been constructed to control her sexuality, widening her expressions of womanhood, even as she reinforces the patriarchal hegemony she seeks to unsettle. I have suggested that the Indo-Caribbean woman matters because she embodies a living example of the uneasy complexities that characterize Caribbean realities. As the chutney soca diva, she represents an indication of just how Indo-Caribbean women are exercising their own agency over their own complicated sexual identities, a process involving negotiations of patriarchal tensions that ultimately presents possibilities for redefining Caribbean femininities.

Discography

Belfon, Denise. "Kaka Lele." MP3 file, 1995.

Belfon, Denise. "Jammette." MP3 file, 2002.

Blue Ventures. *De River.* MC D Knife MDK009BV, 33⅓ rpm, 1999.

Butkoon, Artie. "Pussoongi." MP3 file, 2005.

Butkoon, Artie. "When Ah Come Out To Party." MP3 file, 2012.

Butkoon, Artie. "Chutney Seduction." MP3 file, 2014.

Calypso Rose. *Far From Home.* Because BEC5156519, compact disc, 2016.

Calypso Rose. "Introducing Calypso Rose, Queen of Calypso for 40 years!" YouTube video, 4:31, April 21, 2016. http://www.youtube.com/watch?v=egQ_ap9ucZA&t=6s.

Chutney In Yuh Soca. DVD. Directed by Karen Martinez. New York: Filmakers Library, DVD, 1996.

Chutney Soca Monarch 2000. Directed by George P. Singh Jr. San Fernando, Trinidad: Southex Productions, VHS, 2000.

De Mighty Trini. *Curry Tabanca.* Rohit RIA, 33⅓ rpm, 1987.

Dempster, Sanell. "Cock Back." MP3 file, 2005.

Destra. *Bakanation.* Krazi Music 986872758853, compact disc, 2015.

FOX FUSE. "Olatunji—Wining Good (Bharati Laraki) (Official HD Video)." YouTube video, 3:35. October 31, 2014. https://www.youtube.com/watch?v=kk6a8ZcaPso.

Garcia, Destra. "Proppa." MP3 file, 2011a.

Garcia, Destra. "Welcome Back." MP3 file, 2011b.

Garcia, Destra. "Attitude." MP3 file, 2012.

Hinds, Alison. *Soca Queen.* Black Coral STE7002, compact disc, 2008.

lorraine1606. "CALYPSO ROSE the Lioness of the Jungle TRAILER." YouTube video, 3:16, May 7, 2011. http://www.youtube.com/watch?v=N1D2BFg0°oY.

Mann, Sonny. *Sonny Mann Vol. 1 & 2 & 3.* Unknown, compact disc, 1995.

Ramgoonai, Drupatee. *Chatnee Soca.* M&S MJ0036, 33⅓ rpm, 1987.

Ramgoonai, Drupatee. *Mr. Bissessar / Come Together.* Impredisco D002, 33⅓ rpm, 1988.

Rampartap, Heeralal. *T&T Wonderboy With His Chutney Possy And Basmatee Dance.* Unknown, compact disc, 1997.

Sagram, Sally. "Put Some Love." MP3 file, 2012.

Sagram, Sally. "Wine On Meh." MP3 file, 2013.

Square One. *In Full Bloom.* Square One S098002, compact disc, 1998.

Square One. *Fast Forward.* Square One S099002, compact disc, 1999.

Bibliography

De Freitas, Patricia A. "Disrupting 'The Nation': Gender Transformations in the Trinidad Carnival." *New West Indian Guide* 73 (1/2) (1999): 5–34.

Joseph, Terry. "Soca Divas Defy Ban," *Trinidad Express,* January 30, 2004. http://triniview .com/selfnews/viewnews.cgi?newsid1075492550,13568,.shtml.

Manuel, Peter. "East Indians in Trinidad, Guyana, and Suriname." In *Music in Latin America and the Caribbean: An Encyclopedic History, Volume 2: Performing the Caribbean Experience,* ed. Malena Kuss, 417–24. Austin: University of Texas Press, 2007.

Matroo, Carol. "Sexy Soca divas." *Trinidad Newsday,* March 6, 2011. http://www.newsday .co.tt/carnival_2011/0,136860.html.

Mohammed, Patricia. "Ram and Sita: The Reconstitution of Gender Identities among Indians in Trinidad through Mythology." In *Caribbean Portraits: Essays in Gender Ideologies and Identities,* ed. Christine Barrow, 391–413. Chicago: Ian Randle, 1998.

Mohapatra, Prabhu. "'Restoring the Family': Wife Murders and the Making of a Sexual Contract for Indian Immigrant Labour in the British Caribbean Colonies, 1860–1920." *Studies in History* 11, no. 2 (1995): 227–60.

Munro, Hope. *What She Go Do: Women in Afro-Trinidadian Music.* Jackson: University Press of Mississippi, 2016.

Myers, Helen. *Music of Hindu Trinidad: Songs from the Indian Diaspora.* Chicago: University of Chicago Press, 1998.

Niranjana, Tejaswini. *Mobilizing India: Women, Music, and Migration Between India and Trinidad.* Durham: Duke University Press, 2006.

Noel, Samantha A. "Carnival is Woman! Gender, Performance and Visual Culture in Contemporary Trinidad Carnival." PhD dissertation, Duke University, 2009.

Noel, Samantha A. "De Jammette in We: Redefining Performance in Contemporary Trinidad Carnival." *Small Axe* 14, no. 1 (2010): 60–78.

Reddock, Rhoda. "Freedom Denied: Indian Women and Indentureship in Trinidad and Tobago, 1845–1917." *Economic and Political Weekly* 20, no. 43 (1985): 79–87.

Sen, Sharmila. "No Passports, No Visas: The Line of Control Between India and Pakistan in Contemporary Bombay Cinema." In Alternative Indias; Writing, Nation and Communalism, eds. Peter Morey and Alex Tickell, 197–224. Amsterdam: Rodopi, 2005.

Chapter 8

Caribana in Toronto:
From Male Dominance to Female Agency

—Dwaine Plaza

In 2015, women were encouraged by Destra Garcia to join in the project focused on "girl power" in her soca song "Lucy." In the lyrics, Destra chides women to emancipate themselves from the "slut shaming"[1] with her double entendre lyrics. Destra plays with the word "loose" as something she has agency over, and she does not care about the indecent label that has troubled Caribbean women since the period of emancipation when European gender "ideals" became the coded standards. Destra's lyrics are not a unique call to gender emancipation in Trinidadian culture; they fall in line with a new generation of female soca artists that include Fay Ann Lyons-Alvarez, Alison Hinds, Patrice Roberts, Drupatee, and Nadia Batson. These fifth-wave feminists[2] have been influenced by earlier feminist calypso artists who pushed the boundaries of "morality" policing. These pioneer, trailblazing women include Calypso Rose, Denise Plummer, and Singing Sandra (Smith 2004). The evolution of women's participation in Trinidad Carnival and its cultural industry has precluded the role and participation of Caribbean women in diaspora carnivals in spaces like Toronto, New York, and Miami.

Caribana began in 1967 in Toronto as a showcase of Caribbean carnival music, culture, and art, including costume design and playing steel pan music. The evolution of the Caribana Festival in Toronto parallels the changing social, economic, and cultural role of women in the Trinidad Carnival where bands are increasingly devoid of men as masqueraders. The purpose of this chapter is to examine the current state of Caribbean women's participation in the Caribana Festival in Toronto. Caribbean-origin women in general have, over time, developed transnational identities that are a logical extension of their roles as modern, assertive feminist subjects who are employed full-time, juggle familial responsibilities, and are also actively participating in the Caribana cultural festival each year as spectators, supporters, and dancers who provocatively express their agency and independence.

Women in Carnival

Trinidad Carnival has been the subject of considerable controversy from its beginnings in the late eighteenth century (Green and Scher 2007). Carnival began as an inversion of the hierarchical structure, in the establishment of an upside-down world where people are free and temporarily liberated from fear of societal imposed rules. In Carnival, there is a suspension of all hierarchical rank, privileges, norms, and prohibitions where everyone is considered equal (Noel 2009). The middle and ruling classes of Trinidad (mainly white, socially white, and light-skinned) have used dance and participating in Carnival as a way to differentiate society's haves from its have-nots. African-origin men and women who dance, prance, and provocatively express themselves in Carnival were often regarded as low class, dangerous, and licentious because of their "indecent street behavior" (Green and Scher 2007).

In the late nineteenth century, the Trinidad Carnival came to be known as the "Jamette Carnival,"[3] after those citizens of the underworld, petty criminals, prostitutes, thieves, and pimps, who were all called "Jamettes" (Green and Scher 2007). From the late nineteenth century until the mid-twentieth century, the poor black woman who defied standards of propriety and retaliated against her dehumanizing position in society was referred to as the "Jamette." The Jamette in Trinidad and Tobago was historically seen as an abomination by the authorities and by members of the elite[4] because of her lack of "morality" and fidelity related to the Victorian cultural and sexual standards of the time (Franco 2000).

When Jamettes violated the conservative rules of etiquette in everyday life, and during Carnival, they prompted a re-evaluation in Trinidadian society of the ways in which women appeared and behaved in public, thereby challenging control of their bodies by colonialism (Noel 2009). The legacy of the Jamette label still exists today as a hegemonic unconscious cognitive bias within patriarchal Trinidadian society. However, the difference today is that there is new negative language policing the boundaries of "morally" acceptable behavior for women who participate in Carnival. The new diction includes terms like "Jagabat," "wajang," or "wabean."

The stigma attached to "respectable" women participating in Carnival persisted until the late 1960s in Trinidad. Change only came as a result of a second-wave feminist revolution that was taking place worldwide. Women in general began to question and push back on the narrow gender boxes and prescribed gender roles that restricted their place in society as second-class citizens (Friedan 1963). Caribbean women in general have not had the luxury of being only housewives. North American feminism was not the main factor that liberated them to play *mas'*. It was the fact that, by the 1960s, many were gaining an education and had developed earning power. Carnival came to be embraced as "national culture" and therefore socially acceptable for many to participate in. The development of the big bands (Berekely, Minshall, Poison, Harts, Lee Heung, etc.) also encouraged women's participation. Women have also become less afraid to exhibit their sexuality on the road in Carnival (Green and Scher 2007). By re-enacting explicitly sexual displays of auto-eroticism on the street, Caribbean women today may embody patriarchal stereotypes that depict women as sexually available, but they are also able to maintain agency and control of their circumstance (Barnes 2000, Franco, 2000). It is from this early history of Carnival in Trinidad that Caribbean women in diaspora Carnivals come to participate and find new meaning.

Caribbean Migration to Canada

Caribbean women began migrating to Canada later than the men. Once they began to migrate, however, women soon caught up to the numbers of Caribbean men already in Canada. The early trickle of Caribbean women into Canada began in 1909, with the recruitment of Caribbean domestic workers (Calliste 1994, 140). Since the 1950s, women have consistently outnumbered males in Caribbean immigrant flows to Canada and the United States (Simmons and Turner 1993). This unusual pattern of a female-led chain migration is unique to the Caribbean cohort of migrants. It may be explained by the significant number of women coming to Canada each year as domestics and subsequently having their immigrant status adjusted after spending the required number of years of employment in that field.

There have been three major waves of immigration from the Caribbean to Canada. From 1900 to 1960, Canada accepted about 21,500 immigrants from Caribbean countries. The second period, from 1960 to 1971, corresponded with the "liberalization" of the Canadian Immigration Act.[5] During this period, Canada accepted about 64,000 people from the Caribbean. Since the 1970s, Canada has seen increased migration as part of an international movement to slow European emigration, and Canada began to depend increasingly on skilled and semi-skilled labor from developing nations. The last period, which began in the early 1970s, coincided with the economic recession. Except for 1973 and 1974 (unusual years because of the Addressment of Status Program that helped many persons regularize their status), immigration from the Caribbean declined. Caribbean immigration fell from 10 percent of total immigration in 1975 to 6 percent in 1979, remaining at that level until 1996. Before 1960, most immigrants came from Barbados, Jamaica, Trinidad and Tobago,[6] and Bermuda (Plaza 2001).

According to the 2016 Canadian census, there were 403,550 first-generation persons from the Caribbean and Bermuda now living in Canada. Of these, Jamaica heads the list with 138,345 persons followed by Haitians with 93,480, and Trinidad and Tobago with 65,040. The remainder are from the smaller Caribbean countries. Guyana, which is numerically listed by the census as part of South America but it is always culturally included with the English-speaking Caribbean, is at 87,680 persons. The majority of English-speaking migrants from the Caribbean live in Ontario whereas most French-speaking Haitians live in Quebec (Statistics Canada 2017).

In Toronto, Caribbean migrants have faced a variety of problems with racism in the labor and housing markets. For many Caribbean immigrants, unemployment and labor market segmentation have contributed to relatively low housing ownership and lower median incomes for some Caribbean groups (James 2017).

The population of Canadians of Caribbean origin has grown more quickly than the Canadian population as a whole. Between 1996 and 2001, the Canadian population grew by 4 percent, but the Canadian-Caribbean population increased by 11 percent. Caribbean-Canadians are concentrated overwhelmingly in the major urban centers of Québec and Ontario; in 2001, 91 percent of Caribbean-Canadians lived in one of these two provinces (James 2017).

Caribana in Toronto

Caribana in Toronto has roots in Trinidad's Carnival, the official Canadian multiculturalism policy and a little known black women's organization of the 1950s, the Canadian Negro Women's Association (CANEWA). This group of women were instrumental in initiating the first black history celebration in Ontario schools, and provided the first academic scholarships for black students. From 1952 to 1964, CANEWA members produced, funded, and hosted annual events they called Calypso Carnivals in Toronto (Phillip 2007). Largely serving as fundraisers for scholarships, the Calypso Carnivals attracted attention for a one-day event of Caribbean food, dance, and music. The CANEWA were often criticized for their middle-class values and lack of street level politics (Hill 1996).

The current version of the Caribana Festival began in 1967, when Canada was celebrating its centennial. At that time, the West Indian community was asked by the federal government to make a contribution which would enhance the celebrations of Expo '67. The festival was originally meant to showcase Trinidadian carnival music, culture, and art, including costume design and steel pan music (Trotman 2005).

The highlight of the Caribana Festival was the annual street parade, held initially on Yonge Street in 1970 and then moved over to University Avenue in 1985. In 1991, it again moved to the Canadian National Exhibition Grandstand and nearby Lakeshore Boulevard. Scheduled on the first Saturday in August in commemoration of the emancipation of Caribbean people from slavery in 1834, the parade is a spectacular display of costume, sound, and color that winds its way past more than one million spectators over several hours (Trotman 2005).

Participants in the annual Caribana parade are organized into masquerade "bands" (there were ten big bands in the 2015 parade) each of which is accompanied by live music (usually a DJ or a percussion group). Each masquerade band expresses a particular theme (be it historical, satirical, political, or fantasy) and is led by a "king" and "queen" who appear in lavish costumes. This organization often parallels what happens each year in Trinidad in terms of costume colors, designs, and traditions (Trotman 2005).

Festival events in Toronto include calypso "tents" (shows), "jump-ups" (dances), "fêtes" (parties), "*mas*" (masquerade) competitions, a junior carnival, "pan blockos" or "blockoramas" (steel band street parties), "talk tents" (shows featuring storytellers, comedians, and others expert in the oral traditions), a series of moonlight cruises on Lake Ontario, and a Caribana picnic on Toronto Island (Burman 2001). Once again these events parallel what takes place annually in Trinidad during the build up to the Lenten Carnival. Although Caribana is the official name for events sponsored by the Caribbean Cultural Committee, other organizations and individuals mount carnival-type events during the Caribana season. For example, the Ontario Calypso Performers Association holds an annual Calypso Monarch of Canada Competition featuring the talents of local calypsonians (calypso performers) (Burman 2001).

Theoretical Framework

Participation in Toronto's Caribana can be examined through a number of intersecting theoretical lenses that include: nostalgia, transnational acculturation, mattering, cultural mourning, and potential space. Several theorists (Turner 1997, Stewart 1998, Jameson 1991, Frow 1991) have offered valuable ways of differentiating among forms of nostalgia and have provided models of analysis. Nostalgia is selective, as is memory in general, but nostalgia suggests a certain longing and desire for what was past, lost, and can never be again. Nostalgia is an attempt to recreate what cannot be regained. Nostalgia involves attempts to recreate that past period or condition in some new environment (Frow 1991). Nostalgia encompasses the romanticization of the "home" left behind.

An important aspect of the Caribbean immigrant experience in Canada is coming to terms with feelings of alienation and marginality. These feeling are a result of perceiving that one does not belong or fit in within a certain group or community. This feeling may be permanent, especially if individuals feel that they are trapped between two worlds and must identify by paralleling two cultures. This feeling is particularly magnified when someone is racially different than the group they are living among (Schlossberg 1989).

As a direct result of exposure to systemic and institutionalized racism in spaces like Canada, many Caribbean migrants experience a sense of cultural mourning. The idea of cultural mourning has its origins in the theories of object loss as conceptualized by Sigmund Freud. According to Freud (1939), the loss felt by the infant at the initial break from the mother compels the infant to repeatedly attempt to "fill the gap." The act of "filling a gap," takes many forms and might ultimately result in a perpetual attachment to the mother (Ainslie 1998, 285). In most cases of object loss, however, individuals are able to mourn their loss in a way that prevents derangement. According to Volkan (1981, 18) the mourner eventually finds "linking phenomena" that provide "a locus to externalize contact between aspects of the mourner's self-representation and aspects of the representation of the deceased." Linking objects might include eating authentic Caribbean food, listening to soca music, participating in Caribana, experiencing Caribbean art work, attending a soca fete, and code switching in the use of language (Volkan 1981, 20).

A visual representation of the theoretical framework can be found in the appendices. This illustration shows the psychosocial effects that female masqueraders can derive from participating in the annual Caribana parade. Women can simultaneously experience feelings of euphoria during the street parade. They can rekindle positive memories of nostalgia for a place and time that mattered the most in terms of their self-esteem. Women can also feel a sense of empowerment and a relief from a sense of cultural mourning. Finally, wearing a costume and dancing in the streets in the diaspora allows women to occupy a "potential space" that is safe and not restricted. For second-generation Caribbean-origin *mas'* players, or those *mas'* players who are of Caribbean ancestry but do not come from a Carnival-culture background

(Guyana or Jamaica), these men and women experience a gemeinschaft feeling of belonging in the space.

Methodology for the Research

Data for this research was derived from multiple methods that included ethnography, semi-structured interviews and informal focus groups held in Toronto, Canada, during the period 2010–2015. In order to collect five years of data, I became a "regular" at the Saldenah Mas-K Club camp in Toronto.[7] I chose to collect data at the Mas-K Club camp because I have been an active masquerader with this group for fifteen years. As a "regular" visitor and "limer" at the Louis Saldenah *mas'* camp in Toronto, I had a relatively easy time getting in and fitting in. As a researcher, I also have both ascribed and achieved characteristics that gave me privileged access to the backstage activities of the Mas-K Mas Camp.[8] My ascribed characteristics include being born in Trinidad as a person of mixed African-Indo Caribbean ethnicity, having played *mas'* annually in Trinidad or Toronto for over twenty-five years, and having been an annual fete promoter in Toronto for over ten years. My achieved characteristics include being formally trained in ethnographic research methods and having a long history of carrying out both quantitative and qualitative research on the Caribbean diasporic community in Toronto.

In order to carry out an ethnography of the Saldenah *mas'* camp in Toronto through the intersecting lens of gender, race, and social class, I focused on: (a) the physical setting of the *mas'* camp, (b) the participants at the *mas'* camp, (c) the activities and interpersonal interaction in the *mas'* camp, (d) the conversations in the *mas'* camp environment, and (e) the informal activities in the *mas'* camp. Besides taking written notes of the *mas'* camp events, I also photographed various activities/rituals and audio recorded various subjects in their natural work environment. This research was done with the consent of the *mas'* camp leadership and the verbal permission of the *mas'* camp volunteers. The observations in the *mas'* camp were systematically coded for patterns. An ethnography such as this allows for a better understanding of social phenomena from the user's specific cultural context, aiming at an analytical description of the behaviors that characterize and distinguish cultures or social groups (Walters 1980). Table 1 in the appendices presents a summary of the socio-demographic information about each person interviewed for this study. The ten interview subjects were all first-generation, middle-aged to elderly, Caribbean-born men and women. This cohort is not reflective of the vast majority of Caribana street masqueraders, who tend to under thirty-five years of age. The interview subjects were themselves not so long ago street masqueraders. Many now participate in the building of the costumes and the running of the *mas'* camp. Despite this limitation, the reflections this group provides about the festival, the masquerade trends, and the history of Caribbean-born people in Canada are valid because the interviewees continue to occupy a liminal space that is transnational.

The focus groups were informal, spontaneous gatherings that were recorded on audio and lasted about one hour apiece. The participants which varied from four to six people were led though a series of informal questions about history, gender, race, class, transnational practices, and participation in the Caribana and Carnival events both in Canada and Trinidad. The focus group participants were encouraged to speak about or beyond the issues as the conversation moved them. I provided minimal probes during the focus group meetings and relied on the individuals to engage in relaxed "old talk" as a way to gather data. The focus group sessions included alcohol consumption, soca music blaring in the background, and an overall convivial relaxed environment. I considered this a natural *mas'* camp setting in which to have the women and men speak in mixed groups about issues related to Caribana, women's role in the parade, cultural life in Canada, and the issues surrounding raising families that were engaged with the culture.

The interviews and focus group meetings were transcribed and analyzed using the strategy of the "constant comparative method of analysis," a strategy of data analysis that calls for the continual "making comparisons" and "asking questions" (Strauss and Corbin 1998). Interviews and focus group meetings were coded and sorted according to emerging themes. These themes were then compared to each other for generalizability. According to Patton (2002, 56), inductive analysis allows for "categories or dimensions to emerge from open-ended observations as the inquirer comes to understand patterns that exist in the phenomenon being investigated." Essentially, as Patton (2002) notes, this type of analysis involves identifying categories, patterns, and themes in one's data through one's interaction with the data. After this analysis, similarities and differences were documented based on my personal understanding, professional knowledge, and the literature.

The use of multiple methods of research for studying women's participation in Caribana in Canada has allowed me to accomplish three goals. First, I was able to capture the particular migration, settlement, adaptation, and acculturation process for the Trinidadian population in Toronto. Second, I was able to examine Trinidadian women's feelings about their changing gendered roles in Carnival and Caribana over time. Finally, the data allowed for a better understanding of how transnational culture and feelings of nostalgia, cultural mourning, and a desire to feel a sense of belonging were a major influence as to why women participate in Caribana.

Findings from the Qualitative Data

The following is a discussion of the themes heard in the focus group meetings and during the individual interviews. Overwhelmingly, I heard from the participants that the *mas'* camp is an important "potential space" for connecting and reconnecting people with their Trinidadian family, kin, and friends spread out. The respondents also spoke in endearing terms about the numerous times they were serendipitously reunited with someone from their street, village, or high school in Trinidad. Having these opportunities for spontaneous reunification at the *mas'* camp gave individuals a rekindling of what it meant to be a caring "family." These situations were also recalled as important to individuals because it gave them an opportunity to alleviate some of the cultural mourning they felt in Canada. The environment of the *mas'* camp rekindled a nostalgia for being back "home" because individuals were surrounded by people who cared deeply for them. This feeling was conveyed in the sentiment articulated by Janet.

> The music, food, and drinks in the Saldenah *mas'* camp allow me to feel like I am back in Woodbrook gluing or beading belts in a *mas'* camp. It's the same vibe where people come to the Toronto *mas'* camp after work to lime, socialize, build costumes, and see people who you have not seen in a long while. Normally the winter makes us all hibernate so we don't cross paths. The *mas'* camp in the summer is a place where I can feel a sense of belonging in Toronto where I normally feel like an outsider trying to be someone I am not. (Janet 2015)

For some women, returning to the *mas'* camp occurred due to a a major life change in Canada. The experience of being in Canada for a long time meant that women come to live through times of alienation, bad marriages, divorces, seeing children grow up, or becoming nostalgic about back home. This is certainly what happened to Seeta, who was experiencing a cultural mourning after having lived in Canada for thirty-nine years and, as a result, began visiting Saldenah's *mas'* camp as part of her attempt to reconnect with her Trinidadian roots. Over time, she became an annual Caribana volunteer making costumes. Seeta explains:

I began going to the Saldenah *mas'* camp in the nineties with my youngest sister who was playing in Hayden's section. She was playing in Caribana and she was going back in February and jumping with Poison in Trinidad. She was all about fun and showing off her body. That was before she met Kelvin and had two children. My sister was an international party girl who knew how to have fun and enjoy she life. Looking back, I wish I had been more like her. It's only since my divorce that I returned to the *mas'* camp to build costumes and participate in the king and queen show. I feel it's important for young people to learn how to bend wire and assist in the building of big *mas'* costumes. (Seeta 2015)

While in the *mas'* camp, it is clear that the women tend to follow a typical pattern each time Caribana comes around. Women tend to arrive about 6:00 p.m., working diligently in the camp, and socialize while they work in one area. This work environment is captured in the first and second photographs in the appendices showing a mixed group of workers focused on their task of hot-gluing belts, vests, and wristbands. Men, on the other hand, do not stay in one area and just work. Men tend to float throughout the *mas'* camp, picking up work where it needs to be done while liming with other men. Cheryl comments on this pattern of gendered work and cultural mourning when she says:

Look around Saldenah's *mas'* camp, there are lots of women in for the evening shift. Women come here after work and they stay until around 11 p.m. from July to August. During that time, women work on costumes with a glue gun. Most of them are doing it for nothing. Some do it to get a discount on their own costume. Many also do it for the love of *mas'*. I notice a lot of young women coming to the camp to help out each year. The younger ones come with children who run around and play while mom works. Its therapeutic in my mind, that's why I am in the camp night after night. I get to listen to good music, gossip with the other Trinis, enjoy some food, and reminisce about the good old days back home. . . . We also have a task of making 130 costumes in one month. That will take us right up to the night before the parade—it's kind of exhilarating and exhaustive all at once. (Cheryl 2015)

Despite women's hard work in the *mas'* camp, a common theme that came up in the focus groups was the gendered division of labor in the various costume sections and responsibilities. Angela's observation of the section leaders in Saldenah's *mas'* camp typifies the behind-the-scenes role women play in the administration of the band. Angela notes that women make sure that all the fine details required for success in the band are taken care of. As Angela tells us:

Women in the *mas'* camp are the real brains behind the logistics. They are the ones who handle the registration and the problems in the section. The men, on the other hand, control the money. It's only in the sections where men have their mothers or wives working on the costumes that I see a difference. I see these women controlling the money situation and the area where the costumes are being built. The men are really just a figurehead or the name in the band while the women are controlling the strings in the background. (Angela 2014)

Although women have become more involved in the production of *mas'* costumes at Saldenah's Mak-K Club, there remains a glass ceiling in terms of becoming a section leader. Women who aspire to have their own section often have to spend many years as an assistant to an established male. Eventually they can move away from the established male and come up with their own section by taking some of his clients. Women have to work twice as hard to gain a reputation as being creative and organized before other women will trust them to bring out a good section. There is clearly a situation of horizontal hostility[9] that women must overcome. There also seems to be an unconscious cognitive bias within the Trinidadian community that the leaders of a *mas'* section are naturally men. The third photo in the appendices shows a group of women section leaders in Saldenah's *mas'* camp in 2015 waiting for their patrons to pick up their finished costumes. In reflecting on this pattern, Nadia tells us:

In Saldenah's *mas'* camp over the last five years, I have seen a new group of women who have become section leaders. These women have typically worked their way up the ranks by assisting for years. These women have a hard time dealing with people signing up for their section. There is a tradition of going back to the same section leader year after year. So for women trying to break in as section leaders or attract a following, they need to put in a few years of hard work under a man and hope to develop their own network. . . . Eventually they can use these contacts to set off on their own building a section. (Nadia 2013)

In addition to playing *mas'* with Saldenah's band during Caribana, a number of women reported that they make an annual pilgrimage to Trinidad for Carnival. This is an opportunity for them to revive the nostalgia of the various events of Carnival like J'ouvert, Panorama, Dimanche Gras, or a calypso tent. These events also alleviate the cultural mourning that many of the women reported feeling in Canada. Daphne reflects on her sister's transnational activities in Toronto and Trinidad. She says:

My sister Katie makes an annual two-week pilgrimage to Trinidad. It's her way of dealing with the racism and loneliness of Canada in the winter as she talks about it. She can feel at "home" in the height of winter and get a reprieve from the cold. I have seen her checking on line the costumes from Tribe Band launch in July. She gets excited on Caribana Day and starts immediately after Skyping our cousin and figures out what costume she will play in February. . . . Over the years I have seen the costumes become skimpier and skimpier but Katie does not seem to mind. Actually, she is always asking Louie to get the costume designer to follow the Trinidadian *mas'* trends. (Daphne 2014)

During the Caribana parade there was an annual competition among women to make it into the newspaper while wearing their costume. One of the highest accolades for Trinidadian woman in August is to find herself in one of the collage of photos that appears on Sunday morning after the parade in the biggest newspapers (*The Star* or *The Sun*). Other newspapers that also give women a higher self-esteem is appearing in the *Caribbean Camera* or the *Share Newspapers*. To appear in any one of these publications is a significant badge of honor for women. This trend was captured by Vanessa, who said:

Women playing *mas'* in Caribana are the focal point of the media coverage. I rarely see the photographers taking pictures of men in their costume. It's a showcase of women having fun on the big day. Each year, there is always an image of women wining on a cop. In the *Star*, there is always a collage of color photos with women in all shapes and sizes looking pretty extravagant in their feathers and glitter. On the road, women do all sorts of erratic things to attract the men with cameras to take their photo. I find it hilarious to watch. Everyone dreams about being a feature in a Toronto newspaper and being the talk of the town. (Vanessa 2014)

Through the decades, Trinidadian women have taken over the organization and implementation of Saldenah's annual participation in the junior Carnival in Downsview Park, and more recently in Malvern Park. The junior carnival in Toronto is a transnational event that parallels the children's carnival in Trinidad which has a competitive judging. The junior Carnival takes place on the Saturday before the Caribana jump-up. The event includes all the features of the big band competition with a judging area. Women have been particularly drawn to the junior Carnival event as a way of introducing their second-generation children to authentic Trinidadian culture that includes costumes, music, dance, and food. Trinidadian women will spend exorbitant amounts of money to have their children wear mini-adult costumes in order to participate in the parade. These same mothers will spend the entire day in the hot sun chipping by the side of the road while their kids cross the stage and are judged. Ultimately mothers are trying to involve their children in transnational Trinidadian culture and give them exposure to what it means to be "authentic" and back "home." The event can also be read as women trying to appease their own nostalgia and cultural mourning for participating in the Carnival. By having their children dance and jump-up in the streets of Toronto, the women are clearly living vicariously through their children. Angela's reflection as a mother who has put her two children in the junior Carnival reveals some of these feelings. She says:

> Kiddies Carnival in Toronto is all about women and their children. The section leaders bring out a mini-section of costumes for the kiddies Carnival the week before the big Caribana jump-up. Kiddies *mas'* is also like a competition between the women for bragging rights for the cutest and most authentic young Trinidadian masquerader on the road. I have seen women put their three year olds in a costume and put them on the road. There is a pride Trini women have for their children playing *mas'* and being part of the Caribana culture in Toronto. I, like many of my friends, feel responsible for exposing my children to authentic Trini culture despite living thousands of miles way. This includes giving them exposure to the language, dance, food, and music that is Trini—stew chicken, pelau, calaloo, roti, and curry chicken and things like that. So putting my kids when they were young in a *mas'* costume was really important to me. (Angela 2013)

The role of Trinidadian men in the *mas'* camp and through Caribana Day is multifaceted and diverse. Over the years, the men have become less likely to wear a costume on the road, but many have moved to an organizational and support role for the band members. The men continue to be the main logistical stewards of Caribana in Toronto. As in Trinidad, men during Caribana are not as visible as costumed masqueraders. Men are usually on the periphery in street clothes or they officially join as volunteer marshals. Men are also more likely to be found engaged in behind-the-scenes activities that make Caribana successful. This includes building the music trucks, driving the drinks truck, organizing the food truck, directing the women masqueraders on the road to maintain sections, moving all the king and queen costumes to the parade, and ensuring that at the end of the parade that all equipment is picked up and returned to the *mas'* camp. Men's involvement in Caribana is also about trying to have a feeling of nostalgia for a Carnival that was left behind in Trinidad. The men who do get involved in the *mas'* camp also have a cultural longing to have a sense of Trinidad identity in Canada. Men who participate in Caribana are also more likely to be inclined to live transnational lifestyles. This includes making regular return visits to family and friends in the Caribbean. They are also likely to keep up with politics, news, and sports that are happening in the region. The men often participated in these activities in order to alleviate their feelings of cultural mourning for their imagined ideal lives while growing up. The fifth and sixth photos in the appendices show two typical roles of men during the Caribana parade. A small minority of men put on a carnival costume and dance in the streets. A significant number of men volunteer to be marshals in the band. This role involves older men being responsible for the revelers in the band while it moves along the parade route. The caretaking role for the men is voiced by Dexter who worked for many years as a volunteer in the Saldenah's *mas'* camp. He says:

> On Caribana Saturday, it's the women who are in a costume on the Lakeshore representing our Trini culture. Men like me have left the parade as masqueraders years ago. For the past ten years, I am in the Saldenah *mas'* camp doing odd jobs for Louis or Hayden to make the event a success. I work for free, the only thing I get is a good feeling knowing that I am part of the Saldenah "family." On the parade day, I get a marshal T-shirt for the road and me and a whole group of men maintain the safety of the band. Our main job is to keep non-masqueraders out of band and keep the road safe for the women wearing costumes. I guess another advantage of being a marshal is that we can take a wine on the women and have some drinks on the road. If everything goes well, Saldenah wins another Caribana band of the year title. (Dexter 2015)

Dexter also commented on women's activity taking place Caribana Day that he witnesses annually as a marshal. His sentiment about why the women "get on" seems to follow closely with the ritual of cultural mourning and agency women feel on the parade route. The seventh photo in the appendices shows a group of Caribbean women using their body to occupy the "potential space" on the streets of Toronto. The women are using their body to disrespect a police cruiser parked along the parade route. By wining on the police car with their body in a manner that simulated a provocative sex act, these women are in effect snubbing the hegemonic white male power base that typically uses its hegemony while patrolling the streets of Toronto like an occupying armed force. This is clearly evidence of the women showing their agency towards Canadian authority figures. Dexter tell us:

> If you look at all the bands on Caribana Day, it's like Trinidad, 90 percent of the costumed masqueraders are women who have paid a lot of money to put

on a skimpy costume for just a few hours. Canada is different than Trinidad where it's two days. On Caribana Day, the police in Canada feel threatened by the fact that the streets are under the ownership of black people. By taking over the streets of Toronto on the day of the parade, Caribbean women are able to temporary find a reprieve from a long and sustained history of being ignored and in general excluded from Canadian society. By just being on the road, we can close our eyes and imagine ourselves jumping down Fredrick Street with our friends. We can also find ourselves transported to a place where we can feel like we home. (Dexter 2015)

Conclusion

Caribbean women's participation in the Caribana Festival has evolved since 1967. Then, they were mainly spectators and passive individuals, but in the present, they are more likely than men to be masqueraders on the streets and costume makers in the *mas'* camp. When a Caribbean person leaves loved ones at home, he or she also leaves the cultural enclosures that give them a sense of mattering and belonging. The Caribbean sojourner simultaneously must come to terms with the loss of family and friends, as well as the loss of cultural forms (food, music, art, for example) that have given the individual's world a distinct and highly personal character. For many, this represents a psychological trauma that they endure while living a predominately "white" space that is culturally not like the one they were born and were socialized in.

Participating in the annual parade each year allows Caribbean immigrants in Toronto to occupy a "potential space" and experience a temporary reprieve from the pervasive racism and feelings of alienation in Canada. To be in a costume in 2017 is a badge of honor for Caribbean origin women during the Caribana festival. It's the one time of the year that women of color in Canada flourish and are elevated to the highest status of being desirable as exotic beauties who are admired for their skin color, curves, blemishes, scars, or other age markers that are normally hidden behind clothing or concealed with make-up. This optimistic feeling for women of color manifests itself into a feeling of agency and self-efficacy.

During the festival, both Caribbean-origin first- and second-generation participants have an opportunity to rekindle a nostalgic memory for what they have lost in their migration journey to Canada. For the second-generation participants, in particular, Caribana Day is the one time they get to disrupt the normally sedate streets of Canada by playing loud music, wining, prancing, and provocatively expressing themselves in public. Being in a costume and out in public on the streets is cathartic for some Caribbean-origin individuals who have spent the previous 364 days repressed and feeling like they don't belong in Canada. The opportunity to let off steam and thumb their nose at the Canadian conservative establishment—which is often based on order and space, punctuality, political correctness, and individualism—is often the goal of masqueraders. Occupying liminal space on the streets together in bands full of other young people of color ultimately gives masqueraders a short-term "we" feeling of being dominant and belonging to a welcoming "tribe" for the one day. The second and the third generation essentially use Caribana as a vehicle for expressing the culture that their first-generation parents passed down to them, even young Caribbean-origin people who originate from islands where the Carnival ritual is not institutionalized annually.

The summer Caribana Festival in Toronto is the one day of the year where there is a disruption of "white" supremacy in Canadian society. The Caribana parade allows Caribbean women to have a sense of optimism about their future and that of their children because Lakeshore Drive is temporarily transformed into a "potential space" where they have a sense of belonging. For that day, Caribbean people feel like they "matter" in Canada and that their culture is celebrated as part of the multicultural aesthetic. On the day of the festival, revelers can temporarily feel free and liberated from the fear of being arrested by the police for playing loud music, dancing in the streets, or consuming open containers of alcohol. This temporary reprieve is important for the mental health of Caribbean people in Canada who are often suffering from cultural mourning and object loss from the migration experience. As many Trinidadians often say, "Canada is the place I work and live, but Trinidad with all of its quirks is my 'home' that will never change" (Lisa 2014).

This chapter has demonstrated that Caribbean women in Canada have developed transnational identities that are a logical extension of their roles as modern, assertive feminist subjects who are employed full-time, juggling familial responsibilities, and also actively participating in the annual festival each year as a demonstration of their agency and independence. Some conservative feminists might see Caribana as an example of false consciousness whereby women freely objectify themselves for the pleasure of men on the sidelines watching. I would suggest that other issues are at play, ones that take us to the heart of what is meant by agency as Caribbean women in Canada celebrate their culture and difference from the white hegemonic aesthetic that often relegates them to be less than or reviled. Women dancing on the street are largely in charge of who "wines" on them or who is allowed to intimately touch their most intimate body parts.

Workers in the Saldenah *mas'* camp building costumes are disproportionately women.

The work of fine braiding and beading with a glue gun is most often done as gendered work by women.

Women have become organizers and section leaders in the Saldenah *mas'* camp. This was once a role dominated only by men.

Women feel a great deal of pressure in Canada to be the stewards of culture for the second generation. Women often involve their children in Caribana activities like the junior Carnival parade.

A small proportion of the costumed masqueraders on Caribana day are men. This individual is also displaying his Guyanese ethnic identity with body paint and flag.

Men use the band marshal responsibility as a way to indirectly participate in the street parade. The official marshal T-shirt becomes a costume for males wanting to remain part of the event.

This image shows three women spontaneously grinding and touching a parked police car with their body. These women are in effect showing their agency over the hegemonic white male power base that polices and controls the streets in Toronto.

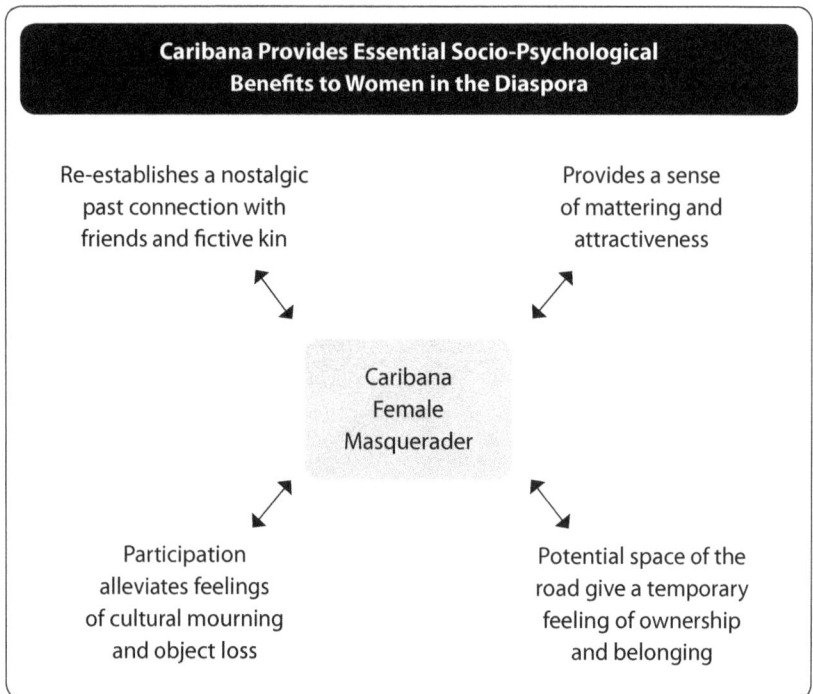

Caribana Provides Essential Socio-Psychological Benefits to Women in the Diaspora

Re-establishes a nostalgic past connection with friends and fictive kin

Provides a sense of mattering and attractiveness

Caribana Female Masquerader

Participation alleviates feelings of cultural mourning and object loss

Potential space of the road give a temporary feeling of ownership and belonging

Theoretical framework explaining women's participation in Caribana.

Table 1

Interviewees at Saldenah's Mas Camp in Toronto

Interviewee Pseudonyms	Age	Generation	Mas-Camp Role	Citizenship Status	Self-Identified Ethnicity	Social Class	Occupation	Country of Birth	Length of Time in in Canada	No. Family in Trinidad	No. Family in Canada	Highest Level of Schooling
Dexter	46	first	Marshal	Canadian	Black	Working	Machinist	Grenada	26 years	30	45	Highschool
Janet	55	first	Mas-maker	Can/Trini	African	Middle	Sales	Trinidad	33 years	60	35	College
Lisa	47	first	Sec-leader	Canadian	Indian	Working	Media/Consultant	Trinidad	27 years	45	40	Bachelor
Roger	50	first	Mas-maker	Can/Trini	Mixed	Upper	Insurance Sales	Trinidad	29 years	50	66	Highschool
Vanessa	42	first	Mas-player	Canadian	Portuguese	Middle	Real Estate	Trinidad	21 years	21	50	Bachelor
Angela	49	first	Mas-player	Canadian	African	Middle	Hair Stylist	Trinidad	22 years	30	25	College
Nadia	55	first	Mas-maker	Canadian	Black	Working	Social Worker	Trinidad	25 years	35	25	Masters
Daphne	43	first	Mas-maker	Can/Trini	Indian	Middle	Manager	Trinidad	22 Years	55	60	College
Seeta	61	first	Mas-maker	Canadian	Indian	Middle	Accountant	Trinidad	39 years	25	30	Bachelor
Cheryl	62	first	Mas-maker	Can/Trini	Mixed	Middle	Nurse	Trinidad	35 years	41	36	Bachelor

Note: All names are pseudonyms. All first generation interviewees are born in the Caribbean and migrated to Canada after age twelve.

Feelings of mattering also promote better coping skills with the many transitions and events associated with immigration and settling into a foreign culture. Schlossberg's (1989) theory offers a rationale for understanding why some Caribbean people participate in Caribana on a regular basis. Participating in the parade tends to allow some Caribbean-origin women and men an opportunity to connect with others and reinforces their humanity and helping of others. Dancing in the streets of Toronto for one day gives the participants a feeling of importance and higher self-esteem because they are being gazed upon by hundreds of thousands of spectators along the parade route. On any other day in Toronto, being gazed upon by strangers is regarded as an "Othering gaze." During Caribana Day, however, the gaze from strangers and law enforcement becomes empowering and raises the self-esteem of the individual masqueraders.

Notes

1. Slut-shaming is a process by which women are attacked for their transgression of accepted codes of sexual conduct, i.e., admonishing them for behavior or desires that are more sexual than society finds acceptable (Ringrose, 2012).

2. First-wave feminism (1910 to 1950s) focused on women's suffrage, property rights, and political candidacy. Second-wave feminism (1960s to 1980s) focused on reducing inequalities in sexuality, family, the workplace, reproductive rights, inequalities, and official legal inequalities. Third-wave feminism (1990s to 2008) focused on embracing individualism and diversity. Fourth-wave feminism (2008 to present) focuses on combating sexual harassment, assault, and misogyny. And fifth-wave feminism is future feminism (Ringrose 2012).

3. The "Jamette Carnival" was a term used by the French and English colonial elite in Trinidad to describe the Carnival celebrations of the African population during the period 1860 to 1896. It comes from the French word "diametre," meaning beneath the diameter of respectability or the underworld (Franco 2000).

4. The middle and ruling classes of Trinidad (mainly white, socially white, and light-skinned) have vociferously denounced the African presence in Carnival as a dangerous and licentious display. The "indecent behavior" of masqueraders, particularly women, has been an issue of great public debate. In the 1800s, critics focused on the behavior of working-class people and felt that their negative behaviors would diffuse on to the middle class (Green and Scher 2007).

5. As a result of the policy shift to a "Point System," in the late 1960s through the mid-1970s, some 8,000 to 12,000 immigrants arrived in Canada from the Caribbean each year (Plaza 2001). Various forces contributed to the size of this flow, including high unemployment and low wages in the Caribbean relative to Canada, and the preexisting culture of migration in the Caribbean.

6. In Trinidad, the 1970s oil boom generated a massive investment on the part of the government in terms of infrastructure. The construction of new roads, schools, telecommunications networks, electricity, and running water all facilitated a more "upscale" lifestyle for the average Trinidadian. For the nation as a whole, the rate of unemployment stayed relatively stable. The rate at which emigration proceeded from Trinidad affected a smaller percentage of the population than in other Commonwealth Caribbean nations, amounting to 10 percent as opposed to 18 and 17 percent, respectively, for Barbados and Jamaica (Plaza 2001).

7. A *mas'* camp is set up as a work space for masquerade costume designers and costume assemblers a month or two before a major Carnival event. Carnival participants can visit the *mas'* camp to view the costume choices, be fitted for a costume, purchase a costume, socialize with old friends, or to put in volunteer labor before the actual Carnival jump-up day(s). The term originates from Trinidad and Tobago, where the *mas'* camp is typically a "liming" spot for locals.

8. Goffman (1959) defines the "backstage" as a place where the actors can discuss, polish, or refine their performance without revealing themselves to their audience. It also allows people to express aspects of themselves that their audience might find unacceptable.

9. "Horizontal hostility" is the term used by feminists since the 1970s to describe infighting, or factionalism, within the women's movement. Instead of banding together, members of subgroups snipe within the group (Penelope, 1992).

Bibliography

Ainslie, Ricardo. "Cultural Mourning, Immigration, and Engagement: Vignettes from the Mexican Experience." In *Crossings: Mexican Immigration in Interdisciplinary Perspectives*, ed. Marcelo Suarez-Orozco. Cambridge: Harvard University Press, 1998.

Barnes, Natasha. "Body Talk: Notes on Women and Spectacle in Contemporary Trinidad Carnival." *Small Axe* 7 (2000): 93–105.

Brereton, Bridget. "The Trinidad Carnival: 1870–1900." *Savacou* 11/12 (1975): 46–57.

Burman, Jenny. "Masquerading Toronto Through Caribana: Transnational Carnival Meets the Sign 'Music Ends Here.'" *Identity* 1, no. 3 (2001): 273–28.

Calliste, Agnes. "Race, Gender and Canadian Immigration Policy: Blacks from the Caribbean, 1900–1932." *Journal of Canadian Studies* 28, no. 4 (1994): 131–49.

Dudley, Shannon. *Carnival Music in Trinidad: Experiencing Music, Expressing Culture.* New York: Oxford University Press, 2004.

Espinet, Ramabai. "Caribana: A Diasporic Dub." *Fuse* 22 (1999): 18–25.

Franco, Pamela. "Dressing Up and Looking Good: Afro-Creole Female Maskers in Trinidad Carnival." *African Arts* 31, no. 2 (1998): 62–67.

Franco, Pamela. "The 'Unruly Woman' in Nineteenth-Century Trinidad Carnival." *Small Axe* 7 (2000): 60–76.

Frankiel, Rita. *Essential Papers on Object Loss.* New York: New York University Press, 1994.

Friedan, Betty. *The Feminine Mystique.* New York: W. W. Norton, 1963.

Frow, John. "Tourism and the Semiotics of Nostalgia." *October* 57 (1991): 123–51.

Glick, Schiller, Nina, L. Basch, and C. Szanton-Blanc. "Transnational Perspective on Migration: Race, Class, Ethnicity, and Nationalism Reconsidered." *Annals of the New York Academy of Sciences* 645 (1992): 1–24.

Goffman, Erving. *The Presentation of Self in Everyday Life,* Garden City, NY: Doubleday, 1959.

Green, Garth, and Phillip Scher, eds. *Trinidad Carnival: The Cultural Politics of Transformational Festival.* Bloomington: Indiana University Press, 2007.

Henry, Francis. *The Caribbean Diaspora in Toronto. Learning to Live with Racism.* Toronto: University of Toronto Press, 1994.

Hill, L. *Women of Vision: The Story of the Canadian Negro Women's Association, 1951–1976.* Toronto, Ontario, Canada: Umbrella Press, 1996.

James, Carl. *Towards Racial Equality in Education: The Schooling of Black Students in the Greater Toronto Area.* Toronto, Ontario, Canada: York University, 2017.

Jameson, Fredric (1991) "Nostalgia for the Present." *South Atlantic Quarterly* 88, no. 2 (1991): 517–37.

Mason, Peter. *Bacchanal!: The Carnival Culture of Trinidad,* London: Latin American Bureau; Philadelphia, PA: Temple University Press, 1998.

Noel, Samantha. "Carnival is Woman!: Gender, Performance and Visual Culture in Contemporary Trinidad Carnival." Unpublished dissertation, Department of Art, Art History and Visual Studies, Duke University, 2009.

Nurse, Keith "Globalization and Trinidad Carnival: Diaspora, Hybridity and Identity in Global Culture." *Cultural Studies* 13, no. 4 (1999): 661–90.

Patton, M. *Qualitative Research and Evaluation Methods,* 3rd edition. Thousand Oaks, CA: Sage Publications, 2002.

Penelope, J. *Call Me Lesbian: Lesbian Lives, Lesbian Theory.* Freedom, CA: Crossing Press, 1992.

Phillip, Lyndon. "Reading Caribana 1997: Black Youth, Puff Daddy, Style and Diaspora Transformations." In *Trinidad Carnival: The Cultural Politics of Transformational Festival,* eds. Garth Green and Philp Scher. Bloomington: Indiana University Press, 2007.

Plaza, Dwaine. "A Socio-Historic Examination of Caribbean Migration to Canada. Moving to the Beat of Changes in Immigration Policy." *Wadabagei Journal of Diaspora Studies* 4. no. 1 (2001): 39–80.

Ringrose, Jessica. *Post-Feminist Education?: Girls and the Sexual Politics of Schooling.* London: Routledge, 2012.

Scher, Phillip. *Carnival and the Formation of Caribbean Transnation.* Gainesville: University of Florida Press, 2003.

Schlossberg, Nancy. "Marginality and Mattering. Key Issues in Building Community." In *Designing Campus Activities to Foster a Sense of Community,* ed. Dennis C. Roberts. San Francisco: Jossey-Bass, 1989.

Simmons, Alan, and Jean Turner. « L'immigraction antillaise au Canada, 1967–1987: contraintes structurelles et experiences vecus. » In *Population, Reproduction, Societes: Perspectives et enjeux de demographie sociale,* eds. Denis Cordell, Danielle Gauvreau,

Raymond Gervais, and Celine Le Bourdais, 395–418. Montreal: Presses de l'Universite de Montreal, 1993.

Simmons, Alan, and Dwaine Plaza. "The Caribbean Community in Canada. Transnational Connections and Transformation." In *Negotiating Borders and Belonging: Transnational Identities and Practices in Canada*, eds. Lloyd Wong and Vic Satzewich. Vancouver: University of British Columbia Press, 2006.

Smith, Hope Munro. "Performing Gender in the Trinidad Calypso." *Latin American Music Review* 25, no. 1 (2004): 32–56.

Statistics Canada. "Immigration and Ethnocultural Diversity Highlight Tables." http://www12.statcan.gc.ca/census-recensement/2016/dp-pd/hlt-fst/imm/Table.

Stewart, Kathleen. "Nostalgia—A Polemic." *Cultural Anthropology* 3, no. 3 (1998): 227–41.

Strauss, Anselm. and Juliet Corbin. *Basics of Qualitative Research. Techniques and Procedures for Developing Grounded Theory*. Thousand Oaks, CA: Sage, 1998.

Trotman, David. "Transforming Caribbean and Canadian Identity: Contesting Claims for Toronto's Caribana." *Atlantic Studies: Literary, Cultural, and Historical Perspectives* 2 (2005): 177–98.

Turner, Brian. "A Note on Nostalgia Theory." *Culture and Society* 4, no. 1 (1997): 147–56.

Vertovec, Steven. "Transnationalism and Identity." *Journal of Ethnic and Migration Studies* 2, no. 4 (2001): 573–82.

Volkan, Vamik. *Linking Objects and Linking Phenomena: A Study of the Forms, Symptoms, Metapsychology, and Therapy of Complicated Mourning*. New York: International Universities Press, 1981.

Walters, J. "What is Ethnography." In *Ethnography: A Research Tool for Policy Makers in Drug & Alcohol Fields*, eds. C. Akins and G. Beschner. Publication no. 80–946, Washington, DC, 1980.

Glossary

Ah—Trini pronunciation of the words "or," "I," or "of" (depending on the context). (Examples: "ah what?" = "or what"; "ah gone" = "I am leaving"; "some ah dis and some ah dat" = "some of this and some of that.")

All-inclusive—section or band in which costumed masqueraders pay for their costumes, unlimited drinks and food, and other accoutrements. Costumed band consists of a group organized around a theme and divided into sections.

All'yuh—Trini term for "everyone."

Bacchanal—the Trini-Creole use of the word can either describe vigorous winin', general commotions, wild parties, or fights between friends, neighbors, and family; it can also be used in a playful sense to describe winin' scenes that are often associated with Carnival revelry.

Baby Doll—a traditional *mas'* character now largely extinct. A young woman carries a white doll and a white baby bottle and accosts men demanding money while claiming they are the father of her child.

Band—a group of players. There are many different kinds of bands, including traditional character bands, Jouvay bands, fancy *mas'* bands, brass bands, calypso bands, and *mas'* bands.

Bajan—Anglophone-Caribbean terminology for "Barbadian."

Ba'John—Trini term for a hooligan.

Bamsee—Anglophone-Caribbean Creole term for "butt." Other spellings: "bomsee" or "bumsee." (Synonyms: "bombom," "bambam," "bumbum," "bumper," "bottom," "behind.")

Baiganee—sliced eggplant fritter.

Bazodi—Afro-Trini creole (from French word "abasourdir," meaning to daze) that describes being in a state of light-headedness or shock as if in a daze or if stunned.

Behavyah—Trini pronunciation of the word "behavior."

Bhojpuri—lingua franca of the Indian indentured laborers, related to Hindi.

Bligh—an opportunity, a chance.

Brek (Trini) or Bruk (Jamaican)—meaning "break."

"bruk out"—means to break away from social mores and expectations. literally translates into "break out," but loosely translates into "do whatever you feel, including dance however you would like." (Synonyms: "brek-free," "free-up," "get-on," and "misbehave.")

Bumper, Bamsee—Anglophone-Caribbean Creole term for "butt."

"Bus' ah sweet wine"—literal translation: burst (open) a (bottle of) sweet wine; general translation: to indulge in winin'.

Calypso—the music and rhythm native to Trinidad and Tobago. The word probably comes from the African Hausa "caiso," a praise singer of West Africa.

Cannes Brulee—a French term meaning "burning canes." It refers to the practice of rounding up slaves to put out fires in the cane fields and to harvest cane before it was destroyed.

Carnival—a momentous pre-Lenten festival found in Trinidad. The season usually starts on Boxing Day (the day after Christmas) and ends at midnight on Ash Wednesday, with the main event (the parading of the bands) occurring on the Monday and Tuesday before Ash Wednesday. During these two days, men and women dance and parade through the streets wearing elaborate costumes.

Carnival Monday—the day before Ash Wednesday. In the early morning, costumed bands come out to play J'ouvert (Jouvay).

Carnival Tuesday—the last day of Carnival before Ash Wednesday. The main bands, many playing pretty *mas'*, come out to parade the streets and enter into the costume competitions.

Chantuelles (chantwells)—praise singers who most frequently use their skills in songs called "lavways" (or "truth") to enhance the performance and reputations of stick fighters. They are often seen as precursors of the modern calypso.

Chip (chippin')—Trini term for how one is forced to walk in the midst of a crowded Carnival. It's a walking shuffle step that is also performed when one needs rest from the high energy dancing; it is sometimes performed to slower Soca as well. Because your knees never fully straighten as you drag your feet along the ground, chippin' is also a way of walking or dancing in rhythm to the music.

Choola—a traditional Indo-Caribbean earthen stove that uses coal or wood.

Chutney soca—the combination of Indian indentured folk and Afro-Caribbean Carnival musical traditions.

Commesse—Trini patois for "confusion."

Crop Over—the festival in Barbados that is similar to the Trinidadian Carnival.

Cyah—Trini pronunciation of the word "can't."

Daal—split peas.

Dame Lorraine—a traditional Carnival portrayal initially performed by men, based on ridicule of the old French planters and played by slaves to mock their masters. "She" is made to look voluptuous through the use of pillows and stuffing.

Da'iz—Trini pronunciation of the term "that is."

Dancehall—a popular genre of dance music specific to Jamaica that originally developed out of reggae music during the 1970s.

Dat—Trini pronunciation of the word "that."

Devi—the sacred feminine in the Hindu religious tradition.

Despelote—term used in Cuba for the dexterous and vigorous rolls of the hip, pelvis, and buttocks (literal translation: "all over the place").

Dey—Trini pronunciation of the words "they" or "there" (depending on the context). (Examples: "he dong dey" = "he is down there"; "dey gone" = "they left.")

Doh—Trini pronunciation of the word "don't."

Dong—Trini pronunciation of the word "down."

Di—Trini pronunciation of the word "the."

Fete (fettin' and fetted)—Trinidian creole term meaning "to party" or "a party."

Free-up ("free-up myself")—see "bruk out."

Fuh—Trini pronunciation of the word "for."

Get-on ("get-on bad")—see "bruk out."

Gouyad—Haitian patois for grinding one's hip, pelvis, and buttocks; literal translation: "grind."

Grief—in the Trini-social context, this means to "give someone a hard time" (usually a lover and usually to cause to them heartache).

Grong—Trini pronunciation of the word "ground."

Gyal—Trini pronunciation of the word "girl."

Horn—meaning to cheat on a significant other. "To get horned" or "to get ah horn" is the phrasing often used when your significant other is seeing someone else behind your back (e.g., "My boyfriend give me ah horn" or "He horned me").

Horner man/woman—the man/woman your significant other is cheating on you with.

Indo-Caribbean—descendants of Indian indentured laborer in the Caribbean.

Iron band—a predecessor to steelbands consisting of brake drums and oil drums.

Ital—a Jamaican patois term that refers to the food that Rastafarians eat. Deriving from the term "vital," ital food often celebrates food that is natural, unprocessed, and from the Earth.

Jacketmen (Lom Kamisol)—Jacketmen were men of the upper classes who, masked and disguised to preserve their anonymity, would participate in the cultural and festive lives of the Jamette world.

Jagabat—Trini patois term for a "loose woman."

Jahajin—female indentured laborers.

Jammet, Jammette—a woman of questionable morals or a woman who adapts an abrasive or aggressive form of communication with the public. Can also refer to a prostitute.

Jouvay (J'ouvert)—a Trini-Creole word that derives from the French word "jour ouvert"—meaning opening day, daybreak, or opening morning, all of which reference the dawn of Carnival Monday. Sometimes referred to as dutty *mas'* (i.e., dirty masquerading), many of the costumes—such as the devil, the bat, the Dame Lorraine, and the pissenlit—and traditions—which include covering oneself in mud, paint, or oil—that are played and preserved during Jouvay were crafted and disseminated by the late nineteenth-century Trinidadian Jametres.

Jumbie—Trini-Creole word for a ghost, spirit, demon, or an overwhelming energy (sayings: "di Carnival jumbie").

"Jump-up with a band"—like the phrases "free-up" and "get-on," "jump-up" can be used to describe the overall dancing, winin', jumping, and waving that occur during Carnival. In other words, this phrase does not necessarily mean that all you are doing is jumping up and down. (Synonym: "play *mas*".)

Kaiso—alternative name for "calypso."

Kalounjee—stuffed bitter melon fritter.

Kompa—a music genre particular to Haiti.

Kutchela—Indo-Caribbean preserve.

Las lap—the very last time for music, dance, and drink before Ash Wednesday.

Lime (limin' and limed)—Trinidadian creole term meaning "to hangout" (verb) or "a hangout" (noun).

Matador—a stylish, independent woman. The term was often applied to entrepreneurial women in the Jamette world who earned money as madams or prostitutes and who often supported men with their earnings.

Mahgah—a Creole term used throughout the Anglophone Caribbean that describes a very skinny person.

Mas'—Trinidadian term for "masquerade"; "ole *mas*'" refers to older traditional forms and characters; *mas'* camp is where costumes are made and distributed and rehearsals held.

Masquerade—to dress in Carnival costume, parade, and dance through the streets.

***Mas'* camp**—the location where the costumes of a specific band are assembled and distributed and where rehearsals, if any, are held.

Matikoor—a prenuptial Bhojpuri-Hindu folk ritual performed only by women.

Midnight Robber—traditional Carnival character wearing extravagant costume and speaking "robber talk."

Misbehave—see "bruk out."

Mulatto, Mulatress—a man or woman with one black and one white parent.

Neg Jardin, Negue Jardin, Negre jardins, Negres Jardins—from French for "field slave." An early masquerade, apparently played by liberated Trinidadians in satiric mockery of their former enslavement and by plantation owners as derisive imitation of the enslaved.

"On di road"—Trinidadian euphemism that refers to Carnival, especially the parade of the bands (when masqueraders are out in the streets showing off their winin' skills and elaborate costumes).

Obeahman, or woman—an individual who practices "obeah," a system of spiritual and physical health and healing practices derived from African traditions. Believed by some to be black magic.

Oui—French for "yes" (commonly used throughout Trinidad, due its high population of French plantation owners during colonial times).

"Outt a timin'"—literal translation: "Out of timing," as in "off putting"; something said or done that offsets the flow of things (e.g., to "put your foot in your mouth").

Pace—Trini talk that refers to one's ability to keep up with the pace and energy of Carnival. For example, with regards to winin', it means that you were able to wine on or with many revelers.

Pan—the instrument unique to Trinidad made from steel oil drums.

Paratha—a type of fluffy, silky Indo-Caribbean flatbread (roti).

Perreando—usually linked to the dancing associated with the reguetón from Puerto Rico and the Dominican Republic; literal translation: "doggy-style." Usually describes a person gyrating their butt onto the gyrating crotch of their dance partner, like the sexual position known as doggy style.

Pholourie—Indo-Caribbean fritter.

Pickney—an Anglophone-Caribbean creole term meaning "children."

Picong—a way of insulting in a jesting manner; a form of verbal warfare, similar to the African American tradition of the dozens, which is most commonly associated with ol'-time calypso. (Synonym: "fatigue.")

"Play *mas*'"—literal translation: to play masquerade. A Trinidadian saying that means to wear a costume and participate in the parading of the bands during Carnival. (Synonym: "jump-up with a band.")

Pretty *mas*', fancy *mas*'—today's main form of the masquerade which focuses on beautiful but scant costumes with elaborate decorations.

Pum-pum—Jamaican patois meaning vagina. (Synonym: "punanny.")

Queen of Carnival—the largest and fancies female costume in the band. Not to be confused with the Carnival Queen, who was the winner of the prestigious beauty pageant (now defunct) called the Jaycees Carnival Queen competition.

Reguetón—a genre of music originally influenced by Jamaican dancehall-reggae. First developed in Panama as an underground style known as "Spanish Reggae," today it is especially dominated by Puerto Rican and Dominican artists and heavily influenced by US hip-hop and other Caribbean musical rhythms, such as merengue, Jamaican dancehall, and salsa.

Rel—Trini pronunciation of the word "real."

Rumba—Spanish term for "party"; in Cuba, this term also describes a type of Afro-folkloric music and dances.

Sketele—Caribbean term for a loose woman.

Slut—women considered to have loose morals.

Slackness—having loose morals.

Soca—a style of music historically linked to the Trinidadian Carnival. It started to evolve during the 1970s as a blend of African American soul music and calypso. Since then, it has developed into a high-energy sound that mixes calypso rhythms with musical styles from all over the world, including East Indian, African, and electronic dance music.

Steel pan—originally made from old, discarded oil drums, steel pan is an iron drum particular to Trinidad.

Steel band—a musical ensemble whose members play on instruments entirely constructed from steel drums. Before the onset of mobile sound trucks, steel bands provided the music for *mas'* bands.

Stick fighting—ritual dance and martial art dating back for slavery when men would fight with sticks (bois) in rings or gayelles.

Storm—a Trini colloquialism that means to enter an event, uninvited.

Tabanca—an intense feeling of jilted love.

Tassa—Indo-Caribbean kettledrums.

Teif (teifin')—Trini pronunciation of the word "thieve" (thieving).

Ting—Trini pronunciation of the word "thing."

Trinbago (Trinbagonian)—portmanteau of Trinidad and Tobago.

Trini—Anglophone-Caribbean terminology for Trinidadian.

Trini-styled Carnival—festivals held both within the Caribbean and throughout the Caribbean diaspora that are heavily influenced by or modeled after the annual pre-Lenten Carnival festivities of Trinidad.

Tuh—Trini pronunciation of the word "to."

Wahbeen—Trini Creole term for a loose woman.

Wais'line—Anglophone-Caribbean pronunciation of "waistline."

Wassy—Trini Creole term for a loose woman.

Wine (winin')—an Anglophone-Caribbean creole term that translates into "winding," which is how the British described the gyrations of the African people during the colonial era. It is a dance that involves dexterous and vigorous rolls, gyrations, thrusts, and shakes of the hip, pelvis, and buttocks area.

"Wine-up" or "Wine-down"—euphemism that describes acts of winin'. Like the phrase "jump-up," the "-up" or "-down" does not necessarily imply the direction that the wine is happening in; it can be a generalized way of stating that a lot of winin' was happing.

Winer—someone who wines.

Winery—Trinidadian slang that refers to one's winin' skills or abilities.

Wotles—Trini Creole term meaning "worthless"; used to describe a person or their behavior as something that is no good.

"Wukk-up stink"—a particularly Bajan way of saying, "to roll your hips skillfully." Literal translation: "worked up stink."

About the Contributors

Editors

Frances Henry is professor emerita at York University and a member of the Royal Society of Canada specializing in Caribbean studies. She is author of *The Equity Myth: Racialization and Indigeneity at Canadian Universities* and *He Had the Power: Pa Neezer, the Orisha King of Trinidad*. Her work has appeared in the *Journal of Canadian Studies* and *Canadian Ethnic Studies*.

Dwaine Plaza is professor of sociology at Oregon State University specializing in Caribbean studies. He is coauthor of *Returning to the Source: The Final Stage of the Caribbean Migration Circuit*. His work has appeared in *Global Development Studies*, *Terres D'Amerique*, and *Revue européene des migrations internationales*.

Contributors

Darrell Gerohn Baksh has a PhD in cultural studies from the University of the West Indies and is currently working in Toronto.

Jan DeCosmo is professor of humanities in the Department of Visual Arts, Humanities & Theatre at Florida A&M University and former president of the Caribbean Studies Association.

Professor **Jeff Henry**, born and raised in Trinidad, was a famous mas player in his time and later became a leading member of The Little Carib Dance Theatre in Port-of-Spain. Years later after migrating to Canada, he became professor of theatre arts at York University, Toronto, specializing in physical movement for actors. He also organized the first Black theatre in the city. A few years ago, his continuing interest in the Carnival led to his book *Under* *the 'Mas': Resistance and Rebellion in the Trinidad Masquerade* (2008) published by Lexicon LTD Limited.

Philip W. Scher is professor of anthropology/media relations at the University of Oregon and specializes in folklore and popular culture with an emphasis on the Caribbean.
(https://uonews.uoregon.edu/philip-scher-department-anthropology)

Samantha Noel is assistant professor of art history at Wayne State University. Her PhD is in art history from Duke University. Her interests are in visual culture and performance in Black society.

Adanna Kai Jones is a postdoctoral research associate at the University of Maryland. Her interests are in Caribbean culture, especially dance, and her PhD is from the University of California, Riverside.

Asha St. Bernard works as a media consultant in Trinidad. She has an MA from Western University (formerly the University of Western Ontario) in class and gender in Carnival.

Index

www.ingramcontent.com/pod-product-compliance
Lightning Source LLC
Chambersburg PA
CBHW030650270326
41929CB00007B/287